A Lutheran Plague

Studies in Central European Histories

VOLUME 55

The titles published in this series are listed at brill.nl/sceh

A Lutheran Plague

Murdering to Die in the Eighteenth Century

By

Tyge Krogh

BRILL

LEIDEN • BOSTON
2012

Cover illustration: Finished Artwork of Woodcut from the ballad about Cicilia Johansdatter ('en meget ynkelig Viise hvorudi en Synderinde...'), 1744 (The Royal Library Copenhagen). The creator of the finished artwork is Tina Madsen, ReklameService, Kalundborg.

This book is printed on acid-free paper.

Library of Congress Cataloging-in-Publication Data

Krogh, Tyge, 1954-
A Lutheran plague : murdering to die in the eighteenth century / by Tyge Krogh.
p. cm. -- (Studies in Central European histories, ISSN 1547-1217 ; v. 55)
Includes bibliographical references and index.
ISBN 978-90-04-22115-4 (hardback : alk. paper) 1. Murder--Europe, Northern. 2. Murderers--Europe, Northern--Psychology. 3. Murderers--Religious life--Europe, Northern. 4. Salvation--Lutheran Church. 5. Pietism--Europe, Northern--History--18th century. 6. Capital punishment--Europe, Northern--History--18th century. 7. Criminal justice, Administration of--Europe, Northern--History--18th century. I. Title.

HV6535.E86K76 2012
364.152'309409033--dc23

2011039830

ISSN 1547-1217
ISBN 978 90 04 22115 4

CONTENTS

LIST OF ILLUSTRATIONS AND TABLES

Illustrations

Tables

ACKNOWLEDGEMENTS

This book has grown out of my broad research into the eighteenth-century Danish punitive system and the beliefs underpinning it, which was published in 2000 in the book *Oplysningstiden og det magiske. Henrettelser og korporlige straffe i 1700-tallets første halvdel (The Enlightenment and the magical. Executions and corporal punishments in Denmark in the first half of the eighteenth century)*. In 2003 I was granted a one-year research fellowship at the Danish Institute for Advanced Studies in the Humanities and benefited from the inspiration provided by my colleagues there. The work was not completed at the Institute, however, and over the following years I was grateful for the sustained support given to me by my employer, the Danish National Archives. In addition to putting up with a somewhat protracted work schedule, they granted me five months' full-time research to finish the book, as well as financing travel and editing of the language. Lillian og Dan Finks Fond has generously supported the final editing of the language.

Several friends and colleagues have helped with critical insights, suggestions and sources. I would like to thank in particular Ning de Coninck-Smith, Signild Valgårda, Karen Arnfred, Jens P. Sørensen, Helga Schnabel-Schüle, Susanne Hehenberger, Erik Midelfort, Thomas Munck and Michael Gelting.

CHAPTER ONE

INTRODUCTION

Criminal justice is an important part of the grand narrative of the genesis of modern society. The early modern period is known for its harsh penalties for acts that are no longer considered even to be crimes. *The Spectacle of Suffering* is the title of one important book on the subject, and *The Theatre of Horror* is another.[1] The punishments were, in the words of Richard Evans,

> cruel, barbarous and sadistic: physical mutilation, whipping, and branding, and everywhere executions on a scale, and by means, from hanging, drawing and quartering to breaking on the wheel, that we now regard with incredulity and revulsion.[2]

The ending of this harsh system of public executions and of the persecution of crimes such as witchcraft, adultery and sodomy, is seen as one of the most important achievements of modernity.

Implicit in this dominant narrative of early modern criminal justice is an almost inevitable tendency to view the condemned as unjustly treated. It is easy to see the people executed in these barbarous ways as victims of a brutal, insensitive and superstitious justice system. This victimization is seen most clearly in descriptions and narratives of cases of witchcraft and of infanticide. In dramatizations of such cases in literature and films there is, moreover, a tendency to attribute to the condemned a modern world-view, so that they act as our eyes on the past. It could be said that they become martyrs in the fight for modern humanity.

This implicit victimization, however, restricts our understanding of the system of justice and of the punishments. The world-view embodying this system of justice is inherently seen as something forced upon the criminals, who thus represent an opposition to that world-view. The solemn and harmonious execution scene, which is described in

---

[1] P. Spierenburg, *The Spectacle of Suffering*, 1984; Richard van Dülmen, *The Theatre of Horror*, 1985.

[2] Richard J. Evans, *Rituals of Retribution: Capital Punishment in Germany, 1600–1987*, 1996, p. 1.

numerous sources, is noted but viewed with suspicion as an apology for the brutalities.

The implicit wish to victimize these barbarously executed criminals is perhaps also the reason why the murderers who are the subject of this study have been overlooked by historians of the criminal justice system as well as by enlightened critics of the grotesque punishments meted out in the eighteenth century. The murderers discussed here cannot be categorized as victims of cruelty or of inhumanity because, simply, they were not victims at all. The punishment was their goal, and provided the motive for the crime. As such, however, the murders have the unique quality of presenting us with executions with no victims, and this freedom can open our eyes to what really took place at the sites of these early modern executions.

As an example of these suicide murders, let us look at the case of Margrethe Christensdatter.[3] In Copenhagen, just before Christmas 1741, she deliberately threw a nine-year-old girl into a canal, where she drowned. A couple of days later, while the search for the young girl was in progress, Margrethe went to the city gaol and gave herself up. She told the court that she only vaguely knew the girl. On the day of the murder she had met her in the street. Margrethe asked after her parents and was told that the girl's father had died. She took the girl by the hand and asked her to go with her, which the child did. When they reached the canal, she pushed the child into the water and then immediately ran away without hearing the child's cries for help. When asked why she had done it, Margrethe said that she had dreamed that she would commit such a murder, and that since she had had the dream she could not stop thinking about it, especially during the fortnight before the murder. Her defence probed deeper into her motives and established that she had been to confession and taken communion three weeks before committing the crime. A week later she had left her job as a housemaid and returned to her parents, claiming that she had a swollen hand. Her mother told the court that she had been depressed when she returned home but that she would not say why. The last few days before the murder Margrethe had wandered around the streets all day, occasionally going to church.

The prosecuting attorney stated that there was ample proof that Margrethe had murdered the girl and that the murder was premeditated. In order to prevent similar crimes he demanded a severe

[3] Appendix, case 1742:1.

punishment, including pinching with red-hot tongs and cutting off her hand and head. Margrethe's defence attorney argued that it was severe temptation by Satan that had caused her to commit the crime. He noted that she had told the court that she was willing to suffer for what she had done, and he claimed that she was now more than happy to be killed for her evil deed. The defence even assumed that her execution—provided the method of execution was not too severe—would help assure the salvation of her soul. The court sentenced her to decapitation by sword, a penalty that allowed her to be buried in consecrated ground.

Another source allows us to come closer to understanding Margrethe's motives. Thirty years later, the dean of the cathedral of Copenhagen, the renowned Pietist Henrik Gerner, published his memoirs.[4] In them he recounted Margrethe's story. She was a gentle creature, he wrote, bright and anxious to be saved. But instead of turning to the Lord and finding comfort there, she made a habit of going around to the Pietist pastors in the town and asking for their help. She had visited Gerner himself several times—the last time was not long before her terrible crime. Gerner recalled that he had spoken seriously to her and asked her whether she really wanted to be saved, since she knew very well whom she had to turn to in order to be absolved. She should not come to the dean so often, as it was not for him to absolve her. When Margrethe was arrested, Gerner's children's private tutor decided to offer his assistance by preparing her for her meeting with God. According to Gerner, the tutor now told Margrethe that Jesus by his sufferings and his death had taken on her sins. He had been following her for a long time, and although she had been faithless and ungrateful to Jesus, and committed a terrible atrocity, He had not changed. Her faithlessness had not destroyed His faithfulness. He had once by His sufferings saved her. All she had to do was to believe in this. According to Gerner, Margrethe immediately believed these words, as though the Holy Ghost had conveyed them directly to her heart. She burst into tears and was almost unable to speak for crying and out of her sense of shame, but she was able to say that she now really believed that all her sins were forgiven. From that point until her execution she had no misgivings or doubts about her salvation and no fear of death. The evening before the execution Gerner visited her and saw that she was cheerful

---

[4] Henrik Gerner, *Nogle Merkværdigheder*, 1772, p. 98–109.

and content. He watched the execution from a building just opposite the scaffold, and saw how his children's tutor prayed with Margrethe and commended her to God, at which point the executioner stepped forward and beheaded her with a sword. Gerner concluded:

> This was of course a revolting event, and God save any honourable person from such destiny; but nevertheless there is something good, evangelical and pleasant in it, and it is a great example of the faithful shepherd's unending forbearance and patience in saving the lost souls.[5]

Margrethe Christensdatter's decision not to kill herself but instead to commit a murder and as a result lose her life with the assistance of the authorities was not an isolated case. In the ten years preceding her crime there had been twelve such murders and nine similar attempted murders in Copenhagen. The objective circumstances were that all of the murderers were motiveless, in that the murderer had no grudge against the victim, that the murderers usually turned themselves in, as Margrethe did, and they usually told the courts that the motive for their crime was a desire to be executed. Women predominated among the murderers, and to an even greater extent children predominated among the victims.

As I have already mentioned, these suicide murders transform completely our view of eighteenth-century public punishments. In such cases, when the person being executed is not the terrified victim of a brutal state apparatus but has actively sought the execution, then it is the attraction of the execution scene itself that needs to be understood, and descriptions of the condemned men and women going happily to their death, such as that given by Henrik Gerner, cannot be dismissed as mere clerical gloss. The case of Margrethe Christensdatter demonstrates that religious beliefs and the religious staging of the executions were at the centre of this attraction. Margrethe, as a Lutheran and a Pietist, believed that she had been tempted by the Devil to commit the murder, but after she confessed in court, Gerner's private tutor managed to open her heart to Jesus, so that she was reborn and felt certain of salvation and so went cheerfully to her execution.

The importance of the Lutheran execution ceremony and the Pietist development of it is underlined by the geographical distribution of the

[5] Gerner, *Nogle Merkværdigheder*, p. 102–3: 'Dette var vel en fæl Tildragelse, og Gud bevare hvert ærligt Menneske fra saadan en Førelse; men imidlertid er der dog noget Artigt, noget Evangelisk og Fornøyeligt deri, og det er et meget stort Eksempel paa den troe Hyrdes uendelige Langmodighed og Taalmodighed i at giøre de Fortabte salige.'

suicide murders. My research shows that such murders were a significant criminal problem only in Lutheran countries and cities. Starting from these findings, this study will argue that it was elements of faith specific to the Lutheran confession that made the religious execution scenario attractive, and that these elements of faith thus played a crucial role in provoking the suicide murders and in their presence in such large numbers. After the Reformation the Christian confessions developed different responses to the challenges in society. For the criminal justice system this meant that the confessions developed different attitudes towards the death penalty and towards the execution ceremony itself. The Protestants were well aware of their peculiarity in criminal justice: they boasted of their rigour in following Mosaic Law as well as their greater care for those sentenced to death. This positioning in turn created a different culture of justice as well as different patterns of criminality, and finally for this reason the abolition of the death penalty had different implications in the Protestant countries from in Italy and France, where Beccaria and Voltaire put forward their famous critiques of the death penalty in the 1760s. It is thus my argument that religious or cultural factors that had developed in the confessional struggles during and after the Reformation created substantial differences between neighbouring countries in penal practice and criminality.

This is a neglected aspect of the history of early modern criminal justice. The influence of religion on definitions of crime, on the penalties and on the execution ceremonies is generally recognized in the literature on criminal justice,[6] but religion is interpreted as having a common impact on different societies, and the confessional differences are seen as less important because—in the spirit of Emile Durkheim—religion is seen as rooted in economic and social conditions. So the influence of religion on criminal justice is primarily explained as a common social construct, not as one of the effects of specific religious cultures. Confessional differences, in execution rituals especially, are noted in the criminal justice studies, but they are not credited with

[6] The main comparative studies are: Lenman and Parker, 'The State, the Community and the Criminal Law in Early Modern Europe', 1980; Spierenburg, *The Spectacle of Suffering*; Van Dülmen, *Theatre of Horror*; and Evans, *Rituals of Retribution*. The absence of confessional explanations is further commented on at p. 115. One might expect that the heightened interest in cultural history in recent years would have led criminal justice historians to make confessional comparisons, but this is not the case. One reason for this may be the popularity of the micro-historical approach. Small-scale studies do not fit in well with comparative history.

having any influence on crime itself or on penal practice. The only exception is studies of witchcraft persecutions, where the impact of confessional differences is frequently discussed.[7]

While a confessional approach is rare in concrete studies of early modern social history, it is a recurrent feature of German meta-historical debate. In particular, the rise of Prussia in the eighteenth century is partly explained by the Calvinist faith of the Hohenzollerns as well as by by Hallensian Pietism.[8] Max Weber took this argument a step further in his famous book *The Protestant Ethic and the Spirit of Capitalism*, in which he discussed the role of the Calvinist work ethic, Pietism and Methodism in the development of capitalist society. After the Second World War discussions of a German historical *Sonderweg* leading inevitably to the horrors of Nazism also cited Protestant culture as a cause. These grand narratives describing the impact of the Protestant confessions on capitalism, on the unification of Germany and on the grandeur of the German empire, and ultimately their possible role in the development of the Third Reich, are, however, characterized by huge generalizations and are highly debatable. Thus as a Danish historian I cannot help noticing that several of the religious developments that are said to have advanced the social and political strength of Prussia in the eighteenth century also took place in the kingdom of Denmark–Norway, which had a fate quite different from that of Prussia.

In the 1980s the German historians Wolfgang Reinhard and Heinz Schilling coined the term 'confessionalization' as a way of placing a new focus on the distinctive characters of Catholic, Lutheran and Reformed religious cultures and their impact on society as well as their role in the development of modernity.[9] This focus is much in line with

[7] See especially Erik Midelfort, *Witchhunting in Southwestern Germany, 1562–1684*, 1972, and Wolfgang Behringer, *Hexenverfolgungen in Bayern: Volksmagie, Glaubenseifer und Staatsräson in der frühen Neuzeit*, 1987.

[8] The explanation was laid out by Otto Hintze in 'Geist und Epochen der preussischen Geschichte', 1903, and 'Kalvinismus und Staatsräson in Brandenburg zu Beginn des 17. Jahrhunderts', 1931 (Hintze, *Regierung und Vervaltung*, vol. 3, p. 1–29, 255–311). More recently the ideas have been advanced by: Thomas Nipperdey, 'Max Weber, der Protestantismus und die Deutschen: Drei Kommentare zu einer klassischen Thema', 1986; Richard Gawthrop, *Pietism and the Making of Eighteenth Century Prussia*, 1993; and Heintz Schilling, *Höfe und Alianzen. Deutschland, 1648–1763*, 1994, p. 378–85.

[9] See W. Reinhard and H. Schilling (ed.), *Die Katholische Konfessionalisierung*, 1995, especially H. Schilling, 'Die Konfessionalisierung von Kirche Staat und Gesellschaft: Profil, Leistung und Perspektiven eines geschichtswissenschaftlicen Paradigmas', p. 1–49.

my approach. The focus of the confessionalization studies, however, has generally been limited to religious institutions and practices and to education. It has not, to my knowledge, generated confessional interpretations of the justice system. Erik Midelfort has developed the idea in a contribution to a seminar on confessionalization.[10] In a discussion of the impact of the Lutheran confession on suicide he described this effect as an 'unintended confessionalization' and thereby suggested that confessionalization was not just a conscious effort to shape society. The development of the suicide murders to a large criminal problem in Lutheran areas can very accurately be described as an unintended effect of confessionalization.

Few scholars have studied the suicide murders. In 1937 the German legal historian Helmuth von Weber wrote an article on the murders in Germany that was based on eighteenth-century juridical publications.[11] The murders provoked a special penalty that was included in the Preussische Landrecht (Prussian general law) of 1794, and this addition was the main focus of von Weber's article. His presentation of the German juridical debate as well as many precise observations on the nature of the crime has been very helpful to me. In 2000 the historian Jürgen Martchukat presented a debate about the murders that took place in Hamburg in the 1780s.[12] He mentions only a few murders but highlights the importance of the execution ceremony for the murderers. Both von Weber and Martchukat point to the religious and cultural causes for the murders.

Recently the American historian Kathy Stuart has published an article entitled 'Suicide by Proxy', based on archival studies in southern Germany and a broader study of contemporary published material in Germany and Austria.[13] Stuart is interested in the role of gender in the murders and in the symbolic meaning the murderers attached to their actions. She thus argues that the murderers in each case imagined the murder as a parallel to their own execution. She recognizes the religious context of the murders, but she gives examples of murders in Catholic areas as well. Although she acknowledges the predominance

[10] E. Midelfort, 'Selbstmord im Urtheil von Reformation und Gegenreformation', in Reinhard and Schilling (ed.), *Die Katholische Konfessionalisierung*, p. 298–310.

[11] Helmuth von Weber, 'Selbstmord als Mordmotiv', 1937.

[12] Jürgen Martchukat, 'Ein Freitod durch die Hand des Henkers', 2000.

[13] Kathy Stuart: 'Suicide by Proxy: The Unintended Consequences of Public Executions in Eighteenth-Century Germany', 2008.

of Lutheran perpetrators, she is sceptical about the role of the Lutheran confession in producing the crime.

A different approach to the murders is taken by the Swedish historian Arne Jansson.[14] Jansson has gone through the Stockholm crime records looking for cases of homicide and suicide in the period from 1600 to 1720. He points to a sharp decline in the frequency of legally prosecuted homicides during this period and a change from almost exclusively cases of unpremeditated manslaughter to more and more cases of premeditated murder. A large proportion of these murders were suicide murders. This change in homicide cases also coincides with a rise in the number of suicides. Jansson groups the suicide murders together with other suicides and explains the growth of both categories by the transition from a traditional society to a modern one, with a diminution in the importance of community (family, work groups and religious congregations) and a greater emphasis on of the individual, leading to an increase in the frequency of suicide. He cites Durkheim as the primary source of this theory.[15]

The same approach is taken by the German historian Vera Lind, who has studied suicides in Schleswig-Holstein between 1600 and 1800. Her focus is on the discourse in which the suicides were understood and the change in this discourse. She describes suicide murders too, but she does not analyse their unique quality. She ranks the murders as a sub-category of suicides, calling them 'hidden' suicides.[16]

The kinship with suicides is obviously present in these murders, and it seems correct to regard them as part of the growth of suicide in early modern society, as Arne Jansson and Vera Lind do. The spread of suicides is also one of the general preconditions for the murders. The kinship with suicides is, however, only one aspect of these crimes. The murderers did not take their own lives: they committed cold-blooded murders of innocent and defenceless children. After the deed, they gave themselves up and openly expected the authorities to fulfil their wish to be executed. Furthermore, as we shall see, in spite of their terrible actions, they had good reasons for expecting to be met with understanding and sympathy by the authorities and the general public, as well as for feeling sure that their souls would be saved.

---

[14] Arne Jansson, *From Swords to Sorrow: Homicide and Suicide in Early Modern Stockholm*, 1998. See especially p. 14–23, 49–50. A substantial number of the murder cases are described in Arne Jannsson, 'Mörda för att få dö', 1994, p. 21–52.

[15] Jansson, *From Swords to Sorrow*, p. 31–48.

[16] Vera Lind, *Selbstmord in der frühen Neuzeit*, 1999, p. 13.

As the motive of the suicide murderers is a desire to be executed, it follows that to understand the motive it is necessary to understand the murderers' interaction with the authorities and the community in the period between the murder and the execution. How did the authorities and the community react to the murders? And what benefits did the murderers expect to obtain? In order to answer these questions, detailed information about the murder cases and information about the attitudes of the authorities and of the communities is needed. It is, however, laborious to search for criminal cases in court records in early modern times. As a result, most early modern studies in crime are limited in time and cover small areas. This study faces the same difficulties. The in-depth archive study is limited to the Danish capital, Copenhagen, where the records of the civil, military and naval court systems have been scrutinized. The cases have been followed from the trial preliminaries to the final verdicts. Debates among the authorities have been searched for. These debates took place in the Supreme Court, in statements by professors and civil servants advising the king in his use of his discretionary power, and in relation to legal initiatives to counter the murder phenomenon. Accounts of the public reception of the murders have been taken from leaflets and other printed matter.

This in-depth study is, however, also used to provide a European perspective on the occurrence of suicide murders and the attitudes towards them. As a result, the study is unusual in giving a view of Europe from the north. Scandinavia is generally seen as one of the outskirts of early modern Europe, an area usually seen as passively receiving impulses rather than actively shaping historical developments. In the case of the suicide murders, however, it appears that Stockholm and Hamburg were among the places where the phenomenon first became a significant criminal problem. In Copenhagen the large number of such murders in the 1750s and 1760s provoked radical government responses, which broke with important Lutheran dogmas but which were also able to combat the phenomenon and which were copied in other parts of Europe later on.

As I have already mentioned, direct research into the suicide murders is sparse, and there is little mention of the murders in general studies of criminal justice. Therefore the European outlook has had to be assembled from various and often indirect pieces of evidence. Many criminal justice studies were undertaken in the twentieth century in various parts of Europe. Although they have other perspectives, they provide details about criminality, penal practice and execution scenarios. I have compared the findings from my in-depth study of Copenhagen with such details and made use of the comparisons to identify similarities and differences. Furthermore, I have consulted contemporary juridical and religious literature touching on the murders or issues in relation to the murders as well as popular leaflets about murder cases.

In the European outlook, I have made extensive use of indirect evidence and undertaken statistical comparisons based on heterogeneous source material to build up a picture of the frequency and topography of the suicide murders and of differences in the penal practice, execution scenarios and religious beliefs behind those differences.[17] This dual approach necessarily results in an imbalance in the descriptions between reasonably certain statements about developments in Denmark and a greater degree of conjecture about developments in the rest of Europe. Research into the murders in primary sources in other parts of Europe would no doubt alter the sketchy picture of this study considerably. I hope, however, to be able to convince my readers that the heterogeneous evidence is sufficiently substantial to validate my conclusions.

***

The study is divided into three parts. In the first part I describe the frequency and spatial boundaries of the murders and try to get as close as possible to the murderers and how they were treated. Who were these murderers? What were their motives for killing? How did the general public react to the murders? What penalties could the murderers expect to be meted out to them? What was the official penal ideology? And how did the pastors prepare the murderers for their deaths?

The second part investigates the confessional origins of the murders through a comparison of relevant elements of faith in the main

---

[17] The use of statistics in early modern social and criminal history is debated. Thus in her study of Wûrttembergian criminal and penal history Helga Schnabel-Schüle is much opposed to their use. See Schnabel-Schüle, *Überwachen und Strafen im Territorialstaat*, 1997, p. 223–5. My statistics should be read in close connection with my descriptions of the source material on which they are based and with the qualifications I give in the definitions of categories used. Statistics are facts in just the same way as citations from documents. The reader can rely on the figures as having a reality in the sources, but when the figures are taken out of their context and used in my description, they turn into arguments. Their complex origin must always be taken into consideration when the validity of the argument is to be judged.

Christian confessions, of penal practices in countries dominated by the different confessions, of the clerical preparation of prisoners sentenced to death and of the execution ceremonies.

The third part traces the painful recognition by the Lutheran states of the relation between the murders and the elements of faith that nourished them, as well as the necessary revision of the elements of faith through legal and intellectual initiatives.

PART ONE

MORPHOLOGY

CHAPTER TWO

FREQUENCY

Before delving into the world of the suicide murders, I will first assess the frequency of such murders in order to estimate the seriousness of the criminal problem with which eighteenth-century society had to deal.

In general, it must be acknowledged that accuracy is difficult to obtain in early modern research. Court records and other material containing information about criminal cases are incomplete in many ways. There are lacunae in the records, and the information about specific cases may be too sparse for purposes of categorization. This study, however, has one advantage compared with other investigations into early modern crime. We are not obliged to take into account any unreported or unsolved cases that, accordingly, did not appear in the court records. For the criminals being studied here the purpose of their crime was to be punished, and as a result they were all brought to trial.

My Own Studies: Zealand and Copenhagen

What is a suicide murder? Basically, it is defined by its motive—a motive that originates in the mind of the perpetrator. On the face of it, the best proof, and a precondition to categorize a murder as a suicide murder, should be the murderer's confession of the motive. One must bear in mind, however, that the motive was of no relevance for passing the sentence until specific legislation against the murders was imposed. Therefore any description of the motive was left to the murderer, and the courts did not try to establish specific categories of motive. Furthermore, even when a suicide motive is given, it should not necessarily be unquestioningly accepted. Human motives are always complex, and in cases where the sources offer a copious description of the circumstances leading to the murder, it is not unusual to find plausible additional motives, especially some sort of revenge on a third party. It is therefore important to take objective circumstances into account as well. There is no concrete objective circumstance that might provide proof of the motive—such as, for instance, possession of stolen goods in cases of murder with intent to rob. But there are characteristics that exclude other motives, and there are characteristics that support (even if they do not not prove) suicide motives. In my own count of suicide murders I have searched for the following characteristics:

1. The murderer stating as a motive a wish to be executed or giving no reason for the murder.
2. The murderer having no reason to want to harm the victim. This is most clear when the victim is a child.
3. The murderer giving him- or herself up or doing nothing to hide the murder.
4. The authorities considering it a suicide murder (i.e., sentencing according to decrees against suicide murders).

Not all these characteristics are present in every case, and there are cases where the suicidal element is not beyond doubt. But rather than discussing whether the exact figures are a bit higher or lower, I prefer to accept the approximate nature of my figures in general. Each of the Copenhagen suicide murder cases is briefly described in the Appendix, making it possible to see how the figures are arrived at.

In a study of crime and punishment in Denmark in the first half of the eighteenth century I made a survey of criminal cases in the area that were appealed to the provincial court of Zealand. A predominantly rural area with only small towns, it contained approximately 100,000 inhabitants, including soldiers in the professional cavalry, which numbered around 2,000. The survey covered the thirty-eight years between 1719 and 1756 inclusive. I found seventeen cases in this period that I would characterize as suicide murders in the terms of the above description. Eight of the seventeen perpetrators were soldiers in the cavalry.[1] In relation to the (again approximate) number of inhabitants, this gives an annual frequency of 0.5 per 100,000 inhabitants. Six attempts at suicide murder should be added to the seventeen actual cases.

The number of suicide murders was much higher in Copenhagen. In the mixed and almost complete source material I found evidence of eighty-three suicide murders in the period from 1697 to 1789.[2] With a population of approximately 60,000, this amounts to an annual frequency of 1.5 suicide murders per 100,000 inhabitants.

---

[1] Tyge Krogh, *Oplysningstiden og det magiske*, 2000, p. 229.
[2] See Appendix.

Stockholm

As already mentioned, Arne Jansson studied the development of homicide and suicide in the Swedish capital in the seventeenth and eighteenth centuries,[3] and he worked hard to find all killings dealt with by the legal system. The lower court record series is, however, not complete, and the records of the high court that issued the final sentences have not been preserved. In total during the period 1670–1773 Jansson found 36 cases of what he calls verified suicide murder, 12 probable cases and 9 verified attempts.[4] Stockholm had an average population of approximately 55,000 during the 100-year period. The 36 verified cases thus amount to a frequency of 0.6 (0.8 when the probable cases are included) suicide murders per year per 100,000 inhabitants.

Hamburg

Suicide murders were well known in Hamburg too. Jürgen Martschukat found seven cases from the 1770s and 1780s as well as public discussions about the subject, but he does not go further into considerations of frequency.[5] We have another type of source material, however, which provides an insight into the relative frequency of the murders in the city. Using a number of lists of executions in Hamburg published in the nineteenth century, the criminal historian Richard Wosnik presented a relatively detailed list of executions in the city from 1390 to 1900. Although the list does not appear to be complete before the second half of the eighteenth century, it seems to be fairly accurate from the second half of the seventeenth century on.[6] The information about

[3] Arne Jansson, *From Swords to Sorrow*. See especially p. 14–23, 49–50. A substantial number of the murder cases are described in Jannsson, 'Mörda för att få dö', p. 21–52.

[4] Arne Jansson does not define what is necessary for a case to obtain the classifications of 'verified' or 'probable'. The distinction is somewhat problematic in that 'verified' motives are a questionable label: motivation is always complex. As mentioned above, rather than using such classifications I prefer to emphasize the generally approximate nature of my figures.

[5] Jürgen Martschukat, 'Ein Freitod durch die Hand des Henkers', 2000, p. 53–74, and Jürgen Martchukat, *Inszeniertes Töten: Eine Geschichte der Todesstrafe vom 17. bis zum 19. Jahrhundert*, 2000, p. 88.

[6] Richard Wosnick, *Beiträge zur Hamburgischen Kriminalgeschichte*, vol. 1, 1926, p. 24–51. Wosnick does not identify the sources of the list, but Martschukat mentions an anonymously printed list from 1824 as the main source. Helmuth Gade states that

the individual executions varies, but the type of punishment is always described and the crime committed almost always given. For the period from 1680 to 1800, 215 executions are listed, of which 73 cases (or 34%) were for property-related crimes[7] and 123 (or 57%) for homicide. The remaining 19 executions were either for sexual crimes or for arson or treason, or for an unspecified crime.

In most of the homicide cases the list gives some details about the crime: the sex of the victim, whether it was a child and whether he or she was related to the killer. Sometimes the victim's occupation is also given. In addition, there is usually a brief description of the method of killing. The descriptions, however, are never full enough to make it possible to state with any great certainty whether or not they were suicide murders. Nevertheless, and knowing some of the outer characteristics of the suicide murders, the list contains sufficient information to give a clear indication that suicide murders were a frequent reason for the use of the death penalty: in 69 of the 123 homicide cases the victim was a child. Of these child murders, 8 were cases where a man killed a child from outside his family, 15 were cases where a father killed his own child, 22 were cases where a woman killed a child that was not her own, and 24 were cases where a woman killed her own child. Of the 24 cases of mothers who murdered their children, in only 9 cases does the list give clear information that the child was newborn and that the reason for the murder was to hide pregnancy and birth. In 4 cases the child was explicitly stated to be one year old or more and to have been killed with a knife. The result is, thus, that between 9 and 20 women were executed for infanticide in the usually acknowledged meaning of the term, and between 49 and 60 men and women were executed for other types of child murder where the motive probably contained a suicidal element. With an average population of around 100,000 during the 120 years from 1680 to 1800, this amounts to a frequency of between 0.4 and 0.5 per year per 100,000 inhabitants.[8] The most common method used to kill the children was cutting their throats

the list is not complete before 1750, but does not provide any argument for the statement. See Gade, 'Hamburgische Strafrechtspflege im 18. Jahrhundert', 1956, p. 111.

[7] This figure includes nine executions where the only information is that the person executed was hanged. Hanging, however, was only used as punishment for crimes against property.

[8] The population of Hamburg is estimated as 75,000 in 1711 and 130,000 in 1794. See Heinrich Rodegra, Mary Lindemann and Martin Ewald, 'Kindermord und verheimlichte Schwangerschaft In Hamburg im 18. Jahrhundert', 1978, p. 279.

with a knife. In 34 cases it was mentioned that the child's throats had been cut.

Of the four frequency studies, the two Danish ones are probably the most complete. Jansson argues convincingly that, if the archives had been better preserved, more suicide cases would be found in Stockholm.[9] The figures from Hamburg are the least certain, but as several of the executions are too sparsely described to categorize, my estimate is that the real number of suicide murders is probably higher than mentioned above. It is, thus, a conservative estimate that the four areas had suicide murder frequencies of between 0.4 and 1.5 per year per 100,000 inhabitants. These are indeed high frequencies and enough to state that the suicide murders constituted one of the dominant criminal problems in the areas described. The frequencies can be compared with the murder frequency in present-day Europe, which amounts to an annual figure of approximately 1 per 100,000 inhabitants. Suicide murders also played a prominent role in the execution scenario of the areas mentioned. In Zealand the death penalties imposed for suicide murders amounted to 17% of all such sentences. In Hamburg the death penalties for child murders amounted to between 23% and 28% of all death sentences.

The frequency studies can be supplemented by normative and literary sources from other areas. In a study of suicide the German historian Vera Lind found 23 suicide murders in Schleswig-Holstein.[10] Her account does not provide any other information about the years in which the murders were committed except that they occurred during her research period, 1600–1820. In addition to these 23 cases, my own research on military cases between 1728 and 1789 has revealed a further 14 suicide murders in Schleswig-Holstein.[11] In Danzig a comment from 1696 referred to by the legal historian Albrecht Meye mentioned as a general problem that some people falsely claiming depression

[9] Jansson, *From Swords to Sorrow*, p. 49.

[10] Lind, *Selbstmord in der frühen Neuzeit*.

[11] Tyge Krogh, *Oplysningstiden og det magiske: Henrettelser og korporlige straffe i 1700-tallets første halvdel*, 2000, Appendix B, describes 9 cases. To these should be added: Eva Maria Heringklee, Rendsburg (NA, Generalauditøren (Landetaten), Justitsprotokol kgl. res. 25.2.1761), Asmus Hinrich Junge, Flensburg (NA, Generalauditøren (Landetaten), Originale relationer til kongen3.6.1761), Peter Tollensen, Gluckstadt (same 18.11.1761), Henrich Eckmeyer, Rendsburg (NA, Generalauditøren (Landetaten), Justitsprotokol kgl. res. 9.11.1775) and Hans Hinrich Schmidt, Rendsburg (same kgl. res. 5.9.1776).

murdered their neighbour so that the authorities would be forced to execute them.[12]

In the middle of the eighteenth century the murders caught the attention of the legal scholars.[13] In this debate the murders were referred to as *Mord aus Lebensüberdruss*: murder because of 'tedium vitae' or depression. In 1738 the professor of law at Helmstedt, Augustin von Leyser, wrote about the murders and stated that he had heard of more than 20 cases in his capacity as legal expert in the principality of Braunschweig-Wolfenbüttel. In 1757 the Thuringian jurist J. Caspar Heimburg published a dissertation on murders committed out of depression or melancholy in which he also cited several such cases. In 1774 and 1778 the well-known legal author and Leipzig professor Karl Ferdinand Hommel spoke of these murders as a great problem in Saxony. I have found evidence of 20 suicide murder cases in Prussia: the 7 from 1717 to 1744[14] and 13 from the 1770s and 1780s (see p. 160).

Suicide Murders Over Time

The frequency studies also reveal something about the development of the suicide murders over time. It appears that the phenomenon of the suicide murder peaked during the eighteenth century. The early development of suicide murders in Copenhagen and Zealand has not been investigated in detail, although two child murders in Copenhagen in 1644 and 1654 indicate the possible early presence of murders with suicide motives in Copenhagen as well. But information about these murders is very limited. In the sixteen years from 1681 to 1696 no such murders were presented to the Copenhagen municipal court.[15]

[12] Albrecht Meye, *Das Strafrecht der Stadt Danzigs von der Carolina bis zur Vereinigung Danzigs mit der preußischen Monarchie (1532–1793)*, 1935, p. 80.

[13] The legal historian Helmuth von Weber has presented the debate in 'Selbstmord als Mordmotiv', p. 161–81.

[14] Friedrich August Herzog, *Sammlung auserlesener responsorum juris criminalis welche von dem berühmtesten juristisch- und medicinischen Facultäten*, case no. 3, p. 15–26 (Magdeburg 1736); case no. 27, p. 149–56 (Magdeburg 1737), case no. 133, p. 528–37 (Magdeburg 1736), case no. 34, p. 178–81 (Magdeburg 1724) and case no. 38, p. 188–9 (legal opinion from the Law Faculty of Frankfurt an der Oder, 1718). Johann Jakob Moser, *Seelige letzte Stunden*, 1753: Catharina Elisabeth Uhlin, Halle, 1736 (p. 161–89), and Gertrud Magdalena Bremmelin, Wernigerode, 1744 (p. 269–326).

[15] Information about the cases up to 1697 derives from the annual accounts of the municipal court of Copenhagen. Information about the cases is thus limited.

On 11 August 1697, however, after a quarrel with her mistress, the housemaid Sidzel Chatarina Siversdatter cut the throat of the three-year-old child in the house while the parents were at church. She gave herself up and confessed to having committed the crime in order to hurt the parents and because she would die for it.[16] After Sidzel's crime, suicide murders became a feature of life in Copenhagen. Another murder occurred in 1699, then one in 1706 and another in 1707. Over the next eighty years the numbers of cases in Copenhagen were as follows:

Table 1. Suicide murders in Copenhagen, 1697–1789[17]

	Murders	Attempted murders	Invented murders
1697–1699	2		
1700–1709	2		
1710–1719	7	5	
1720–1729	9	4	4
1730–1739	14	10	5
1740–1749	10	4	1
1750–1759	15	5	
1760–1769	16	7	3
1770–1779	6	6	1
1780–1789	2	5	1
Total	*83*	*46*	*15*

'Invented murders' were cases where a person claimed to have murdered somebody in order to be executed and was accordingly arrested and taken to court, but where the court subsequently found that no murder had taken place.

In Copenhagen the suicide murders were thus an eighteenth-century phenomenon that peaked after 1730. This pattern is somewhat

The accounts from 1624–63 have been analysed in V.A. Secher, 'Bidrag til Københavns rets- og kulturhistorie, 1624–63', 1907–08. I have searched for suicide murders in the annual accounts, 1681–1789.

[16] Case no. 1697:1. Besides the early murders in Copenhagen I know of a suicide murder committed in Elsinore in 1696; see Krogh 2000, p. 228.

[17] See Appendix.

different from development in Stockholm and Hamburg, where such murders became frequent in the last decades of the seventeenth century.

According to Jansson, a probable suicide murder occurred in Stockholm in 1621, an attempted one took place in 1644 and there was one murder in 1651, in 1667 and in 1668. Then there were 3 in the 1670s, 4–5 in the 1680s, 5 murders and 3 attempts in the 1690s, 6–11 murders and 2 attempts in the first decade of the eighteenth century, and 9–10 murders and 3 attempts in the 1710s. The uncertainty about the exact number of murders stems from Jansson's distinction between 'verified' and 'probable' suicide cases. The source material is very incomplete after 1720. Jansson found only 9–14 suicide murders and one attempt between 1720 and 1773.

The execution list from Hamburg between 1600 and 1659 includes four child murders that could equally be simple cases of infanticide and one case of definite child murder. The latter was a case from 1639 where a man had killed his seven-year-old brother-in-law. There were 5 cases of child murder in 1660–80, and from 1680 to 1779 between 5 and 7 murders were committed each decade, with the exception of 1690–1699, when 10 murders took place, and 1750–1759, when there were 2.

In spite of the differences, the surveys indicate that this type of murder originated in the seventeenth century and flourished in the hundred years from 1680 to 1780.

There is evidence of suicide murders in many parts of northern Germany and Scandinavia, but my own research and historical studies have only been able to measure the frequency for Zealand and Copenhagen in Denmark, Stockholm in Sweden and Hamburg in Germany. In these four areas, however, the figures substantiate the claim that suicide murders constituted one of the dominant criminal problems in the period between 1680 and 1780. In the Zealand survey 17 were executed for suicide murders, whereas 15 were executed for infanticide.[18] It should be noted that the number of unsolved infanticide cases, especially in the larger cities, was high. In Hamburg three times as many people were executed in probable suicide murder cases as in infanticide cases. I do not have the number of infanticide cases

[18] Krogh, *Oplysningstiden og det magiske*, p. 218.

from Copenhagen, but it is my impression that the number of executions for infanticide in proportion to executions for suicide murder is very similar to Hamburg. In terms of the use of the death penalty, the suicide murders thus appeared to be a larger criminal problem than infanticide.

CHAPTER THREE

THE MURDERERS' SOCIAL SITUATION AND MENTAL STATE

My in-depth study of the suicide murders in Copenhagen also allows for a social description of the perpetrators. The figures given in the following description also include the attempted murders.

Most of the murderers were women, and the great majority of them were housemaids working for the families of minor craftsmen and shopkeepers. A few were housewives who murdered their own children.

The Copenhagen Spin-house and other houses of correction were the scenes of no fewer than 19 suicide murders and 13 attempted murders. Some of the inmates in the Spin-house who committed murders had been imprisoned for crimes of immorality and may therefore have earned their living as prostitutes, but many of the female inmates who committed suicide murders came from positions as housemaids in the city.

A last major group comprised soldiers, who were responsible for 17 suicide murders and 17 attempted murders. The great majority of these chose to murder fellow soldiers or used their professional skills combined with their easy access to deadly weapons to kill strangers in the street. Only 8 soldiers chose to murder children. The 10 murders and 5 attempted murders committed by navy personnel are included in the civilian murders, as almost all were perpetrated against children and because the sailors were tried according to civilian law.

Three-quarters of the victims were children under the age of ten. Seventeen of the children were killed by their own mothers and nine by their fathers. The great majority of the murdered children were killed by having their throats cut, but another popular method was to throw the child into one of the canals that run through the city.

The material from Hamburg and Jansson's description from Stockholm give the impression of a rather similar gender composition and social distribution of the suicide murderers, with the exception of one group: there seem to have been more soldiers who committed suicide murders in Copenhagen than in the two other cities. This difference could be due to the source material, but it is also possible that the size of the armies—as well as different attitudes to the soldiers in the armies of Sweden, Hamburg and Denmark—played a role.

Table 2. Suicide murders and murder attempts in Copenhagen, 1697–1789, related to sex, categories of perpetrators and types of victim[1]

	Female perpetrator	Male perpetrator	Total
1 Own child by inmates	1		1
2 Own child by others	16	10	26
3 Unrelated child by inmates	25	6	31
4 Unrelated child by others	23	13	36
5 Child by housemaids taking care of them	3		3
6 Soldiers by soldiers		14	14
7 Adult civilians by soldiers		13	13
8 Adult civilians by others	1	4	5
Total	69	60	129

The primary source for the motives of the suicide murderers is the court records. These were written by the municipal court scribe and took the form of questions asked by the appointed prosecutor and the answers given by the prisoner. Furthermore, the counsel for the defence sometimes asked supplementary questions, and witnesses could be questioned as well. The court hearings were mostly short, as these cases were simple from a juridical point of view. Sometimes, however, a plea of insanity—usually put forward by the defending lawyer on his own initiative and not at the request of his client—could lead to further interrogation and examination.

The prosecutor's questions always followed the same pattern. First, the prisoner was asked for his or her name, parents, place of birth, age, occupation, where he or she worked, and when he or she had last taken Holy Communion. Then the prisoner was asked how the murder had

[1] See Appendix.

taken place, in order to establish both a confession to the crime and proof that the prisoner was actually the perpetrator. These questions were supplemented by the coroner's report. Lastly, the prisoner was asked why he or she had committed the murder.

The answer to this last question was highly dependent on the eloquence of the murderer. Sometimes, without any prompting, he or she told a long story about the events leading up to the murder. In other cases the murderer was very quiet. Sometimes the prosecutor found the explanation given so incomprehensible that he asked supplementary questions. But for the most part he showed little interest in understanding the reasons for the murder. The defence usually explored the possibility of making a plea of insanity and therefore could ask the murderer as well as witnesses about the mental state of the murderer just before the deed was committed.

Many of the murderers only gave the courts very general reasons for their crime. The formulations are often very similar from case to case, suggesting that the courts and the perpetrators were using similar terminology that both parties found adequate for explaining the motives and the states of mind leading to the murder in question: he or she 'had been confused in the head', or had become 'desperate'. In this state of mind he or she had done the evil deed 'in order to take their leave of life'. In the 1730s the expression that the circumstances described had made them decide 'to do a mischief' became common.[2]

An element of revenge on a third party can be seen in a few cases. For example, the above-mentioned Sidzel wanted to hurt the parents by killing their daughter. The Spin-house inmate Anne Marie Nielsdatter cut the throat of a six-year-old girl because she was the daughter of a woman who had informed against her two years earlier.[3] Anne Marie, however, hurried to announce the murder in the work hall of the Spin-house, thus ensuring that she was given the death penalty.

The murderers would most frequently give some social reason for their crimes. These reasons were closely related to the conditions of the three most prevalent groups.

---

[2] Had been confused in the head': *havde været fortumlet I hovedet*; 'desperate': *desperat*; 'in order to take their leave of life': *for selv at komme af med livet*. 'to do a mischief': *at gøre en ulykke*.

[3] Appendix, case 1737:1.

Housemaids

Housemaids in Copenhagen constituted a large proportion of the population,[4] and almost every households had one or more maids. It was a common occupation for a woman in early modern times to be employed as a housemaid from the age of fourteen or fifteen until she got married—if she did ever marry. Many girls came from other parts of the country to seek employment in the capital, attracted by the adventure and the many jobs available in a large city.

Some of the suicide murder cases tell the story of young women being beaten or feeling unjustly treated by her master and mistress and having nowhere to go when the treatment became unbearable. For instance, Sidzel Sivertsdatter, who started the Copenhagen suicide murder wave, told the court that she had come from Sweden on her own a year and a half before the murder.[5] She had worked as a housemaid at two places. She had been happy enough at the second place until the last month, when the mistress and eventually also the master and the older child had started accusing her of stealing and of having had a child. This last accusation could imply that Sidzel was supposed to have given birth in secret and done away with the baby. A week before the murder, the mistress had inquired about Sidzel at her former employer's and had arrived home and said that Sidzel was said to have been stealing there too. The fatal Sunday, just before the parents went to church, the mistress had accused her of stealing two steelyards. After the master and mistress had left the house to attend the church service, Sidzel had found the steelyards, which had simply not been hung up in their right place. The accusations were defamatory and ruinous for Sidzel's future career in the city. This had made her come up with the evil idea that, rather than having to hear such unjust accusations for the rest of her life, she would prefer to die.

Another issue that was extremely important for a young housemaid was marriage. Marriage not only presented the possibility of experiencing love, or at least of having a bearable partner for the rest of one's life; it was also virtually the only possible career path for a

[4] In the census of 1787, 9% of the population of Copenhagen were listed as unmarried housemaids. I would like to thank my colleague Hans Jørgen Marker, Director of the Swedish National Data Service, for this information. Hans Jørgen Marker is working on a statistical analysis of the early Danish censuses.

[5] Appendix, case 1697:1.

woman. In the big city there were also good opportunities for social advancement through marriage. But there were many pitfalls in the game of love and career, not the least of which was the numerous private soldiers garrisoned in the city. They were impressive in their colourful uniforms, but they were badly paid and needed the permission of usually reluctant commanding officers before they could marry.[6] As the soldiers were mercenaries who usually enlisted for periods of eight years, a promise of marriage, if unaccompanied by the consent of the commanding officer, might not be fulfilled for a long time. The number of illegitimate children baptized at the garrison church exceeded the number of those baptized in all the other parishes of the city put together.[7] If the young woman became pregnant and the father of the child would not marry her after all, the shame of having had an illegitimate child awaited her, with public confession of the sin in the church and fines from the authorities combined with a drastic decline in prospects for social advancement.

Such was the sad story of Cicilia Johansdatter.[8] She had worked as a maid at a tapster's and had fallen in love with a royal horse guardsman. Having been promised marriage, she had become pregnant. Her fiancé's commanding officer, however, had denied him the permit (*friseddel*) necessary for him to marry. Cicilia stopped working at the tapster's and went to live with her parents when she gave birth. The child was baptized in the father's church, the garrison church, and named Friedrich Christian, after its father. A few weeks after the birth, however, the father of the child started acting coldly towards her, and he stopped visiting Cicilia at her parents'. Thus, facing a dishonoured life as a single mother, she chose to kill her child.

Anne Knudsdatter had come to the capital from Jutland to work as a housemaid.[9] She was now seventeen years old and had been engaged to a musketeer for two years. Asked why she had killed a five-year-old girl whom she did not know, she explained that the musketeer had made her leave her place, promising marriage. They both went to his commanding officer, but he had refused to issue the necessary permit and

[6] The prohibition was mentioned in the Danish martial law (*krigsartikelbrev*) of 9 March 1683 and repeated several times in the eighteenth century. See Niels Finn Olsen, 'Chr. V.s krigsartikelbrev af 9. marts 1683', 1982, p. 38–9.

[7] See RA, *Reviderede regnskaber, byfogedregnskaber* ('Annual accounts of the city judge'). Fines imposed for extra-marital sex were listed here.

[8] Appendix, case 1744:1.

[9] Appendix, case 1736:2.

had shown her the door. Something apparently happened between her and the musketeer afterwards. Two days later the musketeer had stripped her of a fine cloak belonging to her, and after this she told the court that she went out of her mind and had decided to kill the next child she met. Anna's detailed explanation was incoherent in parts. It seems as though the prosecution and the defence simply allowed her to tell her story and left it to the court scribe to make sense of it as best he could.

Prisoners

Imprisonment was slowly replacing public corporal punishment in the eighteenth century.[10] The sentence of imprisonment with hard labour entered the Danish–Norwegian criminal code just before 1700 as a punishment for theft, but only as a supplement to the main punishment of being publicly whipped and branded. The public punishments humiliated and debased the convicts to such an extent that they were unable to make a living afterwards and thus were forced to continue their criminal behaviour. For this reason the penalty of lifelong hard labour was added. If they were branded, the convicts had no chance of a royal pardon. In the army the less humiliating punishment of running the gauntlet was often supplemented by hard labour for life or for a fixed period. In the civil courts the punishment of hard labour without whipping and branding gradually became more common. Although the number of prisoners was growing, they remained a small proportion of the population of Copenhagen, numbering less than 1,000 in the eighteenth century.

The male convicts were imprisoned at the navy shipyard, Bremerholm, and were later hired out to citizens as so-called 'slaves', to do hard work under army supervision. The female convicts were placed in the Spin-house. In addition to the female convicts, the Spin-house was populated by a mixture of poor and neglected children, beggars caught in the streets and unruly young people sentenced to a period in a house of correction. This mixture of inmates spun and weaved. From the 1720s a small number of male convicts were placed in the Spin-house. They performed the hard and unhealthy task of rasping wood; the

[10] Krogh, *Oplysningstiden og det magiske*, p. 252–67.

resulting dust was used to make colours for dyeing. Beggars with a naval background were placed in the naval infirmary, the Kvæsthus.

Suicide murders were found in all the prisons, but they were most numerous in the Spin-house. The inmates committing suicide murder almost always gave their incarceration, the hard work and the hopeless prospects as explanations for their deeds.

Thus Anna Lovise Pedersdatter, who had been arrested for theft in 1738, was whipped, branded on the forehead and imprisoned in the Spin-house for life.[11] Ten years later she chose to cut the throat of another woman's thirty-week-old baby. After the murder, she went to the work hall, clapped her hands and announced: 'Now I am a free man' (she did not describe herself as a 'woman'). In 1757 three suicide murders took place in the Spin-house within the space of three weeks. As the alleged causes again were hard work, beating and too little food, the defence questioned the actions of the master and of work-mates. The accusations, however, were rejected, and the defence did not get the mitigation of punishment that had been proposed.[12]

The life prisoners were not the only inmates who committed murder. In 1727 eighteen-year-old Anne Margrethe Andersdatter cut the throat of a child and almost killed it. She had one year left of a ten-year sentence of imprisonment for theft. In 1757 seventeen-year-old Marie Johansdatter cut the throat of a three-year-old boy and killed him. She was—at the request of her parents—sentenced to a one-year correction sentence in the Spin-house. But she could not stand the restraint, the beatings and the subsistence allowance, which was in proportion to the daily workload.[13]

Soldiers

Nearly five thousand soldiers were stationed in Copenhagen. The stories of the soldiers committing suicide murders reveal much about the constraints and the tough life in the professional army. Mercenaries in the European armies were poorly paid, and they typically enlisted for eight years at a time. Petty theft and desertions were frequent and were met with harsh corporal punishments, the worst being running the

[11] Appendix, case 1748:1.
[12] Appendix, cases 1757:1, 1757:2 and 1757:3.
[13] Appendix, case 1726:a and 1757:1.

gauntlet for several days. Corporal punishment could be combined with some months or even years of hard labour. A depressing downward spiral followed for many mercenaries. They might desert for fear of the punishment they knew awaited them for petty offences such as selling their army linen. The penalty for desertion, however, was simply harsher physical punishment. Some of these soldiers, when arrested or just before being arrested, chose to kill a comrade or a random passer-by in order to receive the death penalty rather than harsh corporal punishment.

In 1728 the musketeer Philip Schmidt had sold some of his equipment and was waiting in gaol for his punishment, which was to run the gauntlet sixteen times. This involved him walking with his back naked between two rows of soldiers each containing 150 men. Each soldier would give him one blow with a freshly cut wooden stick every time he passed. For safety reasons, the punishment was divided over two days. Thus, over two days Philip Schmidt was to receive 4,800 blows with wooden sticks on his naked back. He feared running the gauntlet to such an extent that for this reason alone he knifed a fellow prisoner in the stomach and killed him.[14] In 1739, in Copenhagen, the musketeer Hinrich Puffvogel had sold some of his equipment and had been accused of stealing a pair of stockings. Facing a stern punishment and then further provoked, he fetched his rifle in order to shoot his sergeant. He could not find him, however, and after a couple of hours he chose to shoot the first person that came along. He followed a sailor who was walking in the street and shot him in the back.[15]

When comparing these social motives for committing suicide murder with the motives for committing suicide presented in studies of suicide in the eighteenth century, many similarities can be seen.[16] Poverty, loss of social honour and romantic problems are pointed out as frequent motives for suicide, just as they are frequent among the people committing suicide murders. It seems, however, that the use of murder as a vehicle for losing your life was almost exclusively a lower-class phenomenon, whereas suicides were found in every strata of society. The high frequency of prisoners and soldiers among

[14] Appendix, case 1728:1.

[15] Appendix, case 1739:2.

[16] Michael MacDonald and Terence R. Murphy, *Sleepless Souls: Suicide in Early Modern England*, 1990, p. 259–300, and Lind, *Selbstmord in der frühen Neuzeit*, p. 219–72.

the suicide murderers is not found in the studies of suicide, but this difference could be a result of the source material used in the studies of suicide.

The Psychological State of the Murderers

The social explanations for the perpetrators' deeds were usually, as mentioned above, combined with a psychological explanation. The only possible defence in these cases was to enter a plea of some sort of mental illness, and so the lawyers appointed to defend the murderers always examined the mental constitution of their clients.

Temporary insanity was pleaded in some cases. Relatives, and more rarely doctors, would testify that the murderers had had epileptic seizures in which they became momentarily insane. Some of the murderers stated that they had been delirious when committing the murder, or that they had had hallucinations that took control of their minds. It is difficult to assess the truth behind these explanations. The courts seldom recognized such pleas of insanity. In only two cases were the murderers judged insane and sentenced to be taken into custody by the authorities, and in both these cases the murderers were already patients at the city's mental hospital.[17]

In several cases relatives testified, or the murderers told the court, that they had been in low spirits or depressed for some time. A few women who killed their infant children said that they had been depressed or not behaving normally. They may well have suffered from what today would be called post-natal depression.[18] Such cases of depression were usually attributed to social circumstances. The reasons given could be poverty, the shame of being a 'fallen woman' with an illegitimate child, or lack of prospects in other ways. Depression was often invoked by the defence as a mitigating circumstance, but it was not until the 1760s that the authorities allowed a plea of depression to influence the verdict.[19]

---

[17] In 1721 Marie Andersdatter killed her own child in the mental hospital at Pesthuset. She had been insane for several years (Byfogedregnskab 1721, bilag 46). In 1764 Mette Friedrich Petersen killed a child who was not her own in Pesthuset with a knife (Byfogedregnskab 1764, bilag 103). I have not incorporated these insanity cases in the statistics concerning suicide murders.

[18] Appendix, case 1710:1 and 1733:1.

[19] Appendix, case 1766:1 and 1772:1.

A third mental state invoked by the murderers and their defence counsels was sudden desperation; some event or chain of events had caused their world to collapse and made them desperate and out of their mind.

The claims about the mental state of the murderers are sparse and inconclusive, but they may indicate that some of the murderers were people who today would be considered mentally ill. In other words, it could be argued that the murders were the result of an inadequate understanding of mental illness in the eighteenth century. I shall return to the question of mental illness in the description of the termination of the suicide murders (p. 166), and merely point out here that the judgement of these murders from the nineteenth century on would tend to make the incomprehensibility and illogicality of the crime part of the evidence for the perpetrators having been mentally ill. In the eighteenth century, however, the murders had a rationality that was based on religious understandings surrounding contemporary penal practice.

CHAPTER FOUR

RELIGIOUS MOTIVES

Alongside the social and psychological framework or discourse presented in the courts, a parallel religious account of the murders flourished among the perpetrators and the spectators at the executions. This discourse inscribed the murders in the grand narrative of the temptations of the Devil and the sinner who finally repents, atones and is saved.

Court Records

The lawyers accusing, defending and judging were not particularly interested in the perpetrators' possible religious motives for committing the murders. Such motives did not affect the charge and could not be used to plead mitigation of sentence. If the court records were our only source, it would be difficult to maintain a dominant religious motivation. Sometimes, however, religious motivations were the only explanations given to the court. In 1736 the tailor Ludvig Jørgen Petersen cut the throat of an eight-year-old girl whom he did not know and gave as his reason the fact that he had doubted God's providence and mercy and his own salvation because he was such a gross sinner.[1]

Margrethe Christensdatter, who, just before Christmas 1741, threw an eight-year-old child into a canal, gave as a reason for her action the fact that she had had a dream that she would do it. After the dream she had left her place of work and for two weeks walked around thinking about committing such an offence. She had taken Communion eight days before she left her place of work, and the defence asked her if, having such temptations, she had not "kept to the word of God",[2] but Margrethe answered that she felt so troubled in her mind that she had not been able to read the word of God. After committing the crime she became very anxious and upset but had not told anybody. She became more troubled day by day, and when she was in church the following

[1] Appendix, case 1736:4

[2] Appendix, case 1742:1. "holdet sig til Guds Ord"

Sunday and heard that the child was being searched for, she finally went to the city gaol and gave herself up. After doing so, she felt very relieved.

The most common religious explanation, however, was to blame the Devil. When asked why he had committed his atrocious crime, the former royal life guardsman Hans Hansen, who in 1736 strangled his own eighteen-month-old child, would only say that he had done it 'at the instigation of Satan'.[3] And seventeen-year-old Kirstine Schiønsted, who in 1749 killed her master's three-year-old son, stated that her sole reason was that 'the Devil had blinded her as she was [only] a young person'.[4]

The choice of a child as victim was not commented on very often, but when, in 1745, musketeer Martin Friedrich Vogel chose to shoot a nine-year-old boy in the street, he said that he had done so because the child had sinned so little, thus implying that he thought the child's soul would rise to heaven, even though the child had not repented of its sins and received absolution before death. The boy's soul would be saved, while only temporal damage would be inflicted on his body. The perpetrator sometimes argued that for some reason the child was expendable. In 1736, when Ludvig Jørgen Petersen chose to cut the throat of an eight-year-old girl, he first asked her if she had a father and a mother, and when she answered 'no' to this question, he killed her.[5] Some of the murderers explained that they had done everything possible to give the child a quick death. Anne Knudsdatter told the court that when she had cut the throat of a five-year-old boy and he did not die immediately, she had wrung his neck in order to put him out of his misery.

When the murderers stated that they had considered committing suicide before their deed, they described the suicide as a temptation (by the Devil) that they had luckily overcome, thereby implying that murder was a better solution.[6]

Public Opinion: Ballads about Executions

These short and randomly registered accounts found in the court records of the perpetrators being religiously motivated to commit the

[3] Appendix, case 1736:1
[4] Appendix, case 1749:1
[5] Appendix, case 1736:4.
[6] Appendix, case 1767:4.

murders can be supplemented, however. Street ballads provide an interesting source material to illustrate how the murders were perceived by ordinary people. It was common practice for ballads to be printed and sold in the streets whenever there were outrageous crimes or an execution. Forty-two ballads have been preserved about criminals and their executions printed in Copenhagen between 1700 and 1789.

The ballads partly mirrored the appearance of a news-sheet announcing an execution. The front page usually described the crime, the punishment and the date and place that it was carried out. The facts of the crimes and the sentences described in the ballads are almost always consistent with my findings in the court records. One exception was a ballad printed in Copenhagen in 1721, telling the incredible story of a woman from Elsinore who had given birth to one child a year for six years and had secretly killed all of them. This led to an investigation by the police, and as the story was found to be untrue, the police tried to find the author of the fictitious ballad. The publisher stated that the author was a student at the university, and the Copenhagen chief of police asked the Academic Council to punish him. In their reply the Academic Council wrote that they would prefer that such 'useless' ballads were not printed at all, but that at least they should be censored by the university.[7] Apart from showing that falsehood in print was taken seriously by the authorities, the case reveals that the statutory censorship of printed material did not cover ballads. The authorities did not approve of the ballads, but they were tolerated as long as they were considered harmless.

A smaller number of the ballads dealing with cases of theft, murder with intention to rob and treason focused on the crimes, their detection and punishment, and were often related in a harsh tone that condemned the malefactors. The majority of the ballads, however, were written about homicides. Five ballads told about killings during a fight, two about killings within the family, two about infanticides and no fewer than eighteen of the forty-two ballads recounted suicide murders.

The ballads about homicides were composed to tunes from burial hymns and usually took the form of a first-person narrative. The social

---

[7] The ballad 'Et ynckelig og uhørlig, et forfærdelig og gruelig Mord er udi Helsingør forøvet af et Qvindfolck', 1721 (Royal Library of Copenhagen). The correspondence RA, Copenhagen University, Konsistorium, kopibog, 1712–27, p. 407–09.

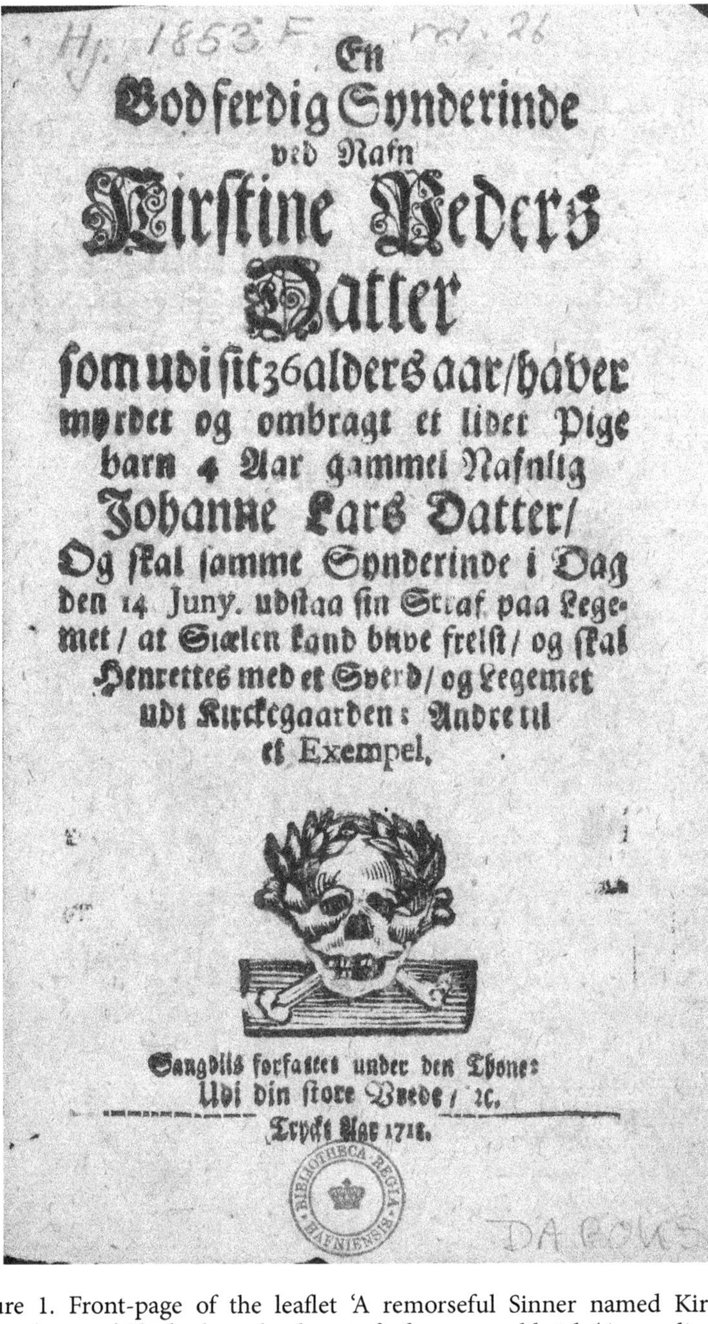

En
Bodferdig Synderinde
ved Nafn
Kirstine Peders
Datter
som udi sit 36 alders aar/ haver
myrdet og ombragt et lidet Pige
barn 4 Aar gammel Nafnlig
Johanne Lars Datter/
Og skal samme Synderinde i Dag
den 14 Juny. udstaa sin Straf paa Lege-
met/ at Siælen kand blive frelst/ og skal
Henrettes med et Sverd/ og Legemet
udi Kirckegaarden: Andre til
et Exempel.

Sangviis forfattet under den Thone:
Udi din store Vrede/ 2c.

Tryckt Aar 1718.

Figure 1. Front-page of the leaflet 'A remorseful Sinner named Kirstine Pedersdatter …'. She had cut the throat of a four-year-old girl. (Appendix, case 1718:1, The Royal Library, Copenhagen)

reason for the murder, which was the dominant theme of the court records, was not important in the ballads. There what mattered most was the criminals' emotional state, their confessions and last words. The murder and execution were inscribed into the grand narrative of the Lutheran faith. Man is tempted by the Devil and sins, but through the intervention of God he repents, atones and is finally saved.

The first part of this grand narrative described the murder as the work of the Devil. An example can be found in the ballad from 1713 about Anna Chatrine Berntsdatter, who wanted to commit suicide but ended up killing her own mother:

> 2.
> In my best age
> I fall into sin
> And make room for Satan
> And do not notice his intention
> Was to throw me
> Into the abyss of Hell.
>
> 3.
> I poor sinner
> Conceived evil on my mind
> Helped by the Devil.
> Soon he put into my thoughts
> That I should go
> And drown myself in water.
>
> 4.
> But God out of pure mercy
> Saved me from that misfortune
> So that unharmed I came home.
> Immediately ready, however,
> Was Satan to hurt me again
> With evil arrows.
>
> 5.
> My own mother I murdered
> Accomplished by my hand
> An unheard-of thing.
> For this I now must mourn
> And be removed from this life
> For such an evil deed.[8]

---

[8] Appendix, case 1713:1. '2: Udi min beste Alder/I Synden jeg henfalder/Og gifver Sathan Rum/ Og mercker ey hans Miine/ Var, at hand mig vild' trine/ I Helvedes Afgrund. 3: Jeg arme Synderinde/ fick Ondskab udi Sinde/ Den Djævel hjalp dertil/

In a ballad from 1751 about Ingeborg Svend Gunnersens, an inmate in the Copenhagen Spin-house who had murdered an eight-year-old girl, the murder is explained by the accumulation of sins from youth:

> 4.
> If in youth we do not think
> Of our beloved Creator
> We easily fall into the chains of Satan,
> And are daily riveted still more.
> By ingrained habit our sinful condition
> Can almost be turned into our nature. …
>
> 7.
> Soon Satan comes and tempts
> Such person with despair,
> Making his catalogue of sins
> Even more gross
> And adds that the door of grace
> Is not open as before. …
>
> 9.
> In mind and heart he soon
> Suggests terrible thoughts,
> Until the sinner obeys his command,
> And falls into the bad thought
> To end his sadness
> In whatever way possible.[9]

These explanations did not depict the perpetrators as dangerous wrongdoers. On the contrary, the ordinary origins of the crimes were stressed. We all have our weak moments when the temptations of Satan are hard to resist, and we all commit the minor sins that can lead to major ones.

After the murder instigated by Satan came repentance. God would not abandon the sinner, and through the Holy Spirit he inspired the sinner to reject Satan and turn to Him:

Snart gaf hand mig i Tancke/ At jeg skulde hengange/ I Vand at druckne mig. 4. Men Gud af idel Naade/ Mig frelste fra den Vaade/ Saa jeg gick uskad hjem/ Strax var igien til rede/ Sathan med Piiler lede/ At saare mig igien. 5: Min egen moder myrdte/ Jeg, og med Haand fuldbyrdte/ Som ey er hørtis før/ Hvorfor jeg nu må klage!/ Og tagis ud af Dage/ For slig en Gierning led.'

[9] Appendix, case 1751:1. '4: Om vi I Ungdom ikke tænker/ Paa vores kiære Skabere/ Let falder vi i Satans Lænker/ Og fængsles daglig haardere./ Lang Vane vores Syndestand/ Fast til Natur forandre kan. 7: Strax Satan kommer til og frister/ En saadan ved Fortvivelse/ I det han ham hans Syndsregister/ End forestiller grover/ Og derhos siger Naadens Dør/ Er ikke aabne nu som før. 9: I Sind og Hierte strax han skyder/ Forfærdelige Tanker ind/ Til Synderen hans Bud adlyder/ Og falder paa det daarlig Sind/ At ende sin Bedrøvelse/ Hvorledes saadant end kan skee.'

8.
Satan indeed relied on
Having won the game
When he got me locked
In such gross vice.
But his bonds did burst.

9.
When God I did not seek
He instead sought to get me out.
For his Almighty Hand
Loosened my bonds
And strengthened me through his Spirit.

10.
This Spirit comforts me so much
That I hardly think
Of all my scorned abjection
Because it will certainly happen
That soon God I shall see.[10]

After repentance came rebirth and the firm belief that for the sake of His wounds Jesus would forgive the repentant and believing sinner and let his or her soul rise to Heaven. This theme was often played out in the ballads' description of the convict's journey to the place of execution, the scene there and the convict's farewell to parents, brothers and sisters. Finally, the ballads would often solemnly describe the happy life in Heaven:

13.
Where my soul can rest
When it goes from me
Through the executioner's sharp stroke
When the heart gets weak
And the neck is stretched
Oh God, open up your door.

14.
So that at the throne of the lamb
With palms and with crown
And dressed all in white

[10] Anon, 'Tvende meget sørgefulde Viiser hvori en ynkværdig Synderinde … Charlotta Claudi, som for begangen Mord', 1744. '8: Satan vel forlod sig til/ At han havde vundet Spil/ Da han fik mig fast/ I saa grov en Last/ Men hans Baand I sønder brast. 9: Da jeg ikke søgte GUD/ Søgte han at faae mig ud/ Thi hans Almagtshaand/ Løsned mine Baand/ Og mig styrked med sin Aand. 10: Denne Aand mig trøster saa/ At jeg tænker neppe paa/ Ald min Spot og Spee/ Thi det vist skal skee/ At jeg snart faar GUD at see.'

I can sing to you, oh Lord,
Laud, praise, honour and glory
And eternally stand in front of you.[11]

The ballads were printed to be sold and must therefore be assumed to reflect the fascination of the public that bought them. It seems, therefore, that what captivated the general public was not the alien nature of an evil being but rather the buyers' own similarity to the murderer and the salvation of the murderer's soul. The faithful feared their inner demons and craved certain salvation. The murderer happily confronting her own death mirrored the spectators' own hopes for a happy death and salvation of their souls.

Some of the printed ballads contained claims on the front page that they were printed at the request of the murderer. A few even stated that they were composed by the murderer him- or herself. These may, of course, have been advertising gimmicks, but looking at the content of the ballads it seems quite probable that the murderers welcomed them. They expressed the murderer's feelings and hope of salvation and thereby helped to make the crowd sympathetic.

In one printed version the ballad was even used to expose the person that the murderer blamed for her misery. Cicilia Johansdatter (see p. 28 above) had killed her own infant child because the father had left her. Two publications appeared at the time of the execution. The first resembled most of the other ballads about executions. The second, however, comprised four 'arias' and was entitled 'A Remorseful Sinner's Swan-Song or Farewell Speech'. At the bottom of the front page it said, 'Printed at the request of the sinner'. The second of the 'arias' dealt with Cicilia's lover:

4. You may have charmed me,
When I was alive
– Help me O Jesus Christ
Through my last short time –
You have forced me
To do that deed
– I shall be buried
But God will hear me.

---

[11] Appendix, case 1713:1. '13: Hvor Siælen min kand hvile/ Naar den fra mig vil iile/ Ved Bødlens skarpe Hug./ Naar Hiertet monne svæckis/ Og Hovedet udstræckis/ Og Gud! din Dør opluk. 14: At jeg for Lammets Trone/ Med Palmer og med Krone/ Og hvide Klæder paa/ Kand siunge dig O Herre/ Lov, Priis, Hæder og Ære/ og ævig for dig staa.'

5. Goodbye then, you worldly friend,
You, Friedrich Christian,
I shall have someone better
In heavenly Canaan
Who will never betray me
But give me Paradise
Then with the crown on my head
I shall face the throne of God.[12]

So it could be argued that the ballads express an understanding of the execution scenario shared not only by the common people in the city who bought the publications but also by the murderers awaiting their execution and meeting with God.

Sweden

Street ballads sold on the occasion of executions were also common in Sweden, where they were called 'prisoner songs'.[13] Like their Danish counterparts, the Swedish ballads focused on the religious aspects of the subject. The temptations of Satan in the shape of drinking, of the wicked lure of the great city of Stockholm or the temptations of the flesh are all described, as are the farewell to family and friends and, of course, the optimistic message of salvation. For example, in a ballad about the penitent sinner Anna Lars Dotter, who had committed infanticide:

To those, who already mourn my decease, these words:
He who goes to ghastly death well prepared, he will be saved;
Away with grief! On the worldly marketplace
For those who blissfully wander, to God's other saints.[14]

---

[12] Appendix, case 1744:1. '4: Du haver gandske vist/ Bedaaret mig i Live/ Hielp mig o Jesu Christ/ Min korte Tid at slide/ Du har mig presset af/ Den Gierning at fuldgiøre/ Jeg leges i min Grav/ Min Gud vil mig vist høre. 5: Farvel du Verdsens Ven/ Du Friedrich Christian/ Jeg faaer en bedre igien/ I Himlens Canaan/ Den aldrig sviger mig/ Men giver Himmerig/ Da jeg med Kronen paa/ Skal for Guds Throne staa.'

[13] Eighteenth-century Swedish street ballads are thoroughly analysed in Margaretha Jersild's dissertation 'Skillingtryck: Studier i svensk folklig vissång före 1800', 1975. Her investigations produced ninety-eight prisoner songs from the eighteenth century. Unfortunately she does not list the ballads in such a manner as to make it possible to identify the prisoner songs. The centre for Swedish Folk Music, Svenskt Visarkiv, however, has kindly helped me with copies of ten prisoner songs about murderers from 1700–70, and three of these were about suicide murderers. This description is based on Jersild's analysis (p. 44–6) and the ten copied ballads.

[14] 'Trenne ganska eftertänkeliga Fånga-Visor, den första: om den botfärdiga Synderskan Anna Lars Dotter, som för begångit barnamord blef halshuggen på

Germany

The number of street ballads about executions preserved (or discovered in the course of my research) in Germany is much smaller than in Denmark and Sweden. I have discovered only a few from northern Germany, and only one of these is from Hamburg.[15] Ballads do not dominate in the German leaflets that have been preserved about executions as they do in Scandinavia. In Germany the preferred description was a prose text about the crime, its detection and the harsh punishment that followed. Some of these descriptions conclude with a few verses.

In his book on capital punishment in Germany between 1600 and 1987 Richard Evans analyses the street balladry on crime in the seventeenth- and eighteenth-century ballads and observes developments over time.[16] Religion dominated in the seventeenth century, with the malefactor being depicted as a penitent sinner going to everlasting peace. According to Evans, this idea of execution was widely shared by state and community in the seventeenth century. In the eighteenth century, however, the ballad went from being something that was bought and read by high and low alike, and something accepted by the authorities, to being a purely popular institution. At the same time the ballads were to an increasing degree shaped by the official censor, who insisted on the portrayal of the malefactor in negative and specific terms. The ballad sheets incorporated a print-out of the official sentence, which described the crimes in detail, and the religious content was gradually replaced by descriptions of the crime and its detection and details of the execution.

Rätteplatsen i Stockholm, d. 17. Julii 1734'. '5: Dem, som redan börja/ At min afgång sörja/ Lemnas thessa ord:/ Den til döden ledder/ Utgår vel beredder/ Den bliver saligt gjord./ Bort med Sorg!/ På werldsens torg/ Öfver dem som saligt wandra/ Til Guds helgon andra.'

[15] I have visited the Deutsches Volkslieder Archiv (German Archive for Folksong) in Freiburg. The copied collections in the Archive, however, did not contain many street ballads about executions from the first half of the eighteenth century. I have discovered some more ballads through references found in the library of the Archive. Some more can be found in German on-line library catalogues, especially the Staatsbibliothek zu Berlin and the Württembergische Landesbibliothek in Stuttgart. In all I have found twelve ballads about murderers being executed dating from the period 1638–1778. Apart from a ballad mentioned by Jürgen Martchukat (*Ein Freitod*, 2000, p. 65), I have not been able to find any ballads about executions from Hamburg and very few from northern Germany.

[16] Evans, *Rituals of Retribution*, p. 150–89.

It is easy, however, to find ballads that do not fit into Evans's characterization. Condemnatory ballads of this sort are found in the seventeenth century too,[17] and religious ballads also appeared in the eighteenth century.[18] Rather than being shaped by the authorities, it is my impression that the ballads differed according to the crimes they described. The fascination provoked by a gang of robbers being hanged or broken on the wheel was different from that aroused by a young mother who had committed infanticide or by a suicide murderer. This difference can also be seen in the Danish ballads. Furthermore, a growing number of the German ballads ceased to be sold at the site of the specific execution that they recounted. Instead, they were written to be sold all over Germany, and over a long period of time. These ballads and prose texts were aimed at being distributed by the so-called *Bänkelsängern* ('bench singers'). This type of street trader became common in the eighteenth century. They travelled around the country with a 'Shocking ballad picture show', as Tom Cheesman calls it.[19] The 'bench singers' presented a show of posters with paintings of the dramatic moments in the crime, and they sang and sold publications about the crimes and executions.

Pious ballads about repentant murderers meeting God did not disappear in the eighteenth century, however. For instance, one of the few examples I have found of German ballads describing suicide murderers is the ballad about Jeremias Bertz, who, having lost the will to live, chose to kill his own daughter and was beheaded in Augsburg on 31 May 1740. The content of the ballad does not differ much from the Danish and Swedish ballads. The main theme deals with Bertz's feelings about committing the murder, his conversion in prison, his farewell to family and friends and his certainty of joining his child in heaven.[20] Thus, although popular prints about executions in Germany

---

[17] 'Ein erbärmlicher Klaglied von einer sehr erschröcklichen That … Michael Rohrbach … der selbig drei seiner eignen Kinder mit seinem Messer die Gurgel abgestochen … zu Wymiss gerichtet hat … wie es dann weiters im Lied gnugsam wird vermeldet', 1638.

[18] 'Bewegliche Abschieds Worte womit Johanna Susanna Riedeln als solche wegen verübten Kinder-Mords', Dresden 1726; 'Moralische Gedanken als Leonhard Fels … Wegen grausamen verübtem Morde seines Sohnes', Augsburg, 1772.

[19] Tom Cheesman, *The Schocking Ballad Picture Show: German Popular Literature and Cultural History*, 1994.

[20] 'Der in der Todt gehende, und seiner eignen Tochter … antwortende bussfertige Vater oder Arme Sünder Jeremias Bertz', Augsburg, 1740. Two more ballads were printed about the murder: 'Reumutiges Klag-Lied des Armen Sünders Jeremias Bertz'

are more diverse than in Denmark and Sweden, the pious ballads focusing on the salvation of the malefactors were present here too.

The religious discourse was rarely expressed in the court narratives, but indirectly it was present. A striking common feature of the perpetrators' explanations to the courts was that they appeared to be utterly candid. The murderers not only freely admitted to the murder; they also told of their wish to be executed and apparently felt confident that the courts would pass the death sentence, despite their admission that they actually wanted to be executed. In addition—insofar as they were able to articulate their motives—they freely related the events and emotions that had led them to the fatal decision. They thus seemed to expect the co-operation of the courts and possibly even expected some understanding on the part of the authorities.

This peculiar candour and expectation of understanding finds its logic in the parallel religious discourse of the murder and its atonement. According to this logic, they could expect understanding and even sympathy for their position as sinful human beings continuously tempted by the cunning Devil and struggling for the salvation of their souls. The brief and random references to religious motives for the murders in the court records are unfolded in the ballads. Here the murders are explained as results of the Devil's temptations, against which man is almost powerless. But when he provoked the murder, the Devil only won the battle and not the war, because God wants to save the sinner's soul. At some point between the murder and the execution, the prisoner's heart is opened to the word of God. When the murderers appeared before the court, they usually had—in their own minds—undergone this change and were eager to testify to their repentant state of mind by admitting their sins as openly as possible.

The penitent then turned to God and, trusting in His infinite mercy, awaited execution, confident in the belief that she would end up in Paradise with a crown on her head. This appealing narrative was the main content of the ballads and seemed to be accepted both by the murderers and by the spectators at the executions.

---

and 'Die aus der Grabe redende nur 15. Wochen alte Martyrin Maria Magdalene Bertzin, welche von ihrem eigenen Vatter Jeremias Bertz ... ermordet worden.'

This interpretation of events was accepted, moreover, not only by the masses. The author Baron Ludvig Holberg, in an epistle published in 1754, told of the attitudes towards the prisoners being executed among his noble and intellectual acquaintances. The general opinion, Holberg said, was that after the execution, 'You should stop such blaming [the malefactor for his misdeeds], because now the malefactor has suffered for his sins, and thereby reconciled himself with God.'[21]

It appears that the murderers could depend on the authorities not only to perform the execution but also, in co-operation with the people, to inscribe the execution in a religious context that allowed the murderer, so to speak, to be reunited with society and save her soul. In the next chapter I will examine the attitudes of the secular authorities and the official religious ideology, and look at how this ideology was administered by the clergy, in order to understand the relation between official ideology and the murders.

---

[21] Ludvig Holberg, *Epistler*, 1748–54, epistle 524, vol. 5, p. 247: 'At man nu maatte holde inde med saadanne Bebreydelser, efterdi Misdæderen havde lidet for sine Synder, og derved var forsonet med Gud.'

CHAPTER FIVE

THE AUTHORITIES AND THE MURDERS

The discussions and actions of the authorities reflect the parallel secular and religious discourses of the murders. The secular discourse was concerned with the just anger of society against the murderer and with the deterrence of possible like-minded offenders; the religious one focused on the salvation of the murderer's soul. Depending on which discourse is consulted, quite different stories of the attitudes of the authorities towards the murders can be written. In the following I shall present the two discourses separately.

Secular Revenge

A premeditated murder was a terrible crime and aroused the anger of the city. This was particularly true of the premeditated murder of a totally innocent victim, as in the case of the suicide murders.

To return to the first suicide murder in Copenhagen, by Sidzel Sivertsdatter in 1697, the city judge was truly horrified. He found the crime a terrible outrage, especially because the victim was a child whom Sidzel had in her care. He therefore asked the king for a change in the law to allow a harsh penalty.[1] This resulted in a new decree on 'The punishment of gross murderers',[2] which for the premeditated murders of a spouse, master, mistress or their children stipulated the penalty of being pinched repeatedly with red-hot tongs and, at the place of execution, having the right hand and the head cut off with an axe, after which the corpse was to be exhibited on the post and wheel.

When this dreadful sentence was pronounced to Sidzel just under a month after the murder, she answered that she now deeply regretted having killed the child. She told the court she was a weak person who had been unable to resist the temptations of Satan. Even if she were to be cut up joint by joint, she would not be able to suffer enough for her misdeeds, she said, so she asked for the punishment to begin as soon as

[1] Appendix, case 1697:1.
[2] Danish National Archives, Danske kancelli, Indlæg til Sjæll. reg. 1697/171.

possible. Her humble attitude induced the city judge once again to turn to the king, asking him to excuse Sidzel from the pinching with red-hot tongs, so that she would not fall into despair. The king granted this petition as well.

The extreme physical punishment laid down in the Danish decree of 1697 was not used very often. It was limited to murders within the household, much like petty treason in English law, and this type of suicide murder was not common. In the courts the penalty stipulated in the decree was imposed five times, but royal pardons always reduced the penalty. Pinching with red-hot tongs was allowed only three times: in 1736, 1743 and 1749.

Danish law did not consider aspects such as premeditation to determine the gravity of different types of homicide, the punishment for which was typically decapitation by sword. Specific types of murder, however, met with harsher punishments. Infanticide was punished by decapitation with an axe, with the head of the perpetrator then being impaled on a pole. Murder in connection with highway robbery and burglary was also punished with decapitation by axe, after which the murderer's corpse was to be displayed on the post and wheel. The 'correct' punishment for suicide murders was thus decapitation by sword. Often, however, the judges drew an analogy with infanticide, in particular, and accordingly imposed the more dishonourable punishment for crimes of this sort.

The essential question confronting the civil courts in the case of suicide murderers in the period up until 1749, when a new decree changed the punishment, was not so much whether or not the murderer was to face the terror of the red-hot pincers, since the use of this punishment was very infrequent. The important question was what should happen to the corpse. This was partly a question of honour and partly one of religion. A penalty involving display of the corpse implied that, after the executioner had struck the fatal blow, the body was left to the night man, who put it in his carriage—the same carriage that was used during the day to move animal carcasses as well as to transport night soil tubs—and transported it to the gallows outside the town, where the post and wheel with the whole body or the pole with the head impaled on it were situated. The bodies could be displayed for several years, until the birds had taken their share and wind and weather caused the stake to collapse.[3] Even if display of the body was

[3] Krogh, *Oplysningstiden og det magiske*, p. 323–5.

not part of the punishment, the decapitated body would normally be left to the night man, who drove it out to the gallows and buried it there. The bodies could also be given to the anatomy theatre for examination before being buried close to the gallows. In a case from 1720, at the request of the medical professor Johan Buchwaldt, the king altered the sentence of decapitation, with the head then being impaled on a pole, so that the display of the head should not take place and the whole body could be given to the professor after the execution.[4]

Figure 2. Some of the Danish ballads contained simple woodcuts, usually depicting the execution. The woodcut above shows a decapitation by axe. The executioner lifts the axe, while the night man, gripping the prisoner's hair, holds the head stretched out on the block. To the left, the head is impaled on a pole. In addition, this murderer had had his hand cut off, and the hand has been nailed to the pole with the knife with which the murder was committed. (From 'Poenitensis Taare udøst af en bedrøvet Misdæder Nicolai Marcusøn', 1716, The Royal Library, Copenhagen)

[4] Appendix, case 1720:3.

Figure 3. Woodcut of a beheading by sword, from the front page of the ballad about Maren Hansdatter, an inmate in the Spin-house, who had cut the throat of a small boy in order to end her own life. (Appendix, case 1720:2, The Royal Library, Copenhagen)

It was, however, possible as a special dispensation for those sentenced to beheading by sword to be granted a quiet burial in consecrated ground. Then the defiling handling by the night man was avoided. Instead, a coffin was placed beside the scaffold, and after the execution the dead body was placed in the coffin and buried by relatives or by municipal officers of the poor.

During the trial the murderers usually asked to be granted this boon of burial in consecrated ground. If the court did not comply with this request, many suicide murderers wrote or had a petition written to the king to request it. The priests preparing the convicts usually helped them to write the petition, and sometimes they wrote a supplementary letter to support it. This is what happened in the case of Karen Andersdatter. In June 1710 she had thrown her own four-week-old child into the canal. She gave herself up and was sentenced to decapitation by sword, with the head then being impaled on a pole. She then composed a most humble petition:

> I, poor and wretched creature, have at the instigation of Satan done the fruit of my womb to death … My most humble sigh and prayer is this, that when my head has been separated from my body by the sword, my body then and my head too may be buried in the plot of the poor in the churchyard. For such a great royal mercy towards me poor grieving sinner, the just God, who is the King of Kings, will bless your Royal Majesty for all eternity.[5]

To this petition pastor Christian Kölichen added:

> What this poor sinner sighs and cries for, I ask most humbly to be granted by your Royal Grace … It could perhaps help her to find more peace in her heart, so that her thoughts might be better collected, in order to receive the holy word of God with greater devotion, which she sorely needs for the comfort of her soul. And therefore I most sincerely cry together with her to be heard, as it is I who must watch over the salvation of her soul.

The Danish Kings often complied with such petitions. In 1737 a decree laid down that the sentence of decapitation by sword should always be followed by quiet burial in consecrated ground.[6]

Soldiers who murdered in order to be executed were punished much more harshly than civilians. The grounds given for the judgement mentioned the cowardliness of shooting a victim from behind or of secretly drawing a knife and stabbing the victim. The murders were referred to as 'assassinations', stressing the scandalous breach of the military code of honour. Often the unhappy soldiers carried out the murder with the rifle or the rapier with which they had been entrusted to defend the country. This made the crime even more outrageous.

---

[5] Appendix, case 1710:1: 'Jeg arme og usle Creatur haver ved Sathans Tilskyndelse ombragt mit Foster … min allerunderdanigste Suck og Bøn er denne, at naar mit Hoved er skilt fra mit Legeme med Sværdet, mit Legeme da tillige med Hovedet maatte nedsættes udi den fattiges Jord. For saadan stor Kongl. Naade imod mig fattige bedrøvede Synderinde, vil den retfærdige Gud, som er Kongernes Konge, eders Kongl. Maj:tt udi ald Evighed velsigne.' 'Hvad denne fattige Synderinde sucker og raaber om, beder ieg allerunderdanigst, deres høy Kongl. Naade vilde høre … Maaskee det kunde tiæne hende til meere roelighed i Hiertet, og Tanckerne da dis bedre kunde samlis til at anname Guds hellige Ord med dis større Andagt, hvilcket hun til sin Siælis Trøst høiligen behøver. Og derfor raaber ieg saa inderlig med hende om Bønhørelse, da det er mig, som skal vaage for hendis Siælis Salighed.'

[6] Decree of 9 August 1737; see Krogh, *Oplysningstiden og det magiske*, p. 298.

Table 3. Forms of execution of civilians in Copenhagen, 1697–1789 (one murderer died in prison)[7]

	Decapitation and burial in consecrated ground	Decapitation and burial by night man	Decapitation and display of body	Defamatory route to execution, pinched with red-hot tongs, decapitation and corpse displayed on post and wheel
1697–99			2	
1700–09			2	
1710–19	3	3	1	
1720–29		3	4	
1730–39	3		4	1
1740–49	3		3	2
1750–59	1		2	9
1760–69		1	3	8
1770–79	1			
1780–89				
Total	11	7	21	20

An overview of military cases can be found in records of the judge advocate general, who presented all serious military cases to the king. The records of the office are rudimentary before 1728. Thus, the suicide murder of his own child committed by grenadier Povel Povelsen in 1720 is known only from two street ballads written about the murder.[8] In the period between 1728 and 30 there were no fewer than ten suicide murders in the army. Most of these, however, took place in the garrison city of Rendsburg, in Schleswig.[9] The penalties meted out were harsh, including pinching with red-hot tongs and the terrible breaking of the limbs with the wheel. After this wave of suicide murders, only a few

[7] See Appendix.

[8] Appendix, case 1720:1.

[9] About suicide murders in the military, see Krogh, *Oplysningstiden og det magiske*, p. 231–5, 238–41.

such crimes were committed over the next six years. But then in 1737 there were three suicide murders and two attempts. This led to the military decree of 1738, which stated that anyone who shot or stabbed somebody in order to kill them, without reason and in cold blood, and whether or not the victim died, should be whipped at the scene of the crime once a week for nine consecutive weeks. Then the offender should be taken to the scaffold and there have his limbs broken with the wheel from below and up, and then with no *coup de grâce*—that, is to say, still alive—be placed on the post and wheel and left to die there.

This decree did not put a stop to suicide murders in the army. In 1739 two soldiers stationed in Copenhagen received this punishment, and over the next fifteen years at least thirteen more suicide murders took place in the army as a whole.[10]

The many suicide murders committed by soldiers in the late 1730s corresponded to a similar wave of civilian suicide murders. Four suicide murders were tried in the municipal courts in 1736. In the two first cases the decree of 1697 was used, although the cases did not fit into the definition of gross murders given within it.

Table 4. Forms of execution of soldiers in Copenhagen 1720–89 (including death penalties for two attempted murders)[11]

	Decapitation and display of body	Pinching with red-hot tongs, decapitation and corpse on post and wheel	Whipping for nine consecutive weeks, breaking on the wheel and corpse on post and wheel
1720–29	2		
1730–39	4	2	2
1740–49			1
1750–59		2	1
1760–69	1		
1770–79			
1780–89	1		1
Total	8	4	5

[10] Krogh, *Oplysningstiden og det magiske*, p. 238–41.
[11] See Appendix.

The fourth murder that year was committed by the tailor Ludvig Jørgen Petersen, who cut the throat of an eight-year-old girl whom he did not know. He was a religious man and had led a pious life until the Shrovetide of that year. He had then fallen into a bout of depression in which he doubted God's providence and mercy and his own salvation because he was such a gross sinner, and he had not been able to find comfort in the Word. Following some months of depression, he committed the murder in late June.

The murders were widely discussed in the city, and this last example was taken as proof of the harmfulness of the Pietist revival movement that was prominent but much contested in the Copenhagen of the 1730s. Religious fanaticism was blamed for the murders. When the case of Ludvig Jørgen Petersen came before the Supreme Court, one of the judges, Jens Wartberg, explained the murder as follows:

> (He) seems to have been one of those people who fall into worries about nothing going their way, and get the idea that it will serve their salvation to fall into despair, and that there is no rescue for them except getting out of this world. Thus they find themselves justified to commit a misdeed for which the punishment is death, as they think that one cannot but be saved when dying at the hands of the executioner.[12]

Wartberg was of the opinion that an example should be made in this case and the murderer punished according to the decree of 1697, even though it did not mention this type of murder. The majority of the Supreme Court judges, however, stated that the penalty in the 1697 decree could not be used except when a murder was in strict accordance with the types of murder specified in it. Petersen was accordingly sentenced to execution by sword. He then wrote a petition to the king in which he stated that he was satisfied with the sentence, believing that God would forgive him his gross sin and misdeed, for which he was to shed his blood, but humbly requesting that his wretched body should be permitted burial in consecrated ground. This request the king granted.

In each of the years 1742, 1744 and 1746 a suicide murderer was permitted burial in consecrated ground—in the last two instances as a result of a royal pardon. Thus, although the logic of the murders was

---

[12] Appendix, case 1736:4 '(en) af det slags Mennisker, som falde i Bekymring over at Verden gaae dem imod, og komme paa de Tanker, at det tiener til deres Salighed vel at fortvivle, og at der er ingen Redning for dem uden at komme af denne Verden, finde de sig beføiede at begaae en Misgiærning, som der er sat Livsstraf for, da de synes at man ey kand andet end døe salig under Bødlens Haand.'

now well known and hotly debated, several of the murderers still managed to get off with an 'honourable' decapitation and burial in consecrated ground. The reason for this leniency was probably concern for the pious and repentant prisoners' souls. As Pastor Kölichen had argued, with an honourable execution the prisoner would be better able to collect her or his thoughts and to be receptive to the Holy Word of God. In the first half of the eighteenth century the king and his judges thus wavered between strict deterrence and Christian concern for the sinners' souls.

When, however, a new wave occurred in 1747–48, with four suicide murders and two attempts, the attitude of the authorities hardened.[13] The courts first drew an analogy with the penalty for murder and robbery on the highway, stating that the suicide murder of children not known to their assailants, and in the streets, was an offence against the king's peace (*vejfred*). Accordingly, the murderers were sentenced to decapitation and their bodies were placed on the post and wheel.

But when the fourth murder in two years came before the Supreme Court, one of the judges proposed that a new decree should be issued making the penalty of the 1697 decree applicable to all suicide murders. The proposal met with general approval. The Supreme Court found that the punishment for these murders up to now had not been strict enough to deter such ungodly people, and argued that the harsh punishment in the military decree of 1738 had had a good effect. But the Supreme Court also proposed an addition to the punishment of the 1697 decree. The judges found that the reason for suicide murders was also

> that the condemned are being led to the place of execution with such ceremony, and executed in such finery, that the ordinary crowd, who are easily impressed by outward appearance, get the impression of a happy death, and this fantasy makes evil mature in many ungodly hearts.[14]

The public appearance of the convict should therefore be made more humiliating and defamatory. The proposal by the Supreme Court led to the decree of 7 February 1749, which stated that when somebody

---

[13] A further reason for the change was probably that the Pietist king Christian VI died in 1746 and was succeeded by Frederik V, who in reality left matters of government to the leading officials.

[14] Danish National Archives, Danske Kancelli, Sjællandske registre 1749/28: 'At Delinqventer med saadan ceremonie bliver førte til Retterstædet, og i Stads og Pynt henrettede, hvilket hos den gemeene Almue, som læt imodtager Impression af det udvortes Anseende, har anseende af en lyksalig Død. hvilken Indbildning giør Ondskabet moden i mangt ugudeligt Hierte.'

> deliberately and aforethought, and without the victim having given occasion or offence, solely with the thought of committing a misdeed, has murdered … an innocent person, … such a gross malefactor shall … be pinched with red-hot tongs by the executioner, first in front of the house or at the place where the murder was committed, then … three times between the scene of the crime and the place of execution, and finally at the place of execution. Then the right hand of … the perpetrator, he or she still being alive, shall be cut off with an axe and after that the head likewise with an axe. Whereafter the body shall be taken out by the night man and his people and placed on the post and wheel, and the head as well as the hand shall be nailed on the pole over the body. And no such murderer may be led from his prison to the punishment with any ceremony or finery, but shall be brought from the prison to the place of execution in the night man's carriage wearing the common or daily clothes worn in the prison, without hat or cap, with naked head, with the halter around the neck, with hands tied, in order to add himself or herself greater insult and in order to deter and disgust others.[15]

The new decree had barely been printed before it came into use, and the following decade in Copenhagen alone eleven suicide murderers were punished according to the decree of 1749. The expected deterrent effect thus did not materialize.

Hamburg and Stockholm

The mixed attitudes shown by the authorities in Copenhagen can also be found in Hamburg.[16] Up until the middle of the 1690s only decapitation and decapitation with the head impaled on a pole were used. But from 1694 pinching with red-hot tongs, sometimes even combined

[15] Danish National Archives, Danske Kancelli, Sjællandske registre 1749/28: 'med frie Forsæt og beraad Hue uden nogen foregaaende dertil af den dræbte given Aarsag eller Anledning, alene i Tanke at giøre en Ulykke, at have myrdet … nogen uskyldig person … skal saadan grov misdæder … af Skarpretteren knibes med gloende Tænger først uden for det Hus eller ved det Sted, hvor Mordet er begaaet, siden … trende Gange imellem Gierningsstedet og allersidst paa Retterstædet, Dernæst skal den Skyldiges højre Haand levende afhugges med en Øxe, og siden Hovedet iligemaade med en Øxe. Hvorpaa Legemet af Natmandens Folk skal henføres og legges paa Steile, og Hovedet tillige med Haanden fæstes paa en Stage oven over Legemet. Og maa ingen … slig misdæder fra sit Fængsel til at udstaae sin Straf, føres med nogen Ceremonie eller i pyntelige Klæder, men den skal udi de gemeene og de i Fængslet brugte daglige Klæder, uden Hat eller Hue, med blottet Hoved, Strikke om Halsen og sammenbundne Hænder, sig selv til desto større Forhaanelse og andre til Skræk og Afskye, fra Fængslet til Retterstedet føres paa Natmandens Sluffe.'

[16] For penal practice in Hamburg, see Richard Wosnick, *Beiträge zur Hamburgischen Kriminalgeschichte*, 1926; his list of executions is at p. 35–48.

with breaking of the limbs on the wheel, was used frequently. In Germany there was an old tradition of denigration on the route to the place of execution. The condemned person was wrapped in a raw, wet ox-hide and, with hair hanging down and a bloody knife tied around the neck, dragged on a hurdle to the scaffold by a horse. This form of humiliation became popular in the second half of the eighteenth century.

Table 5. Forms of executions for child murders in Hamburg 1660–1799[17]

	Decapitation	Decapitation and display of body	Humiliating route to execution and decapitation	Pinching with red-hot tongs (and or breaking with the wheel), decapitation and display of body	Humiliating route to execution, pinching with red-hot tongs (and breaking with the wheel), decapitation and display of body
1660–69	1	2			
1670–79	3				
1680–89	3	2			
1690–99	5			4	1
1700–09	1	2		2	
1710–19	2	1		3	
1720–29	3			2	1
1730–39	4				1
1740–49	3				2
1750–59			1		1
1760–69	3		2		
1770–79	2		5		
1780–89	2		1		
1790–99					
Total	32	7	9	11	6

[17] Wosnick, *Beiträge zur Hamburgischen Kriminalgeschichte*, p. 35–48. The table includes six cases, 1660–79, which were not included in the calculations at p. 18. It also includes the eleven cases where it cannot be determined whether they were cases of child murder or infanticide.

But although many perpetrators of suicide murders were exposed to the terror of red-hot tongs and the humiliating road to the place of execution, half of them still escaped with simple decapitation, mostly combined with quiet burial in consecrated ground.

Penal practice in Stockholm is not known, as the verdicts of the superior courts are missing. The use of aggravating supplements to the death penalty was not much practised in Sweden, so it is probable that most of the suicide murderers were sentenced to decapitation and nothing else. Two royal decrees/letters of 1741 and 1754 mentioned by Jansson show, however, that the Swedish authorities shared the thoughts of their Danish and German colleagues. A decree of 1741 stated that some convicts—child murderers, in particular—had been strengthened in their godless purpose by the manner in which the condemned were taken to the place of execution. For this reason, in future the convicts should be brought to the place of execution in an ignominious way. White or black clothing decorated with ribbons was not allowed; only plain clothing without decoration. Anything that suggested magnificence or which implied a dignified path to the scaffold was forbidden. A royal letter/decree of 1754 issued to all higher courts specifically addressed the problem of suicide murders and permitted the courts to sentence these murderers to being displayed in a pillory and whipping in addition to the death penalty.[18]

I shall return to the secular fight against the suicide murders later. For now it can be concluded that until the middle of the eighteenth century the punitive stance of the authorities was ambiguous. The growing recognition of the appeal of the execution scene led to many cruel and humiliating punishments, but at the same time many of the suicide murderers were granted a relatively honourable execution.

Suicide Motives in Other Crimes

The death penalty was used for crimes other than murder in the eighteenth century, and as the suicide motive was so common in the murder cases, it might be expected that other crimes as well could be used as a vehicle for obtaining death at the executioner's hand. In my studies of criminal cases in Denmark in the eighteenth century I have not met

[18] Jansson, *From Swords to Sorrow*, p. 67–8.

suicide motives in cases of property crime or of sex crimes. In cases of crime against religion, however, the suicide motive was present.

Persecution of witchcraft in Denmark–Norway primarily belonged to the seventeenth century. The last witch was burned in Denmark–Norway in 1693. The death penalty for witchcraft was not abandoned until long into the nineteenth century, however, and its continued presence in the statute book allowed for a short period of severe persecution of people selling themselves to the Devil.[19] A few cases around 1700 of people selling themselves to the Devil in signed contracts were treated rather mildly and punished only with public confession of their sin in front of their congregation. Around 1720 a tightening of religious zealotry took place. In 1718 a soldier who had signed a contract with the Devil was sentenced to death, and the king ordered that at the Sunday preceding the execution the pastors should preach on the case in every church in Copenhagen. The publicity did not have the desired deterrent effect, however. On the contrary, many new cases of signed contracts with the Devil came up. In three of the cases the sources mention a wish to be executed as a motive, and in the other cases depression was often mentioned. Three or possibly four people were executed for signing contracts with the Devil before the death penalty was given up again.

In Sweden suicide motives has been found in cases of bestiality. Prosecution of bestiality was widespread and severely punished. Jonas Liliequist has recorded more than a thousand cases of bestiality in Sweden in the eighteenth century, and nearly two hundred people were sentenced to death for the crime.[20] However, 17% of those charged with bestiality had turned themselves in, and most reported incidents that had taken place many years before the confession. The authorities reacted towards these self-accusations with growing suspicion, and after interrogation many of the confessions were withdrawn. The main suspicion of the authorities was that the people who had confessed to the crimes had done so purely in order to be executed, and in many cases Jonas Liliequist was able to provide document proof of this being the motive of those claiming to have committed bestiality.[21] It is

---

[19] The ending of the Danish witchcraft cases and the cases of people selling themselves to the Devil in contracts are described in Krogh, *Oplysningstiden og det magiske*, p. 119–50.

[20] Jonas Liliequist, 'Brott, synd och straff: Tidelagsbrottet i Sverige under 1600- och 1700-talet', 1992, p. 37–114.

[21] Liliequist, 'Brott, synd och straff', p. 107–11.

important to note that the people who admitted to bestiality in order to obtain a death penalty had not actually committed the crime. As Liliequist writes, they wanted by way of a lie to obtain the death penalty. The cases are thus more a parallel to the cases of invented murder that I have found in Copenhagen.

The cases of supposed signed contracts with the Devil in Denmark and of fictitious bestiality in Sweden as a means to try to obtain a death penalty indicate that it is possible for the suicide motive to be present in any criminal case that carried the death penalty. Of course, not all crimes were, so to speak, suitable for someone in a suicidal state of despression. In that state of mind one would not be likely to commit a sexual crime such as bestiality, sodomy or adultery. Moreover, murder was probably the most certain method to get the courts to impose a death sentence.

Official Religion and the Murders

In their deliberations concerning the penalty, the authorities increasingly pointed to a religious motive for the murders. In the arguments for the decree of 1749 it was stated that the murderers killed their victims because they believed that they were sure 'to die saved at the hands of the executioner' and that the execution scene gave the murderers 'the impression of a happy death'. In a related context, Bishop Peder Hersleb commented on the problem as being caused by:

> the old delusion which leads so many to do harm, namely that it is such a blessed death, and that no one can be better prepared for death, and that salvation cannot fail here, where the pastor accompanies with prayer, singing, the word of God and consolation and so on.[22]

The authorities thus wanted to view the beliefs of the murderers as an old delusion, but what did official religion have to say about the executions and the salvation of the murderers?

In early modern Denmark the death penalty was not only an expression of secular vengeance. It had important religious implications as well. Increasingly the Reformation and seventeenth-century Lutheran

---

[22] Danish National Archives, Danske Kancelli, Indlæg til Sjællandske tegnelser 1751/161: 'den gamle Indbildning, som fører mange til at giøre Ont, nemlig at det er saa salig en Død, og ingen kand være bedre bereed til Døden, og Salighed der ikke kand feile, hvor Præsten gaar ved siden med Bøn og Sang, Guds Ord og Trøst etc.'

orthodoxy had woven together worship of God, the system of punishment and princely powers. The Mosaic Law, with its many provisions concerning capital punishment, was taken more and more seriously, as was the belief that God would punish those countries which did not respect the commands of the Law. In Lutheran countries the prince, being the 'sword' of the Church, had a prominent role in the conduct of religion. By enforcing the Mosaic Law, the prince protected the country against God's wrath and contributed to the people's common salvation.

The king's law and the king's sentences were seen as being dependent on an indispensable divine law. This led to a peculiar practice in cases where the king was to approve death sentences. In the first half of the eighteenth century, especially, the king sought advice on pardons from the Faculty of Theology at the University of Copenhagen. The professors were charged with deciding whether granting a pardon from the death penalty would be against God's law. With five to ten statements each year in criminal cases where the courts had passed a death sentence, the theological professors had a significant influence on the use of the death penalty.

Half of the cases presented by the king to the Faculty of Theology were homicides. The theologians could consider milder penalties if a killing could be judged to have been inadvertent or if the prosecution was not strong enough, but if they found that it was a case of murder or manslaughter they always recommended the death penalty. In their reasoning they often used a biblical blood metaphor, saying that, if the killer was not executed, his blood guilt would extend throughout the land, or they cited the Bible: 'blood defileth the land: and the land cannot be cleansed of the blood that is shed therein, but by the blood of him that shed it' (Numbers 35:33).

The divine wrath present in the demand for punishments carried out by the Christian authorities and the threat of the whole realm suffering if the punishment was not carried out were, however, balanced by another understanding of divine punishment. Parallel with the development of religious juridical practice, the religious preparation of the convicts for their execution and the religious staging of the execution ceremony rose to prominence. In Denmark the preparation of the convicts was meticulously prescribed in the official printed Church Ritual from 1685. The chapter describing the preparation of the condemned for death takes up twenty-eight whole pages.

The arguments to be used by the pastor to prepare the condemned are described in detail. The pastor should admonish the sinner, exhorting him to confess the truth and not 'quell' the sin within him, thus increasing his sinfulness, making room for Satan and rousing God to even greater vengeance and wrath. Instead of denying the truth, he should openly admit his offence so that he would not take his leave of this world hardened in sin.

The pastor should encourage the prisoner to show true and upright repentance and remorse for his misdeeds, not because the misdeeds would cause him suffering in this world but primarily because in committing them he had greatly angered the good God, whose wrath and eternal damnation he therefore deserves.

The prisoner should consider his previous life and see if he had not through drunkenness, immorality, avarice, hatred of his neighbour, disobedience to parents and superiors, breaking of the Sabbath, contempt of the Holy Word of God or other such evils sought out the terrible misdeed.

But the pastor should also explain that, even though it might seem as though God was now completely washing His hands of the prisoner, this was not the case. God was faithful and never abandoned a repentant sinner. On the contrary, the prisoner should know that the calamity leading to his condemnation had actually taken place by the will of God. Because when the Lord could not reach the sinner with His goodness, He had had to resort to plagues and finally the death penalty in order to open his eyes, so that the prisoner could see God and his own sinfulness. But the Lord's grace is really infinite. If the prisoner turned to God again and showed true repentance at the moment of death, then the Lord would open the door to him too.

On the day of execution the arguments should be even more optimistic. This was to be the prisoner's last day of struggle and his first genuine day of happiness, when he would undertake the happy passage from his poor, sinful and miserable life to eternal, blessed and immortal life with God in heaven. Furthermore, the Church Ritual implied a view of the death penalty as an act of atonement for the sins committed by the condemned man: it had pleased God, the pastor should explain, to have the prisoner suffer for his sins here on Earth—implying that the prisoner would escape the torments of hell, which could be the fate of others after death.

The course of the day of execution was meticulously described in the ritual. The pastor should arrive at the gaol a couple of hours before the ceremony and carefully prepare the prisoner. If he was truly repentant, he should receive Holy Communion. The pastor should accompany the prisoner to the place of execution. On the way they should stop a couple of times and sing psalms. One of the suggested psalms began:

> Heartily now I long for a blessed ending,
> As I am wretchedly oppressed by grief and misery,
> I am ready to swiftly leave this world
> For the joys of Heaven; come, Jesus, come soon.[23]

At the place of execution the prisoner's confession and repentance should be made public. The condemned man should confess his faith and afterwards answer the following questions in the affirmative:

> Is this your firm belief and confession of faith in God, in which you intend to end your life in this World?
>
> Then do you believe that you are a gross sinner, and that in many ways you have highly angered your good God, but especially by this your great sin, for which you are now to suffer?
>
> Do you also openly confess that you deserve death for that sin, and that you regret it deeply and with all your heart?
>
> Do you believe as well that for the sake of Christ you have found mercy in the eyes of God for this and all your other sins, and that this death will be an entrance to eternal life?
>
> Have you also with all your heart forgiven everybody who could have done anything against you, so that you have no hard feelings and anger in your heart, neither against the authorities that have judged you by right of office, nor against whomsoever else of your fellow Christians and neighbours?
>
> Are you in the name of Jesus Christ fully prepared to die willingly for the sins you have committed?[24]

---

[23] Anders Malling, *Dansk Salmehistorie*, 1963, vol. 3, p. 322: 'Hiertelig jeg nu længes effter en salig End/ Thi jeg ynckelig trængis aff Drøffuelse oc Elend/At vandre er jeg rede fra Verden med en Fart/ Til Himmeriges glæde: kom Jesu kom nu snart.'

[24] *Danmark og Norgis Kirkeritual*, 1685 (1985), p. 263–4 (in the 1685 edn): 'Er dette eders faste Tro og Bekiendelse, om Gud I hvilken I agter at ende eders Liv her i Verden?/ Troer I da, at I er en grov Synder, og i mange Maader højligen har fortørnet eders gode Gud, men særdelis med denne eders store Synd, hvorfor I nu skal lide. Bekiender og rund ud, at I haver fortient Døden derfor, og at I fortryder det inderlig af eders Hierte?/ Troer I ogsaa, at I for Christi Skyld har fundet Naade hos eders Gud, for den og for alle andre eders Synder, og at denne Død skal være eder en Indgang til det ævige Liv?/ Har I og af Hiertet forlat alle og enhver, som eder kan have giort noget imod, saa at I bær ingen Had eller Vrede i eders Hierte, hverken mod Øvrigheden, som paa Embeds Vegne maa holde denne Ret over eder, ej heller over nogen anden, i hvo det og være

After this the pastor should lead the singing of a psalm together with the public. The pastor was to pray with the prisoner constantly, up to the moment of death.

Figure 4. Woodcut from the ballad about Cicilia Johansdatter (Appendix, case 1744:1)

The death penalty for homicide thus had an important religious aspect for the authorities. They were following a divine commandment when they passed the death sentence, and the Church Ritual provided the pastors with detailed instructions about the correct preparation of the convicts, the aim of which was to save the prisoners' souls. According to the ritual, the pastor should assure the prisoner that if only he was repentant at the last moment of his life, his soul would be saved. The meticulous description of the preparation is evidence of the official importance attached to this struggle for the prisoners' souls.

kand, af eders Jevn-Christen og Næste?/ Er I og i den Herris Jesu Navn fuldkommen bereed at døe villig for eders begangne Synder?'

Compared with the ballads about executions, there are striking resemblances in the themes as well as the general message.

The ritual was, however, only a general guide to the preparation of prisoners condemned to death. In the next chapter I will try to get closer to what happened during the spiritual preparation of the suicide murderers and to the role of the pastors in creating the parallel religious discourse of the suicide murders.

CHAPTER SIX

PIETISM AND THE MURDERERS

The important task of saving the prisoners' souls and conveying the higher meaning of the executions to the community was entrusted to the pastors. They prepared the murderer who was awaiting execution. In the weeks up to the execution their sermons dealt with the crime. On the appointed day they accompanied the condemned person from the prison. Just before the execution was carried out, they expounded the religious meaning of the execution to the crowd in a dialogue with the prisoner, and it was not uncommon for the pastor to make a speech at the scaffold just before or just after the execution.

In eighteenth-century Germany a considerable number of publications were printed by pastors that dealt with the preparation of those under sentence of death. Many of them were in the form of speeches addressed to the crowd at the place of execution or sermons held after the execution. The sermons and scaffold speeches were intended to convey the meaning of the bloody scene. They would make clear why God and the authorities desired the punishment, and explain that the execution was an example by God to warn the people against sinning. The majority of the published speeches, however, told of the successful preparation of the malefactor, which had led to his or her conversion and the subsequent salvation of the soul.

This great interest in the salvation of convicts was inspired by Pietism. This was a movement inside the Lutheran Church that arose towards the end of the seventeenth century and continued into the first half of the eighteenth.[1] It was the German pastor Philip Jacob Spener who outlined the aims of the movement in 1675, in his book *Pia desideria* ('Pious wishes'). He criticized the Orthodox Lutheran Church, accusing it of internal decay with scholastic teaching at the universities and complacency about church attendance, and with too much outward show of respect being paid to the Church by the congregation.

---

[1] The literature on Pietism is comprehensive. A good description of the developments in Denmark is to be found in J. Pedersen, 'Pietismens Tid', in *Den Danske Kirkes Historie*, vol. 5, 1951.

Spener stressed the personal relationship with God. He demanded greater devotion and greater intensity of religious feelings, and greater consistency: faith should be expressed in action. He advocated the priesthood of all believers; the laity should share the spiritual government of the Church. Pietism quickly attracted many influential followers at the north German and Scandinavian courts, but it also met with sharp opposition. At the Prussian university in Halle, August Herman Francke developed a practically oriented Pietism, founding orphanages and schools for the poor.

In theological terms the Pietists came to emphasize the teaching of repentance, conversion and rebirth, in which rebirth meant a state of grace that the truly faithful could attain here on Earth. Francke, in particular, stressed that the state of being reborn had to be preceded by agonies of repentance leading to a genuine change of heart and conversion to the true faith. He believed that it was possible with the aid of certain signals to establish the borderline between the reborn and those not yet reborn.[2] The Pietists did not form a sect. They stayed inside the main Church and participated in the ordinary religious life of their congregation. But the reborn gathered at evening meetings and, among other things, related their own conversion stories. Everybody had the opportunity to be reborn. It was the process of conversion that determined the rebirth, not the previous life.

The Pietists developed the use of the press in pastoral care, and many ordinary pastors published works. A popular genre consisted of conversion stories, which were considered edifying entertainment.[3] The tale might be the sad story of a dying child longing for the joys of Heaven, or of a great sinner relating the terrible sins of her past life and the miraculous experience of rebirth.

The main theme of the printed sermons about executions or scaffold speeches was the conversion story. Let us take as an example the publication about Eva Ellingerin, who had committed infanticide and was executed in Pappenheim, in southern Germany, in 1724. The publication contained the verdict and a scaffold speech by the Lutheran pastor Georg Michael Schnitzlein, given just after the prisoner was beheaded.[4]

---

[2] This aspect of Francke's teaching is pointed out by August Hardeland, *Geschichte der Speciellen Seelsorge in der Vorreformatorische Kirche und der Kirche der Reformation*, 1898, p. 425–6.

[3] Hardeland, *Geschichte der Speciellen Seelsorge*, p. 461–2.

[4] 'Kurtze Relation und Urtheil die von des h. Röm. eichs Erb-Marchall- Amts wegen ob commissum infanticidum zu Pappenheim justificierte Eva Ellingerin Betreffend'

'Here lies the beheaded Eva Ellingerin before our eyes, her body still warm in her blood.'[5] She had suffered a just punishment by the secular authorities, the pastor said, but the spectators should not think that the divine judgement would be the same. Eva Ellingerin had, namely, from the first days of her imprisonment punished herself with true contrition and penance. She had admitted not only to the murder but also to the total abomination of her natural depravity. Her sins, the pastor pointed out, were not extraordinary but the everyday sins of those not yet reborn, such as praying and confessing without true worship.

The agony in her heart was very great while she struggled for repentance. Day and night she had untiringly cried to God for just one drop of his comfort. And God had illuminated her with the light of his mercy so that she was filled with inner joy and peace:

> In her last days it was as if her heart was bubbling and burning with happiness and love of God. This last morning of her life on Earth in this overflowing love, with great emotion of heart, she had sung the true believers' spiritual bridal song, 'Wie schön leuchtet der Morgen-Stern' ['How beautiful shines the morning star']. And she went to God immediately after.[6]

The pastor said that he could not possibly speak highly enough of her true penance, strong faith, passionate love of Jesus and of her neighbour, her calm and peace, her zealousness in prayer, and her heartfelt admonitions and appeals to do good directed at her fellow prisoners. The speech ended with a warning to the public not to sin.[7]

Johann Jakob Moser's Collection

We have the German jurist Johann Jakob Moser to thank for the preservation of a considerable number of descriptive accounts of the

---

(Regensburg, 1724), Royal Library Copenhagen. The speech by the city pastor Georg Michael Schnitzlein covers p. 11–15.

[5] 'Kurtze Relation und Urtheil', p. 11: 'Hier liegt die enthauptete Eva Ellingerin dem Leibe nach noch warm in ihrem Blut vor unser aller Augen.'

[6] 'Kurtze Relation und Urtheil', p. 13: 'Die letzten Tage … es sey als wenn ihr Hertz immer wallete und brennete für Freude und Liebe zu Gott. Wie sie dann in solchem Liebes-Trieb das rechte geistliche Braut-Lied der Glaubigen—Wie schön leuchtet der Morgen-Stern etc. eben an diesem letzten Morgen ihres zeitlichen Lebens mit vieler Bewegung ihres Hertzens am ersten gesungen, und bald darauf hingegangen zu Gott.'

[7] Other examples of published sermons and scaffold speeches are: Georg Matthäus Beckh, 'Die von dem barmherzigen Gott hoch-begnadigte Arme Sünderin und

preparation of those condemned to death. Moser came from Lutheran Württemberg, in southern Germany, and is known for his prolific literary production. In his lifetime (1701–1785) he managed to publish approximately 500 volumes. His best-known publication is *Deutsches Staatsrecht*, a description in more than fifty volumes of the constitutional law of the numerous German territories and free cities. Moser, however, also took a pronounced religious stand. In the 1730s he declared himself a Pietist, and in the 1740s he lived for eight years in a Pietist community in Ebersdorf.

While living there, he collected and published his descriptions. The first edition appeared in 1740, then expanded editions came out in 1742 and 1744, and finally a 900-page edition was published in 1753, with the elaborate but also informative title

> Blessed last Hours of 31 Persons having died by the Executioner's Hand: By the World known as Child and other Murderers, Duellists, Robbers, Bandits, Thieves, Incendiaries, Bestiality Committers, Counterfeiters and other Forgers, and Military Criminals; by God, however, known as justified and cleansed in the Blood of Jesus, or at least as Souls hungering for Mercy. Collected in Praise of God's Merciful Love and for the Saving of even more similar Persons and other Brutal as well as Virtuous Sinners. And furnished with an Introduction.[8]

One of the thirty-one accounts told the story in the Gospel of Luke about the crucified thief to whom Jesus gives a place in Paradise. The other accounts were from Moser's own time, with precise details of time and place. Some of them had been published previously as sermons and scaffold speeches, but many had been provided by Moser's network of like-minded religious jurists. In the introduction he asked the readers to forward additional accounts, and the publication was enlarged with at least twelve accounts between the first edition and the last. The accounts were usually written by pastors, and four of them dealt with suicide murderers.[9]

Moser's introduction to the 1740 collection provides an interesting insight into the general understanding and discussion of the possible

---

Kindes-Mörderin in Nördlingen', 1715, and Johann Melchior Grimm, 'Als Margaretha Ursula Huberin Burgerliche Balln-Binderin', Regensburg, 1734.

[8] Moser, *Seelige letzte Stunden*.

[9] They were Catharina Elisabeth Uhlin, who had killed a nine-year-old child in the bridewell of Halle (p. 161–89), the tobacco spinner Andreas Kronberg, who had killed his own eleven-week-old child in Magdeburg (p. 189–207), Gertrud Magdalena Bremmelin (p. 269–326; see also below) and a soldier called Michel Blödörn, from Copenhagen (p. 593–606; see also Appendix, case 1739:1).

salvation of criminals at the place of execution.[10] He begins by discussing whether one should believe the conversion of a person condemned to death just before the moment of execution. At one end of the spectrum of responses to this question is that of the ordinary uneducated people with a purely external religiosity. They believe that a convict who, at the place of execution, answers yes to the pastor's questions, prays to God and accepts their execution will be truly converted. At the other extreme is the view of the educated, arrogant Pharisees, who make themselves out to be better than murderers and robbers and therefore do not believe that such people can be converted. According to them, the pious conduct of the convict at the place of execution is caused purely by fear of death. Even when they see a condemned man who has sincerely converted to God, to them this is merely simulated Pietist hypocrisy. The adjective 'Pietist' reveals that Moser is arguing in defence of a special Pietist interest in the preparation and conversion of those condemned to death.

Moser's position was between these two extremes: some, but not all, convicts who willingly performed their role in the execution ceremony were true converts. Following the thoughts of Francke, he believed that careful observation of the last hours of a person condemned to death would reveal whether or not genuine conversion had taken place.

Moser continued that the conversion of a person condemned to death was highly possible. First, he said that their conversion was 'ordinarily possible', meaning that no extraordinary divine mercy was necessary. The person condemned to death need do no more and no less than others to attain God's mercy. God condemns all sins, and by our nature we are all cursed. Moser backed this argument with several quotations from the Bible. Secondly, he claimed that it was actually easier for gross sinners to convert because their sins were so great and obvious and therefore easy to recognize.

Moser's purpose in publishing these accounts was to convince readers of the possibility of the conversion of those condemned to death, but at the same time to show that all converts underwent a real change of heart, mind and will, followed by a confident belief that Jesus died for our sins. He stated that when a person condemned to death in this way was reborn, one should not talk contemptuously about him or her, but should rejoice together with the newly reborn. He also hoped that

[10] Moser, *Seelige letzte Stunden*, p. 3–26.

his book could serve as a guide for pastors and public officials and show them the importance of a thorough preparation.

The thirty accounts of conversions of criminals tend to follow a pattern. First comes a description of the criminal's previous sinful life as well as their insolent or indifferent attitude towards the pastors when they first meet them. Then comes the first breakthrough, as the Word of God is read to them or taught them. When their interest is awakened through the Word of God, the pastors explain to them about the divine truths. This leads them to an acknowledgment of the many sins they have committed. After a period of moaning about her or his sins comes the prisoner's rebirth, the confident belief that Jesus will save her or him from the just anger of God. The rebirth finally stands its trial on the day of execution.

Magdalena Bremmels

As an example let us take the account of the preparation of the housemaid Magdalena Bremmels, who in July 1744 murdered her master's four-year-old daughter.[11] Magdalena had tried to make out that her parents were grander and wealthier than they really were, in order to become engaged to the master's son. When this failed, she became depressed and desperate and decided to kill the little girl. After the murder she went to the officials and gave herself up.

The murder took place in the city of Wernigerode, ruled by Count Christian Ernst Stolberg-Wernigerode, who was well known for his work as a Pietist.[12] Four pastors were ordered to take turns preparing Magdalena for her execution. The account relates her ignorance of the divine truths but also her eagerness and willingness to learn and understand them. First she starts repenting of her sinful life. She has been proud, licentious, vain and greedy. It was an execution that inspired her to commit the murder. The tears of penance, however, are followed by the belief that Jesus will bear her sins and by serene, confident happiness.

The account gives the impression that there were people around Magdalena most of the time, and not only the pastors. Women

[11] Moser, *Seelige letzte Stunden*, p. 269–326.

[12] He was the cousin of the Danish king, and the two corresponded intensely on religious matters. See H.L. Møller, *Kong Christian VI og Grev Christian Ernst af Stolberg-Wernigerode*, 1889.

came and had supper with her and prayed with her. On the day of her execution they helped her to dress. Over the last two days she received Holy Communion three times. She made much use of a *Hällischen Spruch-Kästlein*, a box containing slips of paper on which were quotations from the Bible. These were drawn at random and seen as personal messages from God. The last two days and nights two divinity graduates took it upon themselves to write down everything Magdalena said and did. They stayed in the room next to hers and wrote down word for word the numerous prayers that she made up.

The execution took place about four months after the murder. Magdalena herself had chosen the hymns to be sung on the way to the place of execution. She left the gaol, walking calmly and solemnly with the four pastors behind her. When the time came for her to make a public confession of her crime in front of the court building, the account says that 'She stood like a lamb and answered undaunted the questions asked of her. Then with a clear voice and happy gesticulations she led the singing of "Mein Heyland nimmt die Sünder an" ["My Saviour, welcome the sinner"]'.[13]

On her way through the city to the city gate she stopped a few times and prayed quietly. When she neared the place of execution, the crowd cheered her: she should be confident. Jesus would not abandon her in her last hour.

The whole city, led by Count Stolberg-Wernigerode, had gathered to witness the execution. Undaunted, Magdalena went up to the carriage carrying the count and his family. She thanked them for their kindness to her and asked the count to bless the people who had gathered. At the gate to the execution platform she said goodbye to the pastors accompanying her, except the one who accompanied her up to the scaffold. Having arrived on the scaffold, she knelt and prayed in a loud voice. The prayer was written down and took up three pages in the account. Then she walked to the chair where she was to sit during the beheading, said a final prayer with the pastor and was dispatched.

The fifty-seven-page description of Magdalena Bremmels's last days provides a unique insight into the religious attraction of committing murder in order to be executed. It is, of course, related by a pastor and

---

[13] Moser, *Seelige letzte Stunden*, p. 321: 'stand sie wie ein Lamm, und beantwortete die vorgelegte Fragen unerschrocken. Nach Endigung desselben fieng sie mit heller Stimme und freudigen Gebehrden den Gesang mit anzusingen: Mein Heyland nimmt die Sünder an.'

Figure 5. A copperplate depicting the execution in Augsburg of a woman who had committed infanticide ca 1750. (Germanisches Nationalmuseum, Nürnberg, HB 4461 caps 1373a)

is coloured by his wishes for a successful preparation and execution. But Magdalena seems to have actively participated in her own preparation. She did not suppress her sin but openly told the eager listeners of her innermost thoughts and feelings. Her penance and conversion were followed by excitement, and she seemed pleased with the respectful audience witnessing her new state of grace, writing down her prayers and admiring her calm and joy. On the day of the execution the smaller audience of pastors and other firm believers was replaced by the much larger public of the whole city, led by Count Stolberg-Wernigerode himself. Here she displayed an astonishing degree of calm and joy, bearing witness to her pious certainty of being saved. She said that she had been inspired to commit the murder by attending an execution, and her own solemn execution might well tempt others to do the same.[14]

Michel Blödorn

Moser's accounts came from many different places and contained one from Copenhagen as well.[15] The Copenhagen account was shorter than the one from Wernigerode and said little about the conversion, but it provides an insight into the dubious effects of harsh punishments on suicide murderers.

The account describes the conversion and death of the first soldier being broken on the wheel pursuant to the decree of 1738. Moser does not give the name of the storyteller but says that he was a count. The murderer was the musketeer Michel Blödorn, who had shot his landlord. There are some minor differences between the description of the murder in the account and that contained in the court records.[16] According to the latter, Blödorn first tried to explain the murder as a combination of drunkenness and an accident. This may have been an attempt to avoid the harsh new punishment. Later, however, he claimed that Satan had inspired him to commit the murder. In his letter to Moser the count stated that Blödorn had first been so hardened that the pastors could do nothing, but then the pastors' persistence and the

[14] The story of Magdalena Bremmels is followed by another story from Wernigerode that took place three years later. See Moser, *Seelige letzte Stunden*, p. 327.
[15] Moser, *Seelige letzte Stunden*, p. 593–606.
[16] Appendix, case 1739:1.

Word of God had crushed his opposition, and he prayed with devotion and shed many tears of penance. When the sentence with its terrible punishment was read to him, he listened calmly and said that he deserved it.

While Blödorn was being whipped once a week for nine consecutive weeks, the pastors had frequently visited him and were astonished by his calm and cheerfulness. On the day when he was to be broken on the wheel, everybody was surprised that he went to his torture so undaunted and calm. The count explained: 'But what was this? The Good Angels accompanied him, and the Holy Spirit comforted him with such force in his heart that you could sense God working wonders in him.'[17]

At the place of execution Blödorn sang and prayed at length and then undressed and calmly lay down. When his legs and arms were broken, he did not cry out but prayed in a loud voice. Still alive, he was put on the wheel to die, and he continued praying and singing. The pastors took it in turns to climb up a ladder to pray with him, holding a hymnbook for him so that he could sing. A large crowd was watching and joined him in singing hymns. When this had gone on all day and Blödorn was not yet dead, a pastor had a runner sent to the king asking for the poor man to be put out of his misery. As the king was out of town, however, it took until one o'clock in the morning before the runner returned with permission for him to be strangled.

The count found the whole spectacle very edifying. In his eyes the spectators had witnessed divine intervention, which had made the soldier able to endure the pain. This divine intervention was caused by Blödorn's wonderful conversion and his state of grace.

The count attached a brief account by Blödorn's spiritual adviser, Pastor Grothausen. The pastor offered a somewhat different interpretation of the effects of the spectacular scenario. He had his doubts about its edifying quality and concluded his account with these words:

> What lessons are being drawn from the memorable ending of this sinner by desperate souls who are tired of life and in their blind rage are searching for a short cut to heaven? We have a testimony thereof from another murderer, who bluntly confessed to me upon my first visit that he had

---

[17] Moser, *Seelige letzte Stunden*, p. 597. 'Aber was war es? Die guten Engel begleiteten ihn, und der heilige Geist trostete ihn so kräftig in seinen Herzen, dass man rechte Wunder Gottes an ihm spüren konnte.'

Figure 6a and 6b. These two woodcuts, taken from a ballad about three soldiers who had robbed and murdered a whole family, illustrate their cruel punishment. The first depicts, in the background, the murderers being pinched with red-hot tongs. To the right, the hand and the head of a murderer are cut off with an axe, and to the left the leader is being broken with the wheel. The second woodcut depicts, to the right, the heads and bodies of two of the murderers placed on post and wheel. To the left, the leader is still alive and has been put on the post and wheel to die. (From 'En gandske nye Viise om det forskreckkelige Mord, som af trende fod-gardere, Carl Evalt, Baltz Beck, og Frid. Elmhorst.', 1727, The Royal Library, Copenhagen)

> chosen not to kill himself but to murder somebody else, so that he had the time to be converted and obtain an end as good as the previous murderer.[18]

In his foreword to the first edition of the collection Moser had not mentioned this side-effect of the 'edifying' executions he described. But in 1753 he added a new foreword, in which he commented on the misuse by saying he hoped nobody would be so blind, stupid and reckless as to commit a crime for which the law stipulated the death penalty purely in order to achieve an edifying death.[19]

The attitude of the authorities towards the suicide murderers was thus ambiguous, mirroring the parallel discourses of the perpetrators in their court confessions and in the ballads. On the one hand, the authorities expressed their revulsion at the horrific nature of the crime. For this reason the murderers were sentenced to death and to humiliating as well as physically terrifying additional punishments. On the other hand, however, the authorities would also show their compassion for a sinner about to meet his maker. The murderers joined a common category of gross sinners sentenced to death. The Lutheran state paid considerable attention to this category by ordering the pastors energetically to prepare them for their execution and by ordering an execution ceremony that supported the message that divine mercy would finally save their souls. The prevailing Pietist preaching took this compassion a step further through its focus on the transformation that took place when sinful man was reborn as a true believer. The conversion of such gross sinners was a particularly wonderful example of God's infinite mercy, which the pastors thought should receive as much public attention as possible. The jurists in the courts represented the authorities' anger, but God was present in the courts as well. The death penalty was ultimately God's will, and the courts accordingly instruments for divine justice. According to this argument, the judges or the king could show

[18] Moser, *Seelige letzte Stunden*, p. 601–02. 'Was aber die desperaten Seelen, so des Leben Müde sind und in ihren verblendeten Wuth einen kurzen Nebenweg zum Himmel suchen, aus dieses Sünders denckwürdigem Ende vor Lehren gezogen, davon haben wir eine Probe an einem andern Mörder, der mir bey der ersten Besuchung rein aus bekannte, er hätte sich nicht selbst, sondern ein andern, ermorden wollen, damit er Zeit hätte, sich zu bekehren und ein solch gut Ende nehmen möchte, wie der vorige Mörder.' The pastor probably referred to the murder by Hinrich Puffvogel, which took place three months after Blödorn's execution. See Appendix, case 1739:2.

[19] Moser, *Seelige letzte Stunden*, p. 27–8.

their compassion for the penitent murderer eager to suffer for her deed by obeying God's will and carrying out the death sentence while nevertheless granting her a burial in consecrated ground.

The Danish bishop Peder Hersleb was formally correct when he called it a delusion to believe that salvation could not fail when the execution ritual was performed. As Moser explained, it was not enough simply to say yes to the pastor's questions, pray and willingly let the executioner do his job; the convict had to have undergone a true conversion in the days preceding the execution. The convicts, however, had the best clerical help possible in their fight for the salvation of their soul, and, as Moser added, the convict had just as good (and in some ways better) conditions for a conversion as anyone else facing death. The ballads were thus in complete conformity with the message of the Church Ritual and Pietist preaching when they told of the conversion of the murderers and the happy life in Heaven awaiting them. Magdalena Bremmels and Michel Blödorn could equally feel in total agreement with official belief when they expressed their calm and joyful certainty of being saved.

CHAPTER SEVEN

MOTIVES

The social reasons and the psychological state of the suicide murderers were very similar to those generally found among people who commit suicide. They were frequently suffering from unjust treatment by their employer or from their superiors, or from problems in their love life, or being forced to endure unbearable living conditions in prison or the army, or living in fear of punishment. These social motives were usually interwoven with mental instability or depression of some sort.

When these people chose not to kill themselves, but instead to kill an innocent child or a stranger, a basic precondition for this choice was, of course, the existence of the death penalty. The most common motive to which the murderers confessed in the courts was the wish to be executed. The religious discourse in which the executions were understood, however, added a number of attractions to the suicide crime, which enhanced the inclination of those wanting to commit suicide to seek the executioner as the tool for their purpose.

First, a religious person would fear to commit suicide, as suicide was a certain way for the soul to go to hell. To commit a murder was a terrible sin, but when the perpetrator envisaged herself as a weak person constantly tempted by the Devil to fall into misery, her deed became somewhat excusable. It was the fate of all people sometimes to succumb to the Devil's temptations and commit sins. When the murder had been committed, the murderer could focus on the salvation of her soul. The Church Ritual, the ballads, the preparation by the pastors and the religious staging of the executions all unanimously communicated the message that salvation was certain if you honestly repented your sins and truly believed in God when you breathed your last. In this religious understanding an aggravated death penalty would just be a greater ordeal, and in the mind of the count attending the execution of Michel Blödorn, for example, the magnitude of the ordeal endured added to the certainty of the soul being saved.

Secondly, the religious discourse provided a number of what might be termed social benefits. Suicide is often an act of communication. Attempted suicides are often cries for help directed towards relatives or society, and people committing suicide often leave a note explaining their action or blaming others for their suicide. Someone who committed a suicide murder had very good opportunities to communicate with family and friends as well as with society, and by virtue of the religious discourse this communication could moreover take place in a spirit of reconciliation.

Facing the judges in the courts, they were able to be perfectly frank and yet obtain their goal. They could tell the courts about the injustices to which they had been exposed and about their plan to achieve death with the help of the courts. This frankness might meet some understanding even within the court, if the murderer presented herself as a penitent sinner, unable to suppress her sinful nature, which Church Ritual warned against, and who willingly accepted the punishment stipulated by God and the authorities.

Facing the pastors and the people, the murderers could expect considerable attention to be paid to their spiritual development, and they could expect some sort of understanding and even pity as a gross sinner hoping for salvation. The execution became a divine ordeal, a final test of the murderer's faith. If the murderers passed the test by joyfully going to their own death, they would, so to speak, be reunited with society.

Some of the murderers seemed to be especially attracted to the great amount of attention given to prisoners awaiting execution, and to being the key figure at the solemn execution ceremony, attended by large groups of citizens. When one reads the story of Magdalena Bremmels, one senses her joy at being the focus of everybody's attention. Several of the murderers mentioned that they had been inspired to commit the murder by attending an execution. By this they probably meant that they felt attracted to the attention given to the prisoner being executed.

In their confessions in the court the murderers often placed the responsibility for the murder they had committed on someone or something else. Soldiers would blame unjust treatment by superior officers for the murder, prisoners would blame the bad treatment and sense of despair in gaol, housemaids would point to the bad treatment they had received at the hands of their master or mistress, and rejected lovers or mothers of illegitimate children would blame the perfidious lover. In contrast to those who committed suicide, the murderers were able to present their case in court and in public, and thus to put the burden of guilt for the murdered child—as well as for their own execution—on the shoulders of those who had been unjust to them. In 1767 a supreme court judge and senior civil servant, Henrich Hielmstierne, in an analysis of the murderers' motives, argued that some of the murderers acted out of indignation and spite. He mentioned a housemaid who had been badly treated by her mistress and in desperation had killed a child. The maid explained, according to Hielmstierne, 'that she had done it to avenge herself on her mistress, as she would be greatly concerned at being the cause of two persons losing their lives'.[1] Cicilia Johansdatter, in the 'aria' cited above, used the attention that her execution attracted to expose her lover and blame him for her murder of their child.

The religious attitude to suicide, the soteriology of the Church and the social motives stemming from the religious discourse and the religious staging of the executions thus furnished a number of enticements to use murder as a vehicle to obtain death, but nevertheless the simple desire to be executed was often the sole reason articulated by the perpetrators in the court. It must therefore be asked if—and if so, then to what extent—suicide murders can still take place in the absence of religious discourse.

In order to answer this question it is necessary to explore the boundaries of the suicide murders in the eighteenth century. Did they occur all over Europe or only in specific areas? Furthermore, in relation to this question it is necessary to investigate the boundaries of the religious discourse encouraging the murders. To what degree was the discourse specific to the Lutheran confession and to the Lutheran states? Finally the story of how the phenomenon of the suicide murder came to an end will show what happened when the religious discourse encouraging the murders disappeared.

[1] Citation from Krogh, *Oplysningstiden og det magiske*, p. 247: 'at hun havde gjort det for at hevne sig paa Madmoderen, da hun ville blive høystbekymret over, at hun var Aarsag, at to Mennisker mistede Livet.' Hielmstierne presented this analysis as a preparation to the decree of 1767; see p. 149.

CHAPTER EIGHT

BOUNDARIES

The statistical studies as well as the accounts of the suicide murders presented so far all come from Scandinavia and north-eastern Germany, but what about the rest of Europe? Were the suicide murders confined to this corner of Europe, or were they a general phenomenon?

This is not an easy question to answer. Quite a number of studies of crime and punishment are available, but their scope and aims differ considerably. In any case, it is always difficult to prove that something did not take place. For southern Germany and Austria especially, Kathy Stuart's study has been of great help.[1] She has looked for suicide murders in the archives of Nuremberg, Augsburg and Württemberg, and has used execution pamphlets and collections of criminal cases to supplement the picture. In this chapter I will investigate what evidence can be found in studies on crime and punishment, in combination with contemporary pamphlets and collections of criminal cases from southern Germany and the rest of Europe.

Before looking at these studies we must, however, make clear what we are looking for. What circumstances—that are likely to be present in studies of crime and punishment—could argue for the presence or absence of suicide murders? One clear sign is that the authorities acknowledge the murders as a threat by discussing them and taking measures to prevent them. Legislative measures, in particular, are likely to be described in studies of crime and punishment. The absence of such measures, however, does not necessarily prove that suicide murders did not take place. Another type of information likely to contain indicators for the presence of suicide murders is categorizations and descriptions of homicides in an area and a period. Detailed descriptions of the use of the death penalty are informative as well, as execution was the *raison d'être* of the suicide murder. And as has already been mentioned, female perpetrators and children as victims are further

[1] Kathy Stuart, 'Suicide by Proxy: The Unintended Consequences of Public Executions in Eighteenth-Century Germany', 2008.

characteristic features of suicide murders which could be taken as indicators. Furthermore, the use of the death penalty for homicide must be of significance if suicide murders were common. The best material consists of copious descriptions of single cases in samples that would be likely to contain suicide murders if they had taken place.

Lutheran Areas of Southern Germany

Southern Germany was predominantly Catholic, but many of the imperial free cities as well as the Duchy of Württemberg were Lutheran.

The suicide murders were well known in Lutheran Nuremberg. In 1702 the municipal authorities issued a decree stipulating harsh punishments for those men and women who, suffering from acute depression, murdered other people's innocent children, or even adults, in order to be executed. They did this, the decree stated, in the belief that if they showed true remorse at the time of execution God would open His door of grace to them.[2] Kathy Stuart has examined the *Malefizuhrteilsbuch*, a book of judgements from the city, and found eight suicide murders between 1691 and 1745.[3] With Stuart's population estimate of *c.* 25,000 in the early eighteenth century, the frequency is 0.6 murders a year per 100,000 inhabitants.

In the confessionally mixed city of Augsburg, Stuart, using similar source material, has found five suicide murders, one attempted suicide murder and four child murders where the motive could not be established, all dating from the period 1740–83.[4] In addition, she has found two invented murders, where two people accused themselves of child murder but where the authorities were not persuaded by their confessions. Such invented murders were well known in Copenhagen as well. With *c.* 30.000 inhabitants, the frequency is between 0.4 and 0.7 a year per 100,000 inhabitants. In addition, I have found one case in Lutheran Regensburg from 1734.[5]

---

[2] Gustav Bode, 'Kindestötung und ihre Bestrafung im Nürnberg des Mittelalters', 1915, p. 29–31.

[3] Stuart, 'Suicide by Proxy', p. 423–4. The *Malefizurtheilsbuch* ends in 1743, but Stuart has found two additional cases from 1744 and 1745 in other archival sources.

[4] Stuart, 'Suicide by Proxy', p. 424–5. Stuart does not mention whether she has searched for suicide murder cases before 1740.

[5] 'Als Margaretha Ursula Huberin Burgerliche Balln-Binderin … Regenspurg …', 1734.

Helga Schnabel-Schüle has investigated crime and punishment in the Duchy of Württemberg from the sixteenth century to the eighteenth.[6] Besides a thorough analysis of the legal system and the social conditions in the Duchy, Schnabel-Schüle studied crime and legal usage. The latter is based on 4,300 criminal cases found in the central archives and dating from the period 1532–1800. Schnabel-Schüle argues that the samples preserved are fairly representative. Owing to some degree of uncertainty, however—as well as profound scepticism concerning quantitative analysis—she has refrained from statistical analysis.[7] There are no references to suicide murders in her detailed analysis of legislation and the legal debate in the Duchy.

The sample contains 656 homicide cases, of which Schnabel-Schüle has conducted a qualitative analysis. The majority were classified as unpremeditated manslaughter. Some women were killed by men with whom they were in a relationship but who wanted to avoid marriage or as a result of domestic disputes. The few child victims were killed by neglect or as a result of brutal punishments by step-parents. In the eighteenth century Schnabel-Schüle found a number of murders resulting from what she terms 'religious exaggerations', the common denominator being that the perpetrators believed either that they were carrying out the will of God or that they were in the power of the Devil. The authorities, for their part, discussed whether the murders could be excused by insanity. One of the four cases mentioned was a suicide murder.[8] In 1673 sixty-year old Hans Bütz, overwhelmed by self-loathing because he had committed acts of bestiality and believing he was possessed by the Devil, thought of killing himself but in the end killed his sister's baby daughter. After this, he said, God made him confess his sins. He then felt better and only wished to die. The authorities mainly discussed his state of mind and, finding him accountable for his deeds, sentenced him to execution by sword.

Kathy Stuart has found an additional six suicide murder cases from Württemberg, one from 1612 and five from the period 1703–23.[9]

---

[6] Schnabel-Schüle, *Überwachen und Strafen im Territorialstaat*.

[7] Schnabel-Schüle, *Überwachen und Strafen im Territorialstaat*, p. 18–22. As mentioned in the introduction, I do not share Schnabel-Schüle's scepticism about the ability of the reader to understand the limitations of statistics.

[8] Schnabel-Schüle, *Überwachen und Strafen im Territorialstaat*, p. 261–2.

[9] Stuart, 'Suicide by Proxy', p. 425. Whereas Schnabel-Schüle dates Hans Bütz's case to 1673, Stuart dates it to 1678. Stuart says that 'at least' seven murders were committed in Württemberg, but she does not report what material she has examined. It would be

Helga Schnabel-Schüle's thorough study, however, indicates that suicide murders were not considered a criminal problem in the Duchy.

In conclusion, it appears suicide murders were known in the Lutheran imperial cities in southern Germany. In Nuremberg and Augsburg they seem to have been just as frequent as, for instance, in Hamburg. In Württemberg they were known too, but were apparently much rarer than in Zealand in Denmark and in Schleswig-Holstein.

Catholic Areas of Southern Germany, Austria and France

What, then, of the Catholic parts of southern Germany? Karl Härter has studied crime and punishment in the Catholic Electorate of Mainz, bordering on Württemberg. Like Helga Schnabel-Schüle, Härter has used criminal cases from the archives of the central government. He deals with 3,705 cases dating from between 1560 and 1802, but only a minority of these (173) are earlier than 1700. Of the 296 homicides, 85 were cases of infanticide, 173 cases of manslaughter and 38 cases of murder. The cases of murder were primarily murders within the family and murders with intent to rob. Among the 18 murders within the family, Härter points out the murders of spouses but also mentions parricide and murder of children for a sexual or material motive. He does not mention suicide murders, and his study indicates that there were few, if any, in the Electorate of Mainz.[10]

Crime and punishment in the major Catholic territory of southern Germany, Bavaria, have been studied by Wolfgang Behringer. He focuses on Upper Bavaria and the capital Munich in the years between 1500 and 1800. Compared with the studies of Württemberg and the Electorate of Mainz, Behringer's study is not very extensive and based on fragmentary and less copious material.[11] He describes the development of criminal law, the crime pattern and the use of executions in various periods. He has described female crime in a separate

interesting to know if she had searched for suicide murder cases in the criminal cases preserved from the rest of the eighteenth century and found none.

[10] Karl Härter, *Policey und Strafjustiz in Kurmainz*, 2005, p. 548, 567–8. See also Härter, 'Zum Verhältnis von "Rechtsquellen" und territorialen Rahmenbedingungen in der Strafgerichtsbarkeit des 18. Jahrhunderts', 2003, p. 433–66, and 'Kriminalität und Praxis der Strafjustiz im geistlichen Territorialstaat des Alten Reiches', p.101–34.

[11] Wolfgang Behringer, 'Mörder, Diebe und Ehebrecher: Verbrechen und Strafen in Kurbayern vom 16. bis 18. Jahrhundert', 1990, p. 85–132.

article.[12] His studies, however, have not led to any mention of suicide murders.

Nevertheless, two suicide murders have been identified in Bavaria. In a collection of criminal cases Kathy Stuart found a case from 1745 from the small town Hilpoltstein, situated close to Nuremberg.[13] In Munich it was common in the second half of the eighteenth century to publish pamphlets about executions. These had a notably uniform appearance. The titles all began with the same words: 'Wohlverdientes Todesurtheil nebst einer Moralrede der …' ('Well-deserved death sentence together with a moral speech about …'). They contained a description of the case, the confession and the verdict—and a versified moral speech. Some thirty of these appear in search results from German library databases, and one of these, from 1783, describes a suicide murder.[14] The lack of more suicide murder cases in the pamphlet series indicates that the murders were not common in Munich. Influenced by the criminal code of Prussia, the Bavarian government considered incorporating a provision in the Bavarian criminal code on the punishment of suicide murders, which was to have been enacted in 1813. But it was finally decided to omit it, with the argument that such cases were very infrequent.[15] This official estimate that suicide murders were very infrequent is a reasonable conclusion on the findings from Bavaria.

In her description of the Catholic cases, Kathy Stuart notes that almost all were from the second half of the eighteenth century. It is therefore possible that to some extent the suicide murders in Catholic areas of southern Germany were inspired by Lutheran cases. The ballads about suicide murders may have been an important vehicle for the spread of the phenomenon. They were in some cases sold all over Germany, and the stories of young women who murdered to obtain death, and who managed to orchestrate their suicide as a marriage to Jesus in front of the whole sympathetic community, provided fascinating narratives. The tales of these murderers may very well have attracted suicidal people in other parts of the country, with other confessions. There are only few Catholic ballads about executions. Catholic leaflets

---

[12] W. Behringer, 'Weibliche Kriminalität in Kurbayern in der Frühen Neuzeit', 1995, p. 63–82.

[13] Stuart, 'Suicide by Proxy', p. 426.

[14] 'Wohlverdientes Todesurtheil nebst einer Moralrede der Margaretha N. vulgo Schilcheten Grödl, München 1783.'

[15] See Weber, *Selbstmord*, p. 173–4.

about executions were primarily descriptions of the case and the verdict, as with the leaflets from Munich mentioned above. These leaflets focused on the heinous nature of the crimes and on their well-deserved punishment and did not encourage the reader to identify with the perpetrator.

The suggestion that suicide murders in Catholic areas were non-existent or extremely infrequent is, however, challenged by the case of Vienna. In this major Catholic city and capital of the Holy Roman Empire, in two independent studies, Kathy Stuart and Susanne Hehenberger have found a considerable number of suicide murder cases. On the basis of published execution pamphlets, Stuart has found 8 suicide murder cases from Vienna between 1738 and 1767[16]. Susanne Hehenberger has searched for descriptions of criminal cases in the *Wienerische Diarium* newspaper in the period 1703–50.[17] For the period 1733–50 she found the same three cases that Kathy Stuart found through the execution pamphlets. She found 10 cases between 1704 and 1732 of (primarily) women murdering children not known to them and 7 cases of mothers murdering their own children and where it could just as well be infanticide. Finally, she found 2 cases of female child murderers where the familial relation to the victim was not reported. A suicide motive was mentioned in some of the early cases as well, and the presence of suicide murders is further documented by a Lower Austrian edict of 22 March 1706.[18] In the preamble the edict said that a growing number of child murders not only by mothers but also by people with no relation to the child were taking place, and 'weariness of life' was mentioned as a motive. Harsher penalites were imposed

[16] Stuart, 'Suicide by Proxy', p. 425, 427. Actually Stuart counts nine cases, but according to my definitions I have chosen to omit a case from 1769, where Catharina J. was executed. She had confessed to have killed six children in the preceeding six years. Three of the murders had not been verified. Two were verified to the extent that the children had actually drowned, and in one case where she confessed to having battered a child to death, the child was found to have been severely beaten about the head but had recovered. All the verified cases were more than three years old. There might be suicidal elements in her finally confessing to the murders, but at the time of the actual murders she committed them out of hatred of their parents and succesfully hid her involvement in their deaths. Therefore I do not consider these to be suicide murders. See 'Todesurtheil einer ledigen Weibsperson namens Catharina J. … 10. Februarii 1769, Wien'.

[17] Susanne Hehenberger, 'Die beleidigte Ehre Gottes auf das empfindlichste zu rächen, in allweg gesonnen: Blasphemie und Sakrileg im 18. Jahrhundert', 2008, p. 179–201.

[18] Codex Austriacus III, p. 511–2. The edict is mentioned by Kathy Stuart.

for female murders of children who were not their own, and for mothers murdering their own unbaptized, newborn children. The information about the cases from Vienna has the same type of uncertainty as those from Hamburg. By analogy with the Hamburg numbers it can be estimated that in the period 1703–67 between 20 and 27 child murders were committed that were not infanticides. With an average population in Vienna in the period of 140,000,[19] this adds up to between 0.2 and 0.3 child murders that were not infanticide.

Child murders were not, however, the only way in Vienna to obtain death at the hands of the executioner. The main subject of Susanne Hehenberger's article is cases of blasphemy and sacrilege. In the early eighteenth century the Austrian authorities punished blasphemy with the death penalty. In the period 1703–21 Hehenberger has found no fewer than twenty-five cases where women especially—many of these inmates in the local spin-house—committed blasphemous deeds such as breaking or stepping on a crucifix or cutting the Host to pieces and were subsequently executed. Here again the purpose of obtaining their own death by execution was mentioned in several cases and caught the attention of the authorities. An imperial resolution from 1713 imposed more severe punishments, but only two years later a new resolution changed the death penalties to hard labour penalties in cases where the motive was depression or despair. This change of penalty apparently brought about a considerable decline in the number of cases of blasphemy. The attraction of the death penalty for blasphemy was thus analogous to the Copenhagen cases of people selling themselves to the Devil in signed contracts.

It is thus clear that in Vienna the state's propensity to impose the death penalty attracted people wanting to take their own life. Suicide murders were frequent enough to provoke special legislation, and the frequency was high, although it did not reach the levels found in Hamburg, Copenhagen and Stockholm.

I have not been able to find French surveys systematically presenting murders committed in one area in the eighteenth century. The surveys that come closest to meeting my requirements are those of Yves and Nicole Castan, describing the legal system in Languedoc.[20] Their main

---

[19] The population of Vienna is estimated at *c.* 100.000 in 1700 and was 175,000 in the first census in 1754. See Heintz Schilling, *Höfe und Allianzen: Deutschland 1648–1763*, 1994 (1998), p. 356.

[20] Yves Castan, *Honnêteté et relations sociales en Languedoc (1715–1780)*, 1974; Nicole Castan, *Justice et répression en Languedoc à l'époque des lumières*, 1980.

interest, however, is in the social and cultural mechanisms of everyday life, including the role of the legal system. All that can be concluded from their surveys is that suicide murders are not mentioned. A description of one suicide murder can, in fact, be found in a French eighteenth-century text, but the murder described did not take place in France. In his memoirs, written in his old age in 1718, Pierre-Daniel Huet, the celebrated French bishop, describes a journey to Sweden in 1652 and relates a then much-discussed suicide murder.[21] The incident astonished Huet so much that it appeared in his memoirs sixty years later. His astonishment can be taken as indirect evidence of these murders being unknown among the educated élite in early eighteenth-century France.

Reformed Areas

Zurich was a stronghold of the Reformed Church. Zwingli and Bullinger preached there and reformed Zurich's criminal laws. Furthermore, Bullinger obtained the right for the priesthood to give opinions to the magistrate on all matters. This right was, exercised, among other things, to recommend—usually harsh—punishments of criminals whom the magistrate was about to judge. The legal historian Erich Wettstein has studied the history of the death penalty in the city of Zürich as well as in the countryside of the canton. Out of a total of 472 executions between 1600 and 1798, 78 were for homicide, including infanticide. In his description of the homicides Wettstein mentions that very few women committed murder (excluding infanticide), and that the most common method for women was poisoning, or assisting and inspiring men to commit murder.[22] Wettstein does not mention suicide murders. Kathy Stuart has searched for references to suicide murder cases in literature on the history of suicide but has found none in studies of the history of suicide in Geneva and Zurich. In Zurich, Markus Schär has, however, found the practice of people turning themselves in to the authorities and accusing themselves of capital crimes,

[21] It was Helmuth von Weber who found Huet's description (see his *Selbstmord als Mordmotiv*, p. 161). Arne Jansson (*From Swords to Sorrow*, p. 51–3) has a long description of the murder which was committed by a young German goldworker, Paul Wulff, born in Nuremberg. I return to this case on p. 131.

[22] Erich Wettstein, *Die Geschichte der Todesstrafe im Kanton Zürich*, 1958, especially p. 59–71. The right of the priesthood to give opinions is described at p. 138–42.

notably sodomy. The authorities did not prosecute them but had them hospitalized as melancholics. The same pattern of self-accusation of invented crimes with the purpose of being executed was found in Sweden and Copenhagen (see p. 59). Stuart suspects on this basis that suicide murders occurred in reformed areas as well. This may well be a correct suspicion, but if so I assume that instances were very infrequent.

The reformed Church dominated the Netherlands too. Crime and punishment in the major city, Amsterdam, have been the focus of a detailed study by Pieter Spierenburg.[23] Spierenburg was able to identify almost all publicly executed sentences between 1650 and 1750 (almost 3,000), and has, furthermore, studied samples of the much more numerous non-public sentences. He found 101 cases of homicide, of which a majority of 71 were cases of manslaughter. They were all committed by men and usually caused by tavern brawls and the like. The 30 cases of murder included few cases of infanticide. Spierenburg does not go on to describe the motives for the murders but writes that the perpetrators in murder cases, excluding infanticides, were predominantly men.[24] No statutes were passed during this period regarding murder. Here again we must conclude that suicide murders, if they occurred at all, must have been rare.

Anglican England (Surrey and London)

John Beattie has carried out an in-depth study both of crime and punishment and of the court system in England in the period 1660–1800.[25] His empirical base is primarily the county of Surrey, the northern fringes of which bordered London. He has analysed homicide cases between 1660 and 1800. Out of 334 people charged as principals in homicide cases, more than half were acquitted, another quarter were found guilty of manslaughter only, and a fifth were found guilty of murder. Among the cases leading to a murder conviction, a considerable proportion took place within the family, and many as the result of personal hatreds and jealousies. Another group were carried out in connection with robbery and theft. Beattie also mentions a few cases

---

[23] Spierenburg, *The Spectacle of Suffering*.
[24] Spierenburg, *The Spectacle of Suffering*, p. 116–20, 165.
[25] J.M. Beattie, *Crime and Courts in England, 1660–1800*, 1986.

where women murdered their own small children by cutting their throats with knives. These cases would seem to resemble suicide murders if it were not for the fact that two of the mothers who murdered their children were acquitted because they were found insane at the time of the murder.[26] Beattie does not discuss the possibility of a suicide motivation. Therefore, on the basis of Beattie's description it can only be concluded that, although suicide murders may have occurred, they were very rare.

In addition to Beattie's study, there is an Internet source that provides a fascinating insight into crime and punishment in England: the proceedings of the Old Bailey. This court dealt with major offences in the City of London and Middlesex, an area with between 600,000 and 1 million inhabitants during the eighteenth century. The printed proceedings from 1714 to 1799, containing 45,000 trials, are available online and can be searched by crime, verdict and punishment, among other things.[27] In all, 1,212 defendants were charged with one or other form of killing. Of these, more than half were acquitted, 231 received the punishment of being branded on the thumb, indicating a guilty verdict for manslaughter, and 247 received the death penalty, indicating a guilty verdict for murder, infanticide or petty treason (i.e., the murder of a superior in the household). Of the 584 convicted, 50 were women. Of these, 20 were convicted of infanticide; in one case a woman was found guilty of killing her own three-month-old child in order to get rid of it. In 3 cases the murder had resulted from violent treatment of children in the custody of the women. In 21 cases the reasons for the murdering women were robbery, jealousy or quarrels of some sort. Of the last 4 cases, one is described too briefly to classify it in any way, and 1 case has some signs of a suicide murder: a woman killing a child where the judge can find no motive whatsoever. There remain two cases that can more clearly be categorized as suicide murders.

In the first case, from 1718, Mary Price strangled a three-year-old child. She did this because the father of the child had taken a tobacco box that had sentimental value for her, and she wanted revenge for this. She gave herself up after the murder, and at the trial she pleaded guilty. This was strange behaviour in the eyes of the judge, and it induced

[26] Beattie, *Crime and Courts in England*, p. 84–5, 101.

[27] http://www.oldbaileyonline.org/. The trial of Mary Price has reference number: t17180709-36, that of Mary Hindes ref. t17680518-39.

the court to have her examined for insanity, but she was not found to be insane.

In the second case, from 1768, Mary Hindes killed the eighteen-month-old child of a friend of hers. She took the child with her to the Serpentine in Hyde Park one evening, and when no one was near, she threw the child in the water and went off leaving it to drown. When arrested in a tavern, she did not deny the murder. She explained that she was weary of life and had committed an act for which she knew she would receive no mercy from the jury. Suicide murders thus did occur in the London area, but they were extremely rare.

In terms of the discussion of motives for the suicide murders, what can be concluded from this survey of crime and punishment studies is, first, that murders with a suicide motive seem to be present in many European countries in the eighteenth century, irrespective of their religion. Although no examples were found in Reformed Zurich and Amsterdam, exceptional cases may well exist here too. Thus the rare cases in London were found only thanks to the extraordinary helpful Internet source containing the proceedings of Old Bailey. Furthermore the attraction of suicidal people to the executioner as a vehicle for losing their lives was not limited to the crime of murder. As long as the authorities were willing to execute for crimes much easier to commit than murder, such as blasphemy or signing contracts with the Devil, these crimes were also used by people wanting to end their life. Inventing crimes carrying a death penalty was another way pursued by those wishing to die. Not all crimes carrying the death penalty were suitable for persons wanting to die, but it seems likely that a suicide motive will be present in more crimes carrying the death penalty than those found in this investigation. I would particularly suspect a suicide motive to be present in witchcraft cases and in cases of infanticide. The executioner's sword was indeed a two-edged means to deter crime. As much as death was feared by the great majority, a minority were attracted by the opportunity to obtain death without having to perform the act themselves. The customary view of the subjects of early modern death sentences as the victims of an inhuman and superstitious justice system thus needs to be modified, and, as I shall show later, the suicide motive in murder cases is not restricted to the early modern period.

Secondly, it is also clear that the frequency of suicide murders differs considerably in countries of different religions. It seems evident that there were only very rare cases in Anglican London and Surrey and in

Reformed Amsterdam and Zurich. The surveys from Catholic areas are more inconclusive. It appears that suicide murders were very rare in Bavaria and rare, if present at all, in the Electorate of Mainz, but in Vienna such murders were frequent and provoked special legislation. Nowhere, however, were suicide murders as frequent and widespread as in Lutheran Scandinavia and northern Germany or some of the Lutheran free cities in southern Germany. It is therefore obvious to look for confessional differences that might encourage or deter such murders. This will be done in the next chapters.

PART TWO

ORIGINS

CHAPTER NINE

DIVINE DEMANDS

The important religious issues for the potential suicide murderers were the consequences of suicide, on the one hand, and of murder, on the other, for the destiny of their soul after death. But just as important were the attitudes of the authorities and of ordinary people towards the murderer awaiting execution.

As for the consequences of suicide for the soul hereafter were concerned, there were no major differences among the religions. The Catholic Church condemned suicide as a mortal sin, and although the reformers did not acknowledge the distinction between mortal and other sins, all confessions condemned suicide as a certain way for the soul to end up in hell. Suicide was a crime to be punished. People committing suicide were denied a Christian burial and their bodies were treated in humiliating ways and were interred at the gallows, or at least not in the churchyard.[1]

The consequences of murder and execution for the destiny of the soul were, however, interpreted differently among the different confessions. These differences originated partly in soteriology, partly in the religious position on the death penalty. And these differences resulted in different attitudes on the part of the authorities and of ordinary people towards the murderers. In the following chapters these differences will be examined at a theoretical, theological level as well as at the practical level of death sentences and of the execution ceremonies.

Interpretations of Mosaic Law

Looking at crimes and the punishments ascribed to them in early modern Europe, it is obvious that a majority of the death penalties for

[1] On official attitudes towards suicide, see: Jansson, *From Swords to Sorrow*, p. 28–30; Krogh, *Oplysningstiden og det magiske*, p. 230; Lind, *Selbstmord in der frühen Neuzeit*, p. 21–2; and MacDonald and Murphy, *Sleepless Souls*, p. 15–6. Kathy Stuart undertakes a comparison between Catholic and Protestant attitudes towards people committing suicide and concludes that the condemnation of suicides in practice was the same, although minor differences can be seen in scholarly treatments of the subject. See Stuart, 'Suicide by Proxy', p. 415–7, 427–8.

serious crimes were motivated more or less directly with reference to the Bible. There were, however, important differences among the confessions in the interpretation of the divine commands concerning death penalties found in the Bible.

The Old Testament is rich in statutes, and large parts of the Pentateuch take the form of legal texts. The laws are explained as having been revealed by God and communicated to Moses, partly at Mount Sinai on the way to the Promised Land, partly immediately before the conquest of Canaan. The laws concern what is clean and unclean, sacrilege, priests, the Sabbath, sexual offences, violence, murder and so on. In a number of cases God demands that the people execute the sinner in order to calm his wrath. The Old Testament prescribes the death penalty for no fewer than 36 crimes.[2] These mortal sins involve blasphemy (1), idolatry and sorcery (10), breaking the Sabbath (1), adultery, (2), incest (12), bestiality (2), homosexuality (1), homicide (1), kidnapping (1), rape (1), violation of filial duties (3) and bad administration (1). Furthermore, the Old Testament is full of examples of God punishing society for not obeying the statutes. He sent the Flood to punish the whole of depraved humanity. The two sinful cities of Sodom and Gomorrah were burned to ashes. Egypt was exposed to the ten plagues, and the ungodly original inhabitants of the Promised Land were expelled.

Even the New Testament mentions the use of the death penalty, but more indirectly. Paul demands that everyone submit themselves to the governing authorities, because God has established the authorities: 'But if thou do that which is evil, be afraid; for he (the authority) beareth not the sword in vain' (Romans 13).

In the first centuries AD several Christian writers argued against the death penalty, but as soon as Christianity became a state religion in the Roman empire this attitude changed. The Fathers of the Church generally approved of the execution of heretics. St Augustine initially rejected this but later came to approve of it.[3]

---

[2] James Megivern, *The Death Penalty: An Historical and Theological Survey*, 1997, p. 10–11. Megivern is a Catholic and an opponent of the death penalty. From this perspective he analyses the foundations of the support of the Catholic Church for the death penalty, primarily through a description of the use of the death penalty by the Vatican state and the historical development of Catholic attitudes towards the death penalty.

[3] Megivern, *The Death Penalty*, p. 35–6.

The influential Christian philosopher Thomas Aquinas discussed the problem with scholastic cogency. He also approved of the execution of heretics, and in a discussion of whether the authorities were allowed to kill sinners, he formulated a general attitude towards the use of the death penalty:

> Now every part is directed to the whole, as imperfect to perfect, wherefore every part is naturally for the sake of the whole. For this reason we observe that if the health of the whole body demands the excision of a member, through its being decayed or infectious to the other members, it will be both praiseworthy and advantageous to have it cut away. Now every individual person is compared to the whole community, as part to whole. Therefore if a man is infectious and dangerous to the community, on account of some sin, it is praiseworthy and advantageous that he be killed in order to safeguard the common good.[4]

Aquinas thus legitimized the use of death penalty through Natural Law. He did not, however, substantiate his argument with reference to the Bible. Aquinas considered the laws of the Pentateuch in the following way:

> We must therefore distinguish three kinds of precepts in the old law: viz. 'moral' precepts, which are dictated by the natural law; 'ceremonial' precepts, which are determinations of the divine worship; and 'judicial' precepts, which are determinations of the justice to be maintained among men.[5]

The moral precepts were eternal, but the ceremonial and judicial precepts were specific to the time and to the people to whom they were given. Today, Aquinas said, the ceremonial precepts were dead, and it would be deadly to observe them, because they were fulfilled in the coming of Christ. To observe them would thus be to deny the coming of Christ. The coming of Christ also annulled the judicial precepts, but they were not deadly to observe:

> For if a sovereign were to order these judicial precepts to be observed in his kingdom, he would not sin: unless perchance they were observed or ordered to be observed, as though they derived their binding force through being institutions of the old law: for it would be a deadly sin to observe them thus.[6]

---

[4] Thomas Aquinas, *Summa theologica*, II, ii, Q. 64, art. 2; an online version in English is at www.newadvent.org/summa.

[5] Aquinas, *Summa theologica*, II, I, Q. 99, art. 4.

[6] Aquinas, *Summa theologica*, II, I, Q. 104, art. 3.

Aquinas articulated what came to be the Catholic understanding of the matter. Accordingly, the death penalties of the Old Testament did not acquire any direct importance in Catholic countries. It was seen as a part of the natural law that the authorities should defend the health of their countries by cutting away (i.e., executing) those that threatened the moral health of society. These criminals could have offended against God, sexual mores, their fellow human beings or property rights. God demanded that the people lived according to the moral law, but the punishments that the authorities enacted to obtain this goal, including the death penalty, were based on appropriateness; they were not based on a divine demand.

The Protestant reformers generally wanted to return to the Bible as the authority in all matters of faith. Accordingly, the literal reading of the Bible obtained great importance. But they also acknowledged the historicity, and therefore the less authoritative character, of the Old Testament.

Martin Luther, like Aquinas, stated that the ceremonial and juridical precepts of the Old Testament were abrogated, and he made the Ten Commandments the essence of the eternal moral law. In spite of this principal viewpoint, however, in several cases Luther advocated the death penalties prescribed in the Pentateuch, and justified them with references to the Old Testament. He thus advocated the death penalty for blasphemy, idolatry and witchcraft by referring to the precepts of the Pentateuch. When Luther justified the power of the authorities, he at the same time justified the execution of killers: the authorities were right to base their rule on the express demand of God. Originally, before the Flood, God had reserved all justice in the matter of crime for himself, but afterwards he stated (in Genesis 9: 6) that 'Whoever sheds the blood of man, by man shall his blood be shed'. According to Luther this meant:

> God had given mankind, that is the authorities, a share in his authority over life and death. When the authorities, following the godly demand stated in Genesis 9: 6, execute a man, then in reality it is God himself, who through human hand kills the murderer.[7]

With this reasoning the authorities were made the instruments of God's justice and of the punishments ordered by God in the Bible. Whereas

---

[7] Paul Althaus, 'Die Todesstrafe als Problem der christlichen Ethik', 1955, p. 6. Translated from the Latin original after Luther, vol. 42, p. 360 (Genesis lecture 1535).

Aquinas argued that God judged society by its success in preventing crime, Luther argued that God wanted the execution of the individual sinner and did not leave it to mankind to estimate the expediency of the penalty. The use of judicial precepts of the Pentateuch to legitimize criminal justice was even more pronounced in the writings of Philip Melanchthon. P.D.L. Avis, moreover, speaks of a tendency in the second generation of Lutheran thinkers to seek a synthesis of the old law and the Gospel.[8]

The creators of the Reformed Church were close to the Lutherans in this question. Calvin advanced the same instrumental view as Luther of the implementation of the death penalty by the authorities. In response to the argument that the death penalty could itself be proscribed by the Fifth Commandment ('Thou shalt not kill'), he answered that the authorities did not execute on their own behalf; they were only enacting the justice of God.[9] And Zwingli and Calvin invoked the Mosaic death penalty for adultery and witchcraft.[10] To these Henry Bullinger added the death penalty for incest, sodomy and bestiality.[11]

The Anglican Church, however, did not follow the continental Protestant churches in this respect. The question was discussed in relation to the punishment of adultery and incest, in particular. In response to the Puritans' demand for the use of the death penalty, the official view of the Church was that so grave a step could not be taken on biblical grounds, but only for reasons of state.[12] The position of the judicial law of Moses as not binding on the Christian state was explicitly expressed in the Articles of Religion of the Anglican Church from 1662 (Article VII).

There was thus a clear tendency for Lutheran and Reformed thinkers to regard a number of the death penalties in Mosaic Law as part of God's eternal commandments, the most important being the death penalty for taking another person's life. In Luther's and Calvin's formulations the Christian authorities were reduced to instruments for God's punishment. It could be said that criminal justice in these cases represented a theocracy in which God was directly ruling society.

---

[8] P.D.L. Avis, 'Moses and the Magistrate: A Study in the Rise of Protestant Legalism', 1975, p. 158.

[9] Althaus, 'Die Todesstrafe als Problem der christlichen Ethik', p. 7.

[10] Avis, 'Moses and the Magistrate', p. 159, 163–4.

[11] Avis, 'Moses and the Magistrate', p. 165.

[12] Keith Thomas, 'The Puritans and Adultery: The Act of 1650 Reconsidered', 1978, p. 269–70.

The Catholic and Anglican churches, on the other hand, rejected the notion that the Mosaic death penalty was binding. This rejection, however, did not imply that the churches opposed the use of the death penalty. In the rest of this chapter I will investigate what influences these differences in the exegesis of the juridical precepts in Mosaic Law had on penal practice.

Death Penalties in Practice

The different biblical readings produced important differences in penal practice especially for homicide, but more than that I shall argue that the theocracy in criminal justice endowed the executions with a religious meaning, which helped to provide a role model for the suicide murderers.

Before we look for differences in the use of the death penalty for homicide, a brief outline of some general legal developments in Europe is necessary. The development of the European legal systems in early modern time was, in general, characterized by growing state intervention. State law, as Bruce Lenman and Geoffrey Parker term it, replaced community law.[13] In murder cases, community law aimed at putting an end to family feuds. The offended family was urged to make a settlement with the offender and his family involving payment of money to compensate for the killing. Composition (a court settlement) involving financial compensation was an integrated part of European medieval justice in murder cases. This system gradually lost ground to state law, in which murder was seen not only as an offence against the offended family but even more as an offence against the sovereign, who guaranteed the peace of the land. In the laws and statutes of the city-states and territorial states, murder and manslaughter were always punished by death. Likewise, composition in the court as well as outside was increasingly forbidden in homicide cases. The introduction of state law and consequently the abrogation of the composition system did not follow confessional lines. In England and France it had already taken place in the twelfth and thirteenth centuries. In Germany the same development took place in the fifteenth and sixteenth centuries, and in Scandinavia it happened in the sixteenth and seventeenth centuries.

---

[13] Lenman and Parker, 'The State, the Community and the Criminal Law in Early Modern Europe', p. 11–48.

In spite of the clear statutory texts, the rise of state law, however, did not necessarily lead to executions in homicide cases. The aim of state law was to place control of the verdicts in the hands of the central authority, not necessarily to impose harsher punishments. The courts would pass sentence according to the law, but the princes had the right to pardon criminals, and this discretionary power was an important part of the royal communication with the subjects.

In addition, it was a more or less general feature in state law—if not in the statutes then in practice—to distinguish between three categories of homicide. The first category comprised killing by accident, killing in self-defence and killing by a person not responsible for his actions. Killings of these sorts only carried the sentence of fines and compensation to the family of the victim. The second category was murder, meaning premeditated, cold-blooded killing or killing committed in the course of a burglary, robbery or other serious crime. Murder almost invariably carried the death sentence in every country. The third category of homicide was manslaughter–unpremeditated killing committed in anger. Manslaughter typically arose from quarrels or fights getting out of hand, not infrequently under the influence of alcohol. Manslaughter was the by far most frequent type of homicide, and it was for this category that the important differences along confessional lines are found.

In the Lutheran countries the introduction of state law more or less coincided with the Reformation. This was the case in Denmark. Here the use of composition in homicide cases had been encouraged in the provincial laws of the thirteenth century. The unconditional death penalty for homicide appears in municipal statutes from the second half of the fifteenth century onwards. Following a civil war in 1533–36, the Reformation was introduced in 1536, and the following year the king issued a statute for the whole kingdom ordering the death penalty for homicide unless committed in self-defence or by accident. The statute blamed composition for encouraging homicides and forbade the victim's family to accept compensation for the killing. Furthermore, it was stated that it was the duty of bailiffs (*lensmænd*) and landowning noblemen to apprehend the killer. These provisions were repeated and further elaborated in statutes from 1539, 1547, 1551 and 1558.[14]

[14] The statutes are printed in J.L.A. Kolderup-Rosenvinge (ed.): Samling af gamle danske love, vol. 4, 1824 p. 176–7, 191–3, 219–21, 239–41, 263–6.

The provisions, however, specifically excluded noblemen. Not until the Danish Law was issued in 1683 was the death penalty for homicide made general.

How, then, was the death penalty used in practice? There are no broad studies of Danish penal practice in the sixteenth and seventeenth centuries. The best study for my purposes is an analysis of the accounts of the magistrate in Copenhagen 1625–51 carried out by V.A. Secher.[15] Here the expenses involved in the great majority of the executions in Copenhagen are accounted for, but of course the crimes and the penalties are mentioned only very briefly. The accounts mention 63 executions in all. Of these, at least 17 had received the death sentence for what seems to have been manslaughter, typically stabbing. As for the eighteenth century, my own survey of criminal cases in the area that were appealed to the provincial court of Zealand in 1719–56 can provide some data. Out of 51 unpremeditated killings 12 were judged as accidental killing or killing in self-defence and 14 perpetrators escaped the death sentence because there was insufficient evidence. Typically, it could not be proved that the accused had dealt the fatal blow or that the blow had been lethal. Four suspects escaped before trial. In 3 cases the king chose to pardon a killer sentenced to death by the courts, and 18 perpetrators were executed.

To sum up, the use of the death penalty for manslaughter was common in Denmark in the seventeenth century, and in the first half of the eighteenth century it was the dominant punishment for manslaughter. As described earlier, the use of the death penalty for homicide in the eighteenth century was deeply inscribed in a religious understanding, with the Faculty of Theology of the University of Copenhagen acting as the interpreter of the divine will emanating from the Bible (see p. 61).

In Sweden, composition in homicide cases was common throughout the sixteenth century, although prominent theologians warned against this disobedience to God and stated that not even the king had the right to pardon a killer.[16] In 1563 and again in 1578 royal statutes forbade the nobility to accept fines in cases of murder and manslaughter as well as blasphemy, adultery, incest and rape. Only the king had the

[15] V.A. Secher, 'Bidrag til Københavns rets- og kulturhistorie 1624–1663', 1907–08, p. 333–84, 569–98.

[16] The prehistory of the Mosaic appendix to the law of 1608 is analysed in Jan Eric Almquist, 'Karl IX och den Mosaiska Rätten', 1942, p. 1–32.

right to pardon a person sentenced to death, the statutes stated. The development of a system of justice that was in better accordance with Mosaic Law was intermingled with power struggles between king and nobility. In the first years of the seventeenth century Karl IX rather unsuccessfully tried to have a new law book passed through parliament. When this failed, he had a slightly revised law book printed, to which was added an appendix with new statutes on blasphemy, parricide, homicide, adultery and rape. The appendix was composed solely of quotations from the Pentateuch. The article on homicide began 'Whoso sheddeth man's blood, by man shall his blood be shed: for in the image of God made he man' (Genesis 9:6) and continued: 'He that smiteth a man, so that he die, shall be surely put to death. And if a man lie not in wait, but God deliver [him] into his hand; then I will appoint thee a place whither he shall flee (Exodus 21:12–13).' The appendix continues to cite statutes describing the free cities to which a killer could flee. The revised law book with the appendix was official Swedish law from 1608 to 1734.

The historian Rudolf Thunander has conducted an in-depth study of the legal practice of one of the two Swedish courts of appeal, the Göta Hovrätt, in the seventeenth century. His findings show that in spite of the strict application of Mosaic Law, composition still played a role in penal practice. The royal court of appeal frequently converted death sentences for manslaughter to fines on the grounds that the offended family interceded for the killer and even argued that they needed the fines. It also appears that an offence against someone's honour was often accepted as a mitigating circumstance.[17]

The Mosaic concept of free cities was interpreted so that a person who had killed and fled to a safe place or out of the country afterwards was granted safe conduct for his return to the country to stand trial. If he nevertheless was found guilty, he was allowed half a month to get away again before the authorities would try to catch him. This application of Mosaic Law, unique in a European context, became an important part of manslaughter cases. Thunander has discovered that almost half of the people sentenced to death for manslaughter had been granted safe conduct. The authorities later apprehended some of these, but the majority fled the country, and some of them received

---

[17] Rudolf Thunander, *Hovrätt i funktion: Göta Hovrätt och brottmålen 1635–1699*, 1993, p. 146–50.

a pardon after some years in exile.[18] In spite of the numerous examples of people guilty of manslaughter avoiding the death penalty, Thunander also documents that sixty people found guilty of manslaughter were executed. This amounts to 26% of those executed in the sample.

Probably nowhere else was Mosaic Law as immediately present in legislation as in Sweden. Statutes composed of quotations from the Pentateuch and the unique practical use of the concept of free cities testify to the literal reading of Mosaic Law as a divine mandate to the Swedish state. As in Denmark, the practical use of the death penalty for manslaughter was common in the seventeenth century, although it appears that the practice of composition, and accordingly an often much-needed compensation to the family which had lost a father or a grown-up son, was hard to overcome.

There are only few studies of German criminal justice addressing quantitative penal practice, and they do not take on comparisons over confessional lines. In Germany taken as a whole the development from community law to state law took place somewhat earlier than in Scandinavia. Susanna Pohl describes as a common German feature the fact that the city magistrates tightened the restrictions over who could use the composition system in homicide cases from the second half of the fifteenth century. A distinction was made between 'ehrliche Totschläge'—honourable killings, where the authorities permitted the families to make a settlement—and 'unehrliche Totschläge'—dishonourable killings, where composition was forbidden. Killings committed by accident or in self-defence but also those committed after defamatory provocations or under the influence of alcohol were considered as 'ehrliche Totschläge'. 'Unehrliche Totschläge' were premeditated killings in cold blood.[19]

A milestone in the general abrogation of the composition system in Germany was the promulgation of the Constitutio Criminalis Carolina, the criminal code of the Emperor Charles V, in 1532. Although it coincided with the Reformation, this unifying initiative by the Catholic

---

[18] Thunander, *Hovrätt i funktion*, p. 150–1. It should be noted that Thunander's research area is a county bordering Denmark. Accordingly it was easier to flee the country from there than from most other parts of Sweden.

[19] Susanna Pohl, '"Ehrlicher Totschlag" – "Rache" – "Notwehr": Zwischen männlichen Ehrencode und dem Primat des Stadtfriedens (Zürich 1376–1600)', 1999, p. 239–83.

emperor was not part of the confessional struggles at that time. In the Carolina, premeditated, cold-blooded killing received the harsh penalty of breaking on the wheel. Unpremeditated killing, which by definition had much in common with 'ehrliches Totschlag', was punished by decapitation by sword. This was considered an honourable execution in Germany as well as in Scandinavia. The perpetrator avoided the death penalty only for killings committed by accident or in self-defence. The Carolina was, however, only a guide and was to be co-ordinated with local practice, especially in the larger territories and free cities.

When looking at the Lutheran territories, a sign of the influence that the Bible had on Lutheran jurisprudence is the use of the Ten Commandments as a model for systematizing criminal law. In Saxony a book of legislation on misdeeds from 1572 was organized according to the Ten Commandments. In the Electoral Palatinate the new Landrecht of 1582 equally followed the Ten Commandments in organizing the criminal statutes, and the Prussian Landrecht of 1620 did likewise.[20] The Danish Law of 1683 followed suit, organizing the 6th Book on misdeeds according to the Ten Commandments.

There are only few studies of penal practice in homicide cases from Lutheran territories and cities, and the religious influence on the verdicts has not been the focus of research. Karl Ernst Meinhardt has analysed criminal justice in the Lutheran free city of Frankfurt am Main from 1562 to 1695. He notes the many special features of the manslaughter cases compared with other criminal cases. The use of torture was very uncommon, the accused could choose his own defence, and his conditions in gaol were better than those of other criminals. This lenient treatment, however, did not mean milder punishments. Out of 74 people tried for manslaughter, 50 were sentenced to death. They were, however, always sentenced to the honourable beheading by sword.[21] In Hamburg the use of the death penalty for manslaughter was common as well. There are numerous decapitations for manslaughter in the list of executions presented by Richard Wosnick. Between 1570 and 1597, 19 decapitations are mentioned for the offences of stabbing or manslaughter (*Totschlag*). Another 23 people were decapitated for

[20] Helmuth von Weber, 'Der Dekalog als grundlage der Verbrechenssystematik', 1949, p. 44–70.

[21] Karl-Ernst Meinhardt, 'Das peinliche Strafrecht der freien Reichstadt Frankfurt am Main im Spiegel der Strafpraxis des 16. und 17. Jahrhundert', 1957, p. 213–5.

unspecified offences.[22] Between 1680 and 1780, 10 people were beheaded for stabbing and another 10 for killing 'in the heat of the moment' (*im Eifer*). It thus appears that in Lutheran Germany, just as in Scandinavia, the general punishment for manslaughter was the death penalty.

The same penal practice is found in Reformed areas and countries. Eric Wettstein, in his study of the death penalty in Reformed Zurich, notes a rising number of executions from the 1530s and ascribes this development to the influence of the reformers Zwingli and Bullinger. The two reformers preached against the use of composition and in favour of the unconditional implementation of the death penalty for homicide. Just like Zwingli and Bullinger in Zurich, Jean Calvin in Geneva contested the traditional understanding that God had granted the authority—meaning the magistrate—the power to issue a pardon in cases of killing and adultery. Calvin stated that the death penalty for manslaughter in anger was a divine demand and therefore such acts of grace were not permitted to earthly powers.[23] Pieter Spierenburg, in his analysis of penal practice in Reformed Amsterdam, does not mention religious motives for the penalties, but the pattern is the same as in the Swiss cities: in the period 1650–1750 homicide was generally punished by beheading; thus only 5 of 68 persons tried for homicide were allowed to live.[24]

What, then, of the Catholic territories in Germany? Here again the studies of penal practice dealing with the penalties for manslaughter are sparse. Wolfgang Behringer provides a presentation of the executions that took place in Munich in the eighteen years from 1574 to 1591. In this period 48 executions took place in the Catholic city, which had *c.* 20.000 inhabitants. The great majority (31) were executed for property crimes, and only 4 of these executions were for the combined category of murder and/or manslaughter.[25] The reason for the small

[22] Wosnick, *Beiträge zur Hamburgischen Kriminalgeschichte*, p. 25–31. From 1530 to 1569 the list appears to be very incomplete. Thus no executions are reported between 1544 and 1554 and between 1558 and 1567. From this period three decapitations are mentioned for the offence of stabbing (*erstechen*). From 1570 to 1597 the list appears to be more complete, with no year without executions and several executions in most years.

[23] Nathalie Zemon Davis: *Fiction in the Archives: Pardon Tales and their Tellers in 16th Century France*, p. 60–3.

[24] Spierenburg, *The Spectacle of Suffering*, p. 119.

[25] Behringer, 'Mörder, Diebe und Ehebrecher', p. 95.

number may of course be that manslaughter was very rare, but when compared with the number of executions for manslaughter in Hamburg in the same period, it is much more likely that the death penalty was seldom given for manslaughter in Munich in the late sixteenth century. In the Catholic Electorate of Mainz in the eighteenth century the use of the death penalty for manslaughter was very rare. Karl Härter has found 173 cases of manslaughter (*Totschlag*) primarily from the eighteenth century, and only 5 of the perpetrators were sentenced to death.[26] So it appears that the death penalty for manslaughter was much more common in the Lutheran and Reformed areas than in the Catholic areas of Germany.

In France the law made no distinction between murder, manslaughter and killing by accident or in self-defence. The penalty laid down by law for all homicides was death. I have not found descriptions of the frequency of the use of the death penalty for manslaughter. Nathalie Zemon Davis, however, provides a picture of the ways killers could avoid the scaffold. In spite of the statutory death penalty for homicide, it was common knowledge as described in the juridical literature that the 'parlements' could reduce a death sentence to whipping and banishment or the galleys if there were extenuating circumstances. These could cover murders caused by accident or in self-defence, but also killings during a game, in drunkenness or in a quarrel. Furthermore, it was common to seek remission from the king in homicide cases, and the king would often pardon accidental manslaughter or manslaughter committed in anger or under the influence of alcohol, and thus free the killer of all punishment.[27] These royal pardons seem to have been of major importance in homicide cases. Spokesmen of the Reformed Church in France contested the use of the royal pardon in manslaughter cases, but the practice was not changed in the period of the Reformation and Counter-Reformation.[28]

In England the royal prerogative to pardon criminals was used as well, but here another institution rose to prominence in the fourteenth and fifteenth centuries–the system of benefit of clergy. The original meaning of this was that churchmen who were tried and convicted

---

[26] Härter, *Policey und Strafjustiz in Kurmainz*, p. 567–8.
[27] Davis, *Fiction in the Archives*, p. 11–5.
[28] Davis, *Fiction in the Archives*, p. 60–3.

in the king's court could claim benefit of clergy and be delivered to the Ordinary to be punished according to ecclesiastical law. In the fourteenth century, however, this benefit was extended to all who could read. Those successfully claiming benefit of clergy were simply discharged after being convicted. From 1487, killers granted benefit of the clergy were to be branded on the thumb in order to ensure that the benefit was granted only once. From the sixteenth century a rising number of offences were made ineligible for benefit of clergy in order to maintain a certain justice, but manslaughter remained eligible throughout the eighteenth century.[29] The lenient punitive practice for manslaughter did not seem to arouse opposition after the Reformation. The Puritans advocated the death penalty for adultery and incest but did not oppose benefit of clergy for manslaughter.[30] As a result, in seventeenth- and eighteenth-century England manslaughter was almost never punished with death. The offender could appeal for benefit of clergy and was consequently merely sentenced to be branded on the hand and then discharged.[31] J.M. Beattie's study of the distinction between manslaughter and murder in the seventeenth and eighteenth centuries shows that most killings resulting from fights in alehouses, at workplaces and so on only received the verdict of manslaughter. This was the case even if deadly weapons were used. In addition, duellists who killed their opponent in a fair fight usually received the verdict of 'clergyable manslaughter'.[32]

It is a shame that more and better studies are not available, but although the studies I have consulted are few and not always precise in answering the questions I posed, they suggest a marked difference in the punishment for manslaughter following confessional lines. On the one hand, there was a Lutheran and Reformed Europe with a harsh penal practice in homicide cases. If it could be established that the blow or stabbing was fatal, that the accused had done it and that it was not accidental, then the perpetrator was pretty sure of a death sentence. This harsh practice had a religious motivation, as God's will. On the other hand we have a Catholic and Anglican Europe, where the death penalty for manslaughter was scarcely in use at all.

---

[29] Beattie, *Crime and Courts in England, 1660–1800*, p. 141–5.

[30] Thomas, 'The Puritans and Adultery: The Act of 1650 Reconsidered'.

[31] Beattie, *Crime and Courts in England, 1660–1800*, p. 77–88 and (concerning the development of benefit of clergy) p. 141–3.

[32] Beattie, *Crime and Courts in England, 1660–1800*, p. 91–8.

Divine Executions

Unlike in the Catholic and Anglican countries, in the Reformed and Lutheran countries the death penalties for homicide were seen as divine demands. Luther and Melanchthon may have had their reservations about following the juridical precepts of Mosaic Law, but such reservations were lost in the orthodox Lutheran world-view that emerged in the sevententh century. Here the literal reading of the Bible was the distinctive mark of their confession, and the strict application of Mosaic Law was the realization of this in criminal law. This religious difference created a dramatic difference in the use of capital punishment for homicide in seventeenth- and eighteenth-century Europe between Lutheran and Reformed countries on the one hand and Catholic and Anglican countries on the other.

But how could this difference influence people suffering from depression to commit suicide murders? The difference concerned the punishment of manslaughter and not murder. It was the case throughout Europe that a person committing premeditated murder would receive the death penalty. The difference may have influenced the inclination of the authorities to excuse murder where the murderer was judged to be of unsound mind, however. John Beattie, in his study of penal practice in Surrey, mentions two cases from the 1690s where mothers murdering their children were acquitted because they were found to be insane.[33] It may have been easier to acquit a murder on grounds of insanity when the death penalty was not seen as a divine demand and when the majority of the killers did not receive the death penalty. If this is true, and consequently a suicide murderer was less certain of receiving the death penalty, then this would reduce the inclination of anyone in the throes of depression to use murder as a means of obtaining their own death. Further investigation is needed, however, to find out whether or not the authorities had different attitudes towards excusing murderers with insanity.

The difference could, however, also influence our general understanding of the executions. Secular vengeance and the secular needs for society to protect itself constituted the logic of the executions for offences against property. This secular justification dominated the reasoning behind the executions in areas where executions for offences

[33] Beattie, *Crime and Courts in England, 1660–1800*, p. 84–5, 101.

against property predominated. This can be seen in studies of the English execution scenario, which will be presented below (p. 123). The situation was different, however, in areas where executions for homicide dominated. Here the religious justification would add new meaning to the executions.

The demand emerging from the Reformation, that persons who had committed manslaughter be executed, must have been hard to grasp. It was a slow process to have the strict new provisions implemented. The composition system was deep-rooted, and the economic compensation to a family that lost a male member was so adequate that it was difficult to erase these practices. The authorities would feel uncomfortable with the insensitive and inexorable death sentences that they passed on God's behalf, and would therefore resort to the claim that they were carrying out God's will. A dialogue between a master builder condemned to death in Lüneburg in 1656 and the magistrate exemplifies the religious atmosphere that marked these cases.[34] The master builder, Johann Toppe, had beaten his wife two or three times with a heavy yardstick. When she fell to the ground, her head hit the stove, knocking her unconscious; she died some hours later. Toppe was then sentenced to death by decapitation. When the magistrate had pronounced sentence, the following dialogue took place:

> Johann Toppe:
> I did not deliberately kill my wife. She provoked me by much mocking and scolding, and she lifted her fur coat and turned her bottom towards me and thus made me angry and furious so that I beat her. I beg for mercy.
>
> The magistrate:
> By the good Lord there is mercy.
>
> Johann Toppe:
> But doesn't the verdict take into consideration that she had caused me to do it?'
>
> The magistrate:
> Yes all that you have said and submitted in writing to the court has been taken into consideration.

[34] The case is described in H.W. Laffert, *Vermehrte relationes et casus criminales cum rationibus dubitandi et decidendi, ingleichen einigen dazugehörigen Königl. Chur- und Fürstlichen Rescriptis sambt andern Beylagen und zugefügten Urtheilen*, 1721, p. 257–61. The case took place outside the area where the other cases in the collection took place and happened thirty years earlier. Dialogue is not quoted in the other cases described. It therefore seems likely that Laffert included it for its exemplary value.

Johann Toppe:
Is there no mercy then?

The magistrate:
By the good Lord.

Johann Toppe:
Then it must be so.[35]

The magistrate of the small town probably felt uncomfortable with the harsh penalty. He did not tell the master builder that he had got his just deserts. Instead, he resorted to the argument that the magistrate was just performing the will of the divine lawmaker. This made it possible for the magistrate and the citizens to reconcile themselves to the sentence. When he accepted the verdict as a divine demand, Toppe accepted that the community was obliged to sacrifice his life in order to protect itself from the wrath of God. The community, for their part, honoured the willing participant in the execution ceremony. By refraining from blaming the community for his death and accepting the divine sacrificial content, he endowed the execution with a higher meaning.

I would thus argue that the understanding of the death penalty as a divine demand contributed to the creation of an extremely solemn execution ceremony dominated by reconciliation and even admiration for the repentant sinner. The solemnity and reconciliation were significant attractions for the suicide murderers.

[35] Laffert, *Vermehrte relationes et casus criminales*, p. 258: 'Ich habe meine selige Frau nicht vorsetzlich geschlagen. Sie hat mit vielen Schmähen und Ausschelten, und dass sie mit Aufhebung des Peltzes mir ihren Hintern zugekehret, zu Eifer und Zorn gereitzet, dass ich sie also geschlagen. Ich bitte Gnade!/ Judex./ Bey dem lieben GOTT ist Gnade./ Johan Toppe./ Ist denn nicht in der Urtheil mit begriffen, dass sie mich dazu verursachet;/ Judex./ Ja alles, was du ausgesagt, und schriftlich übergeben ist referieret./ Johan Toppe/ Ist denn keine Gnade./ Judex./ Bey dem lieben GOTT./ Johann Toppe/ So mags dann seyn.'

CHAPTER TEN

SALVATION OF THE SOUL

The people of the sixteenth, seventeenth and early eighteenth centuries were extremely concerned with the idea of life after death. Philippe Ariès, Pierre Chaunu and other historians have described this obsession.[1] The concern had two elements. On the one hand, the blissful life in Heaven awaiting the souls that were saved was described as immensely better than their poor, painful life on earth. On the other hand, the torments of hell were described no less vividly, ensuring that the believer would do anything to be saved. In the soteriology of all confessions, perhaps with the exception of the Reformed Church, the state of mind in the last moments of life was especially important. For the good of the eternal soul, it was of crucial importance to die in a state of mercy. A good death meant that just before death you made your peace with the world, were given absolution and took Holy Communion, and for the Catholics that they had received the sacrament of Extreme Unction. Numerous books were printed about 'ars moriendi', the art of dying, and unexpected death was feared as it left no time for repentance.[2] Worst of all was a death associated with a sin. To take one's own life was a terrible sin. Suicide inevitably led to everlasting torments in hell.

This preoccupation with the afterlife was an important precondition for the religiously motivated suicide murderers. The torments of hell and happiness in heaven were expounded in sermons, sung about in hymns and depicted in paintings, so that for the murderers they became realistic alternatives to life on Earth.

The Christian confessions had in common the care of all souls of the community, including the souls of those sentenced to death. Jesus had said: 'Naked, and ye clothed me: I was sick, and ye visited me: I was in prison, and ye came unto me' (Matthew 25:36). Clerics of every branch

---

[1] Philippe Ariès, *The Hour of our Death* [1977] 1987, and Pierre Chaunu, *La Mort à Paris XVIe, XVIIe et XVIIIe siècles*, 1978.

[2] See Ariès [1977] 1987, p. 99–110.

of the faith prepared the convicts and taught them about God's infinite mercy, gave the Eucharist to the penitent and were present at the execution. Nevertheless, there were differences in the preparation and in the execution ceremonies themselves.

Comparisons of execution ceremonies along confessional lines have been undertaken but are only cursory. Pieter Spierenburg made an early attempt to compare the religious aspects of the execution ceremonies in Europe.[3] As he himself points out, his comparison is based on very few examples when he goes beyond the Netherlands. He points out that in France and Spain the religious aspects of the execution ceremony seems to be a little more pronounced than in the Netherlands, and he suggests that this reflects a difference between the Catholic and the Protestant countries. As I shall demonstrate below, it is rather the Reformed execution ceremony that lacked a strong religious content. Gustav Radbruch, Richard van Dülmen and Richard Evans have described early modern punishment rituals in Germany.[4] They all have given detailed descriptions of the religious aspects of the execution ceremony, and they use examples from Lutheran as well as Catholic executions. Radbruch states that there were no confessional differences. Van Dülmen agrees, but adds that it was only after the Catholic Counter-Reformation (which took place between 1560 and 1648) that the Catholic ceremonies became as elaborate as the Lutheran ceremonies,[5] thus indicating the later development of the Catholic execution ceremony. Evans describes a number of differences in rituals in Lutheran and Catholic areas but does not use them to elaborate on the confessional differences.[6]

I will argue here that the execution ceremonies did vary along confessional lines and that these variations arose from the different soteriologies in connection with the different understanding of the death penalties described in the previous chapter. The Lutheran Church was more engaged than the other confessions in the clerical preparation of the prisoners sentenced to death.

[3] Spierenburg, *The Spectacle of Suffering*, Chapter 3 and esp. p. 46–53.

[4] Gustav Radbruch, 'Ars Moriendi: Scharfrichter—Seelsorger—Armesünder—Volk', 1945, p. 460–95. See also van Dülmen, *Theatre of Horror*, and Evans, *Rituals of Retribution*.

[5] Dülmen, *Theatre of Horror*, p. 89.

[6] Evans, *Rituals of Retribution*, p. 80–6.

The Soteriology of the Medieval and Catholic Church

The sources preserved do not allow a description of executions in Scandinavia before the Reformation. Developments in the execution ceremony in Germany between the fourteenth century and the sixteenth century have been analysed by Peter Schuster and Gustav Radbruch.[7] The findings from medieval times are very sparse, but they indicate that, despite accepting the right of the secular authorities to execute (the acceptance was expressed by Thomas Aquinas and in papal bulls as well), the Church was hesitant about executions. Gustav Radbruch mentions numerous legends about saints saving convicts from execution as part of their pious deeds.[8]

The clerical attitudes caused suspicion on the part of the secular authorities. In 1312 Pope Clement V warned the secular authorities about the reprehensible abuse of hindering those sentenced to death from receiving Holy Communion. In the fifteenth century it was common for clerics to visit convicts after the death sentence had been passed, but Peter Schuster has found several examples of magistrates who were reluctant to let clerics visit the convicts. The authorities preferred to execute the convict immediately after sentence had been pronounced.

The opposition of the secular authorities to clerical preparation caused the emperor to intervene. The criminal law of Bavaria, the so-called 'Bambergensis' of 1507, as well as the Carolina of 1532, explicitly stated that three days had to elapse between the publication of the death sentence and the execution. During this time the convict's confessor should be allowed to prepare him.[9] The two law books, however, also warned the clerics not to encourage the convicts to withdraw their confession. Thus, according to Carolina, 'In their preparation several confessors adopt the misuse of instructing the sinner to withdraw their true confession at the last minute.'[10]

---

[7] Peter Schuster, 'Hinrichtungsrituale in der Frühen Neuzeit: Anfragen aus dem Mittelalter', 2003, p. 213–33. And Radbruch, 'Ars Moriendi'.

[8] See Radbruch, 'Ars Moriendi', p. 472.

[9] Schuster, 'Hinrichtungsrituale in der Frühen Neuzeit', p. 226–7.

[10] F.-C. Schroeder (ed.), *Die peinliche Gerichtsordnung Kaiser Karls V. (Carolina)*, 1532 (2000), article 31: 'jedoch so haben etlich beichtuätter eyn missbrauch, dass sie die armen inn der beicht vnderweisen, jre sag so sie mit warheyt gethan haben, am letsten zu wiederruffen'.

The Carolina, however, not only allowed the clerics to visit the convicts in the three days between the publication of the death sentence and the execution; it also indirectly allowed the authorities to isolate the convict from all visitors during investigation and trial. It seems as if both these precepts in the Carolina were still taken literally in many parts of southern Germany in the eighteenth century. Johann Jakob Moser complains that it was usual to forbid anybody, including clerics, to visit the convict until the day when sentence was pronounced, and the execution followed three days after the pronouncement. The count relating the story of Michel Blödorn's execution in Copenhagen points out as something special that the pastors were allowed to visit the prisoners before sentence was pronounced.[11]

The disagreement between the pre-Reformation clerics and the secular authorities arose partly from the reservations of the Church about the death penalty, but it was also connected to the understanding of sin, repentance, atonement and salvation. The ordained clerics were important in the soteriology of the medieval Church and later, the Catholic Church.[12] The Church had the key to power. Through the sacraments it opened the gates of Heaven and safeguarded the believer from the everlasting torments of Hell. If you had sinned, the cleric as a representative of the Church could administer the sacraments and thus save your soul. For this reason it was of great importance for the believer to receive the sacraments immediately before death. Then no more sins could be committed and the soul would be saved—but only eventually.

The sacraments could only secure salvation from the everlasting torments of Hell. After death, purgatory awaited. The Church could not free the believer from purgatory, but the believer could shorten his or her stay in purgatory by taking up good works, by buying indulgences from the Church, through prayers and a pious life. A believer who had committed a grave sin would go on a pilgrimage, make a donation to the Church or go on a crusade. A person condemned to death could repent of his grave sin, but he could not atone for it. Furthermore, the preparation of a person condemned to death differed from the preparation of other people about to die. The convict could not be given Extreme Unction, as this was a sacrament given to the sick.

---

11 Moser, *Seelige letzte Stunden*, p. 16–17, 595.
12 The Catholic soteriology is described in Chaunu, *La Mort à Paris*, p. 116–61.

The length of the sojourn in purgatory depended on the believer's life, but even after his or her death it could be shortened through prayers for the dead and through Masses held for the dead. Donations to churches and monasteries in return for the monks saying Mass for the donor's soul after death were common, and confraternities with the purpose of praying for the souls of deceased brothers were widespread.

If the medieval cleric preparing a convict found a truly repentant sinner willing to change his or her life and take up good works, then he would find it to be a Christian deed to save the convict from execution, and thus allow him or her to atone for the grave sin. Priests and monks would often request a pardon for truly repentant convicts, believing that they would take up good works and thus make atonement for their past sins. In Italy, Spain and France confraternities were formed with the task of preparing the condemned spiritually for their death, offering them religious assistance on their way to the gallows and, after the execution, burying the corpse. In some places these confraternities had the privilege of having one prisoner freed from the death penalty each year.[13] Opposition to executions was only a feature of the medieval Church, however. The Catholic Church of the seventeenth and eighteenth centuries did not question the verdicts of the secular authorities.

There exists a Catholic counterpart to Johann Jakob Moser's collection, making it possible to compare the preparation of convicts sentenced to death in the two confessions. In 1738, two years before Moser, the Jesuit P. Jacob Schmid published a book with the title:

> *Grapes of holiness from the thorns of evil. Or wondrous conversions of all sorts of murderers, robbers, sorcerers as well as many criminals and malefactors condemned to death, who either earlier or at least before their death have performed a wonderful penance. Especially for the benefit of convicts and malefactors. Together with a manual for the ordinary to lead the poor sinners to a good death.*[14]

---

[13] See Radbruch, 'Ars Moriendi', p. 474–5.

[14] P. Jacob Schmid, *Trauben der Heiligkeit aus denen Dörnern der Bossheit, oder vervunderliche Bekehrungen allerhand Mördern, Raubern, Zauberern, auch vieler zum Tod verurtheilten Übelthätern oder Maleficanten, welche eintveders noch frühzeitig, oder wenigst vor ihrem Tod herrliche Buss gewürcket. Zu sonderem Nutz der Gefangenen und Ûbelthätern, sambt einer Weiss für die Seelsorger, die arme Sünder zu einem guten Tod anzuleiten*, 1752 (1738).

Nothing indicates that Moser knew of Schmid's collection.

Although he is not very well known, a biography has been written about Jacob Schmid.[15] The author calls him a Bavarian hagiographer, thereby indicating that most of his publications were collections of legends. Besides malefactors, they focused on other poor and despised groups in society, such as farm workers, gaolers and executioners, and described their conversions and good deeds.

Just like Moser, Jacob Schmid collected stories about conversions of malefactors, and like Moser he included the story of the good thief crucified beside Jesus. But with this exception the stories in the two collections are entirely different. Twenty-two of Jacob Schmid's stories are about official Catholic saints and martyrs, and the remaining thirty-four stories had some miraculous aspect as well. Most of the stories had the character of legends taking place in the Middle Ages. The most recent story was thirty years old. Many stories told about robbers and murderers whose lives were saved by a miraculous event and who therefore amended their conduct, taking up good works or the like. In one case a murderer had promised to go on a pilgrimage if saved from execution. He was hanged but afterwards miraculously woke up and fulfilled his promise.[16] Another told of a pirate who was sentenced to death in a Muslim country. He was promised a pardon if he gave up his faith and convert to Islam. He refused and thus, Schmid wrote, became a martyr.[17] In a third story a Jew converted to Catholicism just before being executed.[18]

All the malefactors in Schmid's stories had the opportunity to prove their faith by taking up good works, sacrificing their life or the like. As such, they are in good accordance with Catholic soteriology, but they did not offer a particularly good example for the person about to be executed for some crime, who did not have the time to take up good works and who had nothing to sacrifice. In fact, Schmid states in the introduction that, although the boundless mercy of God towards heinous malefactors exists, it is very rare.

Schmid's stories are followed by a manual for Ordinaries to lead the poor sinner to a good death.[19] He notes that such a guide is missing in

---

[15] Marianne Kendler, *P. Jacob Schmid S.J.: Ein bairischer Hagiograph des 18. Jahrhunderts*, 1974.

[16] Schmid, *Trauben der Heiligkeit*, p. 269–72.

[17] Schmid, *Trauben der Heiligkeit*, p. 276–9.

[18] Schmid, *Trauben der Heiligkeit*, p. 261–9.

[19] Schmid, *Trauben der Heiligkeit*, p. 283–344.

Catholic literature.[20] The guide describes how the Ordinary should meet the convict, starting from the day when the death sentence is pronounced and ending with the execution three days later. It has several similarities with the Lutheran guides: the key passages from the Bible are the same, and so are the main events of conversion and confession of sins, the Eucharist and the preparation for the decisive moment of death. But there are differences as well. The Catholic Ordinary could not avoid the fact that purgatory awaited the convict, and, taking his or her terrible sins into consideration, every Catholic would know that a long stay awaited him there. Schmid suggests that the Ordinary should argue that a willing and penitent participation in the execution ceremony was a great sacrifice to God, which would considerably shorten the time in purgatory. The convict should not be afraid of the crowd. On the contrary, the people present at the execution could pray for the convict and donate money, which could be used to pay the church for Masses to be said for his soul.[21] The message, however, could never be as optimistic as that of the Lutheran pastors.

The Reformed Soteriology

The Reformers reacted to several elements in the medieval and Catholic soteriology. Both Martin Luther and Jean Calvin denied that the Church held any power; there was only the believer and God. They also rejected the whole system of penance through indulgences and good works, as well as the idea of Masses and prayers for the dead. Man had to acknowledge his own total depravity and hence turn remorsefully to God. Man could only be justified through faith. The true believer would take up good works not in order to obtain salvation but because of his faith.

Another radical change took place in relation to convicts condemned to death. Medieval death penalties were the work of secular justice. The Church might approve of the right of the secular authorities to carry out the death sentence, but the penalty had nothing to do with God's justice, which was waiting after death. With Luther's and Calvin's understanding of the secular authorities as the sword of God and the

[20] Schmid, *Trauben der Heiligkeit*, p. 285.
[21] Schmid, *Trauben der Heiligkeit*, p. 305-7.

death penalty as God's punishment, the executions became part of God's justice.[22]

The soteriology of the Reformed confession, however, differed from the Lutheran soteriology in some aspects of relevance for the convicts condemned to death.[23] First, besides the idea of depravity and justification through faith, the Calvinist believed in predestination—that is, the belief that a certain and not very large number of people were pre-elected by God for salvation. This teaching held that the few who were elected at some time in their lives would sense the Lord's mercy, and from then on they would live according to their status. The elected could commit small sins, repent and receive absolution, but it was not likely that one of the elected would commit a grave sin such as murder. If a person presumed to be one of the elected committed a grave sin, this would imply that the person was not among the elected after all. Secondly, the Reformed Church had the most consistent rejection of the magical or supernatural nature of the sacraments and rituals. These were only symbolic, and therefore no divine message could be found in the minister's absolution or in Holy Communion. Accordingly, the Reformed Church rejected the idea that ministers should necessarily be involved in a person's preparation for death. There was no special importance connected to the final absolution and the last participation in Holy Communion.[24] The Reformed Church thus did not have the same focus on the last moments of life. The Reformed ministers would also visit the prisoner sentenced to death, offer consoling words, give them absolution and administer the Eucharist, but, just as for Catholic Ordinaries, the message of the Reformed minister could not be as optimistic as that of the Lutheran pastor.[25]

What, then, of the Reformed execution ceremony in practice? Pieter Spierenburg has made a thorough description of the execution ceremony in Reformed Amsterdam. He does not go into the content of the religious message, however. The death sentence was normally pronounced only a day or two before the execution.[26] After sentence was

---

[22] This is the conclusion of Peter Schuster's article. See Schuster, 'Hinrichtungsrituale in der Frühen Neuzeit', p. 227–31.

[23] The Reformed and the Evangelical Lutheran soteriologies are contrasted in Max Weber, *The Protestant Ethic and the Spirit of Capitalism*, 1958 (1904), Chapter 4.

[24] See Heinrich Bullinger, *Seelsorge mit Schwerkranken und Sterbenden (Bericht der Kranken 1535)*, trans. Siegfried Müller (http://www.solideogloria.ch/Bullinger/seelsorge.htm), especially Chapter 9.

[25] Bullinger, *Seelsorge mit Schwerkranken und Sterbenden*, Chapter 15.

[26] Spierenburg, *The Spectacle of Suffering*, p. 46–9.

passed, the convict was visited by a preacher and a 'comforter of the sick', but it appears that the preacher used to visit the prisoner before sentence was pronounced too. On the day of execution the convict was declared a 'child of death'. For murderers this formula declared that God wanted the blood of those who had themselves spilt blood. After this the magistrate, as the judicial power, together with the prisoners and the preacher knelt in prayer. Then the prisoner was led out of the city hall, where the crowd waited, to the scaffold erected just outside. Here the execution took place. Although half of the citizens in Amsterdam were Catholic, only Reformed priests were allowed to accompany the criminal to the scaffold.

The authorities of Amsterdam considered it important that the criminal co-operated and was convinced of the righteousness of his punishment.[27] The criminal should die repenting of his sins in the hope of saving his soul at the last moment. On the scaffold the criminal was allowed to sing or to say a prayer but was not allowed to deliver a speech. Spierenburg also relates stories of pious deaths on the Amsterdam scaffold.

Another source of the religious message of the Reformed Church at the executions can be seen in the sermons held at executions. Ronald A. Bosco has analysed sixty-two published sermons held before executions in Puritan New England between 1674 and 1798.[28] The main theme of the sermons was to explain how the crime in question was an affront to God, which the community had to answer quickly. The crime was seen as a divine message pointing at some general sin. Thus a servant who had killed his master was seen as God's warning that men must respect authority. It was very common to warn youth not to sin. The criminal was told that the death penalty was God's will, and he was not given much hope in the life hereafter. For example, in one sermon the criminal was told that, when she opened her eyes in the next world, she would see the real price of her crime: either the joys of heaven, which was a possibility given the abundant goodness of God, or, more likely, the miseries of hell.[29] There is a striking difference between these Puritan sermons and the Pietist sermons described above (p. 67–8).

[27] Spierenburg, *The Spectacle of Suffering*, p. 59–66.
[28] Ronald A. Bosco, *Lectures at the Pillory: The Early American Execution Sermon*, 1978, p. 156–76.
[29] Bosco, *Lectures at the Pillory*, p. 173.

Although the possibility of salvation is present in the Puritans' sermons, their message to those about to be executed is a far cry from the joy and optimism with which the Pietist pastors met the penitent malefactors.

The English Execution Ceremony

The soteriology of the Anglican Church looked much like that of the Reformed and Lutheran churches. The belief in predestination was one of the 'Articles of Religion' of the Church, but it did not have the same position in the creed as in the Reformed Church.

J.A. Sharpe has investigated the religious aspects of the English execution ceremony in the seventeenth century.[30] He takes as his point of departure the numerous publications of 'dying words' of, in particular, murderers sentenced to death. The speeches are usually reported and put into print by the preacher preparing the criminal. The speeches contained warnings to the crowd not to follow his or her example, and several of the criminals told how vices such as Sabbath-breaking, heavy drinking and swearing had led them to commit the crime, admonishing the spectators to avoid such minor vices. These speeches and the accounts of the priest provide a picture of an English execution ceremony much like that of Scandinavia and northern Germany. The 'dying words' were however primarily a seventeenth-century phenomenon. Although clergymen were still present at the scaffold, executions in the eighteenth century were, according to Sharpe, becoming more of an embodiment of secular power. Furthermore, Sharpe tells of several criminals who were executed without uttering any last words and without repenting. Most of the pamphlet accounts dealt with murderers, but the overwhelming majority of those executed died for offences against property. This is supported by the findings of John Beattie. In his study of criminal justice in Surrey Beattie writes that out of 111 executions taking place in the period 1722–48, 103 were for crimes against property.[31]

Thomas W. Laqueur criticizes the functionalist view dominating historians' descriptions of the execution ceremony as expressing the

[30] J.A. Sharpe, '"Last Dying Speeches": Religion, Ideology and Public Execution in 17th Century England', 1985, p. 144–67.

[31] Beattie, *Crime and Courts in England, 1660–1800*, p. 515.

purposes of the state.[32] He focuses on the numerous accounts of criminals who did not want to participate in the religious staging of the ceremony and the many descriptions of disorder at the executions. He cites two German visitors who noted the much smaller official presence at the executions in England than at home. The German visitors noted the lack of any strong contingent of soldiers or police maintaining order at the execution, and commented on the poor presence of important officials. Laqueur finds that the English authorities failed to create a coherent state theatre. Instead, the crowd took over and staged executions that were almost like a carnival.

Thus, in spite of similarities in the religious message, it appears that, at least in the eighteenth century, English executions lacked the solemn religious character that marked the executions in Lutheran countries. One reason for this difference may be that executions in England were predominantly for crimes against property.

The Religious Staging of the Lutheran Execution Ceremony

As already described, the soteriology of the Lutheran Church was the one that provided the most optimistic message to the person about to be executed. The Catholic Church had purgatory, and the Reformed Church had the doctrine of predestination. In Lutheran doctrine, however, the person condemned to death had exactly the same possibilities of salvation as anyone else. He or she was depraved and had committed a grave sin. But sinfulness was a human condition, and the infinite mercy of God depended not on the number and seriousness of one's sins but on the ability to acknowledge one's sinfulness and turn to God for forgiveness.

It could even be argued that in some respects the person condemned to death had better opportunities than others to obtain salvation. First, it was difficult for ordinary people to know the hour of their death. The convict knew exactly when he or she was to die and had all the clerical assistance needed to repent and confess his or her faith, and all the spectators needed to make peace with before dying. Secondly, as Johann Jakob Moser wrote, the person condemned to death possibly

[32] Thomas Laqueur, 'Crowds, Carnival and the State in English Executions, 1604–1868', 1989, p. 305–55.

had an advantage because his or her sin was so great and obvious and therefore easy to recognize.

The fight for the salvation of the malefactors' souls was regarded as an important part of the official execution ceremony. The theologians and secular authorities in the Lutheran territorial states and city-states had placed God in the judgement seat of the courts, and now they had to make certain that the divine meaning of the death penalty was made clear to the criminals. God wanted the salvation of all penitent sinners; this was the optimistic message.

Each of the Lutheran territories had its own independent Church headed by the territorial prince or the secular authorities of the city-states. And each of these churches had its own church ritual worked out and printed in several editions. It was a common feature of every ritual to describe how to prepare those condemned to death.

The detailed instructions of the Danish–Norwegian Church Ritual of 1685 have already been described. The earliest Lutheran rituals merely said that the convicts had to be educated, and if they turned to God and showed true remorse, they should be given communion. If not, they should be commended to God. This was the content of the short paragraph 'Van Misdederen to Besokende' in the Church decree for Hamburg, written in 1529 by Johannes Bugenhagen.[33] Bugenhagen also participated in writing the first Church decree of Denmark–Norway, printed in 1539. The paragraph on how to treat convicts was very similar to Hamburg's, but it added that, given the convicts' lack of knowledge of religious subjects, the pastors should not try any in-depth education. Furthermore it was stressed that, despite the reluctance of the convict, the pastor was to persevere in educating him or her and not give up until the convict had been executed.[34]

In the second half of the sixteenth century the instructions became more elaborate. In the Church decree of 1569 for the principality of Braunschweig-Wolfenbüttel, the chapter entitled 'About visiting, warning, admonition and consoling the convict, who had forfeited his life' took up several pages. Initially, the decree complained, at some places within the papacy such poor people were not visited by men of the Church, and thus were brought to think:

---

[33] Emil Sehling (ed.), *Die Evangelischen Kirchenordnungen des XVI. Jahrhunderts*, vol. 5, 1913, p. 510.

[34] Martin Schwarz Lausten, *Kirkeordinansen 1537/39*, 1989, p. 196–7.

> That they were cast off by God and cut off from every communion with the Christian churches. But because no sin is so grave that the penitent cannot be forgiven, and no conversion is too slow and late, when only it is done in this life—even in the last moment. [...] For this reason the pastors are above all to take care of such poor people, and because the Devil has caused them to fall in this way; and moreover they now only have little time and opportunity for a Christian conversion, the ministers shall use all diligence to bring them to true penitence, to comfort and strengthen them in the belief in Christ, so that patiently and obedient as children they will endure the punishment that their misdeed has brought upon them, and thus be a good example for others. Furthermore it behoves the Christian authorities not only to punish the felons corporally, but also to strive for the salvation of their poor souls, so that both body and soul may be sacrificed to the good God.[35]

The text goes on to explain in detail what the convicts should be taught. First, they should acknowledge their sinfulness and repent their sins; secondly, they should be comforted by the cleric, saying that God does not like sinners to be executed. God has led the sinners to this last ordeal in order to give them a last chance for conversion. If the convict showed true signs of remorse and belief, then as a confirmation and certainty of the comfort they should be given absolution and communion. Thirdly, they should be admonished to submit themselves to the punishment with patience, humility and obedience.

A decree regulating the Swedish Church was not issued until 1571, but already in 1529, as one of the first Lutheran countries, Sweden had its own official liturgical handbook. It was written by the reformer of the Swedish Church, Olavus Petri. Petri had studied in Wittenberg and was thus well acquainted with the new teaching, but the handbook was written without many German sources at hand or contacts with

---

[35] Sehling (ed.), *Die Evangelischen Kirchenordnungen des XVI. Jahrhunderts*, vol. 6, 1955, p. 172–4. 'Als ob sie derhalben auch von Gott verstossen und von aller gemeinschaft der christlichen kirchen abgeschnitten weren. Weil aber keine sünde so gross und schwer, die den büssfertigen nicht möge vergeben werden, auch keine bekehrung zu langsam und spat, wenn sie nur in diesem leben, auch am allerletzten, geschicht. ... derhalben sollen die prediger solche arme leute ihnen fürnehmlich lassen befohlen sein, und weil sie der Teufel also zu falle gebracht, sie auch nun nicht mehr lange zeit und gelegenheit zur chrislichen bekerung haben, sollen die prediger allen vleiss anwenden, das sie zu wahrer buss gebracht, durch den glauben an Christum getröstet und gestercket, sich mit gedult und kindlichem gehorsam in die straff, so sie mit ihrer missethat verwirket, andern zum exempel ergeben mögen. Auch gebühret christlicher oberkeit nicht allein, am leibe die übeltheter zu straffen, sondern auch dahin zu trachten, dass die arme seele gerettet und also beide, leib und seele, dem lieben Gott aufgeopfert möge werden.'

reformers in other countries.[36] It contained a long chapter entitled 'A way to deal with those who are to be executed or killed'.[37] The text mainly takes the form of speeches that the pastor was supposed to deliver to the convict: one speech in the prison, one to the convict at the place of execution and one to the crowd at the place of execution. The speeches are dominated by a providential understanding that everything is God's will. God had had the miscreant arrested and sentenced to death in order to save him from eternal damnation, which would be certain if he had remained in the hands of the Devil until his death.

The Swedish handbook was revised in 1614,[38] but the chapter about convicts remained almost unchanged. In another revision from 1693 the chapter about the preparation of those sentenced to death was expanded and took up twenty pages.[39] Petri's speeches to the convict were maintained but revised. Among other things, the providential view was made less prominent. The instructions for the day of the execution were more detailed, with suggestions for hymns to be sung at the place of execution. Furthermore, the chapter was extended with a parallel 'Other way' to prepare the convicts. The 'Other way' supported a dialogue with the convict and was more in line with the German and Danish rituals. As in the Danish ritual of 1685, the arguments became more optimistic as the day of execution approached. The convict should understand that it was a great mercy on the part of God that the convict was not taken away in the midst of his impenitence and dreadful sins. Because God, in just revenge, allows innumerable thousands to die immersed in their sins, and for this reason to suffer eternal degradation, scorn and derision in the torture chamber, but the convict can avoid all this through penitence, faith and temporal punishment.[40]

---

[36] Oscar Quensel, *Bidrag til svenska liturgiens historia I*, Uppsala, 1890, p. 3–6, and Olavus Petri, *Samlade skrifter*, vol. 2, Uppsala, 1915, intro. by Knut B. Westman, p. x–xii.

[37] 'Itt sett huru man skal handla medh them som rättas eller aflijffuas skole', p. 359–65, in Olavus Petri, 'En handbock påå Swensko, 1529', in Petri, *Samlade skrifter*, vol. 2, p. 311–69.

[38] *Handbook ther uti är författadt huruledes Gudstiensten medh Christelighe ceremonier och Kyrkiosedher uthi wåra Swenska Församblingar skal bliffua hållin och förhandlada*, Uppsala, 1614.

[39] *Handbok ther uti är författadt huruledes Gudstiensten med Christelige ceremonier och Kyrkioseder uthi wåra Swenska Församlingar skal bliffwa hållen och förhandlad*, Stockholm, 1693 (1716), p. 177–97.

[40] *Handbok ther uti är författadt huruledes Gudstiensten med Christelige ceremonier och Kyrkioseder uthi wåra Swenska Församlingar skal bliffwa hållen och förhandlad*, Stockholm, 1693, p. 193.

Just as decreed in the Danish ritual, a dialogue should be held at the place of execution.

The official elaboration of the preparation of prisoners condemned to death culminated in the Danish and Swedish Church rituals of the late seventeenth century. In the eighteenth century the authorities and the pastors not only offered the criminals the possibility of conversion; they expected it. When the criminal was unwilling to convert, the pastors would ask for postponement of the execution. In Denmark this took place on the initiative of pastors.[41] In Sweden the state advised the local authorities to allow a postponement, but not for too long,[42] and in Brandenburg in the kingdom of Prussia the 'Criminalordnung' from 1717 stated:

> As it is the responsibility of a Christian authority to do as much as possible to prevent the prisoner from dying without repenting, then the Christian authority, in the case when only a little or no repentance or penitence is seen in the prisoner, should postpone the execution for some days.[43]

The intense official interest the preparation of the prisoners condemned to death and orchestrating the execution ceremony was a distinctive feature of the Lutheran Church. The rituals of the medieval Church did not contain such instructions.[44] The *Rituale Romanum*, the official book of the Catholic rite, printed in 1614, did not mention prisoners

---

[41] For Danish examples see Krogh, *Oplysningstiden og det magiske*, p. 288–9.

[42] Spierenburg, *The Spectacle of Suffering*, p. 63. For a German example of postponement in practice see the account of the preparation of Andrea Kronbergen from Magdeburg. In 1736 she had killed her own ten-week-old child. The pastors asked for postponement of the execution because there had been a set-back in her conversion. Moser, *Seelige letzte Stunden*, p. 202.

[43] Kurmärkische Criminalordnung, 'Da auch einer christlichen Obrigkeit oblieget, soviel möglich dahin zu sehen, damit der Gefangene nicht in seiner Unbussfertigkeit sterbe, so soll dieselbem im Fall der Gefangene annoch wenig oder gar keine Reue oder Busse spüren läst, die Exekution einige Tage aussetzen', quoted in van Dülmen 1985, p. 90.

[44] Examples of medieval ritual books are: Joseph Freisen (ed.), *Manuale Curatorum secundum usum ecclesie Rosckildensis. Kaholisches Ritualbuch der dänischen Diözese Roeskilde im Mittelalter*, Paderborn, 1898; Joseph Freisen (ed.), *Liber Agendarum ecclesie et diocesis Sleswicensis: Katholisches Ritualbuch der Diözese Schleswig im Mittelalter*, Paderborn, 1898; and Joseph Freisen (ed.), *Manuale Lincopense, Breviarium Scarense, Manuale Aboense. Kaholische Ritualbücher Schwedens und Finnlands im Mittelater*, Paderborn, 1904. Only in the ritual from Schleswig was the preparation of convicts condemned to death mentioned in the form of a prayer for the penitent's reconciliation with God, preceding confession and absolution (p. 76). There was, however, no description of how to prepare the convict.

condemned to death either.[45] As Jacob Schmid stated, the Catholic Church lacked instructions for the priests about the preparation of criminals condemned to death. The Anglican *Book of Common Prayer* did not mention care for prisoners either.

The Reformed Church had the divine origin of the death penalties in common with the Lutheran Church. This is probably why instructions on the preparation of criminals for their execution are here too, albeit in much less detail. Thus the Church ritual of the small Reformed German county of Lippe-Detmold from 1684 took only five lines to say that the minister should visit imprisoned malefactors, especially those condemned to death, help them to conversion and comfort them.[46]

Martin Luther taught the total depravity of mankind, but he also had the happy message that at any time of their life all sinners could save their soul if they just repented their sins and opened their hearts to God. This optimism was essential to the Lutheran faith.

The most striking feature differentiating the Lutheran preparation of prisoners sentenced to death from that of the other confessions was the personal providential view. The prisoner was told that Satan's temptations leading to the crime and the execution were parts of God's plan for saving the prisoner's soul. God had led the sinner to this last ordeal in order to offer the sinner a last chance. By converting, repenting and dying piously, the prisoner fulfilled God's personal plan for her salvation.

There are examples of pious and edifying execution ceremonies in every confession, but this happy message gave the Lutheran execution ceremony a special optimism. Moreover, the Lutherans were the first to focus on the salvation of the malefactors, taking pride in this work and making the work a distinctive feature of the confession. When Johan Toppe accepted his death as a divine command, he could look forward to intensive preparation for his death by the pastors in Lüneburg. The feeling that the city might have found another way to punish him, had it not been for the divine command, made it absolutely necessary in Lutheran thinking that his soul was saved. God's harshness in this life had to be balanced by his mildness towards the repentant sinner and his wondrous promises of a blissful afterlife.

---

[45] *Rituale romanum Pauli V. pontificus maximi jussu editum et a Benedicto XIV auctum et castigatum*, Ratisbon, 1872.

[46] *Kirchen-Ordnung der Graffschafft Lippe auf Befehl des Grafen Simon Heinrich*, Lemgo, 1684, p. 135.

CHAPTER ELEVEN

A LUTHERAN PLAGUE

The precise origin of the suicide murders is opaque. Kathy Stuart mentions a suicide murder in Württemberg in 1612.[1] Arne Jansson cites an early example from Stockholm in 1621. A journeyman imprisoned for theft was told that he would be publicly pilloried. He believed that this would prevent him from returning to his master. He then murdered a fellow prisoner with the intention of being executed.[2]

In Hamburg a possible suicide murder occurred in 1639. The journeyman shoemaker Johann Kardener had stabbed his seven-year-old brother-in-law. We do not know anything else about the circumstances of the murder, but the source tells the following about the execution:

> The remorseful sinner walked to the place of execution in a long coat with a black armband, prayed, said farewell to the crowd with blessings, and embraced the executioner, pleading with him to perform his official duty well.[3]

This behaviour unfortunately confused the executioner so much that he twice failed to cut off the head. The crowd, probably deeply moved by Kardener's behaviour, became furious at this disgraceful and humiliating ending. They chased the executioner back into the town, and he was only saved by the soldiers on guard, who fired into the crowd in order to stop them.

Arne Jansson has also found an attempted suicide murder in 1644, and then in 1651 we have the first example of what is clearly a religiously motivated suicide murder. It was committed by Paul Wulff in Stockholm.[4] Wulff was a German goldworker born in

[1] Stuart, 'Suicide by Proxy', p. 425.

[2] Jansson, 'Mörda för att få dö', p. 37.

[3] Wosnik, *Beiträge zur Hamburgischen Kriminalgeschichte*, p. 33: 'Der reumütige Sünder ging in einem langen Mantel mit einer Trauerbinde zum Richtplatz, betete, nahm von den Zuhörern mit Segenswünchen Abschied, fiel den Frohn um den Hals, mit der Bitte sein Amt wohl zu verrichten.'

[4] Von Weber starts his article with Huet's account of this murder ('Selbstmord als Mordmotiv', p. 161). Arne Jansson (*From Swords to Sorrow*, p. 51–3) describes the case too and, as well as Huet's account, makes use of the court records and Paul Wulffs

Nuremberg, and had lived in Stockholm for six years. In May 1651 he lured a widow from her house and then with a pistol shot her four-year-old son, who was lying asleep. After visiting the German pastor in town and telling him what he had done and asking for consolation, he was arrested. In court he freely confessed to the murder. He said that he had been depressed and had wanted to die ever since he was a child; he had thought of killing himself, but had hesitated, thinking of the salvation of his soul. He then decided to kill somebody else. The judges found him sane and sentenced him to death.

The murder was much publicized in Stockholm. More than a year later the French cleric Pierre Daniel Huet visited Stockholm and heard of the incident. The story fascinated Huet so much that he incorporated a description in his memoirs, published more than sixty years later. Huet's description of the motive for the murder focused on Wulff's intriguing and disturbing religious argument. It was written in the form of the murderer's own confession to the judges:

> 'I know', said he, 'that I have deserved death, and I employed this artifice to obtain it from you, satisfied that there could scarcely be a safer way of securing eternal salvation than to quit the world with the senses entire, with a body not debilitated by disease, the soul being lifted to God by the pious prayers of religious men and aided by their counsels and exhortations.'[5]

Huet's elaborate description of the religious motives for the murder is not supported by the court records. They probably represent the explanations circulating at the Swedish royal court, which he was visiting. But Huet's description shows that Wulff's case was extraordinary and much talked about. The case might be expected to have attracted followers, but it was sixteen years before the next suicide murder took place in Stockholm.

The early suicide murders thus seem to be isolated cases. Although the executions were solemn and attracted many spectators, something was lacking in terms of inspiring imitators. Between 1670 and 1680,

---

written confession. Jansson's spadework made it possible for me to acquire a copy of the court records and the confession; see *Stockholms Stadsarkiv, Magistratens og rådhusrättens arkiv, Tänkebok i renskrift 1651*, p. 225–35.

[5] Huet wrote his memoirs in Latin. This text is from the English translation: *Memoirs of the Life of Peter Daniel Huet, Bishop of Avranches, written by himself, and translated from the original Latin, with copious notes, biographical and critical,* by John Aikin, London, 1810, p. 155–6.

however, suicide murders became frequent in Stockholm and Hamburg, and they reached an early peak in both cities around 1700. This development of the suicide murder coincided with the rise of Pietism. Before looking into the contributions of Pietism to the development of the execution scenery, though, some other factors should be mentioned.

First, the number of executions in general declined. All over Europe, the last decades of the sixteenth century and the first decades of the seventeenth were marked by an extraordinarily high number of executions. Figures of around 20 executions per year per 100,000 inhabitants were not unusual. From around 1620–30, however, the number of executions fell drastically, and in the last decades of the seventeenth century the frequency had fallen to 2–4 per year per 100,000 inhabitants.[6] The relative rarity of the executions heightened the interest in the single execution on the part of the people as well as the authorities.

Secondly, the religious wars in the first half of the seventeenth century sharpened the orthodoxy of the confessions. The divine origin of the death penalties as well as the careful preparation of the prisoners sentenced to death were distinctive elements of the Lutheran Church, and they were increasingly elaborate. The Lutheran princes were God's agents here on Earth. They legitimized their power by using it to create a Christian realm, and the fulfilment of the divine obligation to execute murderers and other criminals was part of this work. The decision whether or not to use the death penalty was ultimately one where the Lutheran princes could jeopardize their own and their countries' salvation by an incorrect verdict. The practice of the Danish kings of seeking advice from the theological professors of the University of Copenhagen when considering whether to pardon someone under sentence of death, originated in the sixteenth century. The practice did not, however, become common until the last decades of the seventeenth century. The comprehensive guides in the Danish and Swedish church decrees of 1684 and 1693 have already been mentioned in connection with the preparation of prisoners sentenced to death. The orthodoxy preceding Pietism thus shaped the formalities of the religious execution.

[6] See: Van Dülmen, *Theatre of Horror*, p. 113–5 (for Germany), Philip Jenkins, *From Gallows to Prison: Execution Rates in Early Modern England*, 1986, p. 51–71 (for England); Thunander, *Hovrätt i funktion*, p. 21, 166–8 (for Sweden); and Krogh, *Oplysningstiden og det magiske*, p. 39–42 (for Denmark).

The age of orthodoxy, however, was also an age of intellectual self-sufficiency on the part of the pastors and of dogmatic learning. Gustav Radbruch tells of Pastor Hagendorn from Nuremberg, who prepared several prisoners for death in the period 1605–20. He worked on their salvation, as the Church rituals taught, but instead of devotion he focused on the prisoners' religious knowledge. He tested their knowledge of the Catechism and the Bible and used the short time they had left to make good the vast gaps in their knowledge.[7] Thus although the orthodox pastors preached the possibility of salvation, they probably often doubted that the criminals were in fact saved.

Pietism added a focus on the devotional conversion and rebirth to the orthodox preparation and execution ceremony. Salvation was dependent not so much on scholarly learning of the divine truths as on true, heartfelt repentance and the emotional experience of divine mercy. The blissful conversion of a prisoner going to his or her death was a magnificent example of the great mercy shown by God to all true believers. The instructive value of these conversions was greatly enhanced by the public attention surrounding the executions. It probably became more and more common to see prisoners walking to their death not just humbly and in a spirit of obedience to the authorities in the hope of salvation but happily singing psalms and expressing their certainty of salvation in appearance and words. This blissful appearance was taken by the clergy as well as by ordinary spectators as proof that the angel of mercy was beside the prisoner and that the Holy Spirit comforted her or him, as the count from Copenhagen explained when he witnessed Michel Blödorn walking happily to his terrible punishment.

Pietist pastors and popular prints united in celebrating these spectacular incidents of divine punishment and divine mercy. The result was the establishment of the popular conviction that nobody could be more certain of salvation than those who, well prepared, walked to their death accompanied by a pastor.

The narrative of the suicide murderers was fascinating. They were seduced by Satan to commit a terrible sin, and in doing so they evoked God's righteous wrath and demand for their death. After the murder the malefactors came to their senses. In great agony they repented their wrongdoings and at last they found comfort in the belief that Jesus had

[7] Radbruch, 'Ars Moriendi', p. 481–2.

taken on their sins and that God, in spite of their terrible sin, would open the gates of heaven to them too. In this belief they walked happily to their terrible death. The narrative was made all the more powerful by the fact that it was supported in practice as well as theory by the authorities.

Figure 7. Woodcut depicting Karen Corneliidatter and God, from the ballad 'En bodfærdig Synderindes Samtale med sin Gud … Karen Cornelidatter', 1756 (The Royal Library Copenhagen). Karen Corneliidatter had murdered an eight-week-old baby in the Spin-house and was to be pinched five times with red-hot tongs before having her head and one hand cut off. The ballad was constructed as a conversation between the 'Doomed and forlorn sinner' and 'The indignant and just God'. As depicted, it ends with the sinner being reconciled with God through the intercession of Jesus. (Appendix, case 1756:2)

When the narrative was first created, it was difficult to combat. It fed on central and distinctive elements of the Lutheran creed. Pastor Grothausen saw with terror how his successful preparation of Michel Blödorn caused a new murder. But he had to prepare the new murderer for his death in the same way. Moser was also terrified when he realized how the logic of the suicide murderers was nourished by the Pietist preparation of prisoners sentenced to death, but his project of destroying the kingdom of Satan and spreading the kingdom of God was too important to stop the new edition of his book.

PART THREE

DEMISE

CHAPTER TWELVE

THE DANISH DECREE OF 1767

The phenomenon of the suicide murder began later in Copenhagen than in Stockholm, Hamburg and probably other German cities, but the murders soon became popular, and in the middle of the eighteenth century the Danish capital was heavily burdened by them. With 55 murders and 26 attempted murders between 1730 and 1769, Copenhagen must have been one of the cities most severely afflicted by the crime. The Danish state was the most active in using legal initiatives to combat the murders. With the decrees of 1697, 1738 and 1749 the state laid down painful additions to the death penalty and ordered the murderers to be paraded in a humiliating manner on their way to the execution place. The decrees were partly due to the comprehensive Danish Law of 1683, which limited the legally sanctioned punishments and necessitated new legislative action in order to use such harsh penalties. The harsh and humiliating penalties, however, did not deter the murderers; on the contrary, the number of suicide murders increased in Copenhagen after 1749. This provoked a final Danish decree to combat the suicide murders. The decree of 1767 was revolutionary in laying down a new type of punishment in the European penal arsenal and, more importantly, in the way it broke radically with the religious foundation of criminal law in the Lutheran countries. Before discussing the decree and its prehistory, it is necessary to give a general overview of the position of Mosaic Law and of penal practice in the Lutheran areas in the middle of the eighteenth century.

Religious and Mental Changes

As we have seen, the Reformation led to penal practices in the Lutheran and Reformed countries and cities that were strongly influenced by Mosaic Law. The cornerstone in this influence was the belief that God's law demanded the death penalty for witchcraft, adultery, bigamy, incest sodomy/bestiality and homicide. From an exegetical point of view the foundations of the mandatory death penalty were not beyond dispute. The line between the forensic parts of Mosaic Law which need not be obeyed after the coming of Christ and the parts which were seen as belonging to Natural Law and thus eternal was difficult to draw. Nevertheless, the death penalty was written into the criminal laws of the Lutheran countries, and its divine nature was canonized in the way the death penalty was communicated to the public. It was presented as an inevitable consequence of the literal reading of the Bible that was so important to the Lutheran confession and which in its own understanding was the core of the distinction between it and the Catholic Church.

During the late seventeenth century and the eighteenth century the belief in the mandatory character of the death penalty for these crimes was gradually questioned. But changes in religion were a sensitive question for the Lutheran states and churches. Matters of faith came directly from the word of God, and no authority could do anything about that. The religious edifice was seen as unchangeable, and it was feared that if one stone was removed it would endanger the whole building.

Around the year 1700 the mandatory character of the death penalty was taken up in learned literature in Latin. The reform jurist Christian Thomasius and the orthodox theologian Philip Ludwig Hanneken had both argued in dissertations that the Christian prince was not bound to retain the death penalty under Mosaic Law.[1] In 1733 the leading juridical professor in Halle, Justus Henning Böhmer, in his work on Protestant church law, called the mandatory death penalty an illusion that was just one of the errors of some Protestant theologians and jurists of recent years.[2] A critical position was thus articulated in learned circles from the beginning of the eighteenth century, but its way into penal practice was slow, and its introduction into the law even slower.

The following discussion refers mainly to developments in the Danish penal practice, with references also to developments in Sweden and Germany where such information is available. The Danish Law of 1683 maintained the death penalty provisions for witchcraft, adultery/bigamy, incest and homicide which had been issued in the preceding

[1] Christian Thomasius, *Dissertatio inauguralis iuridica, de jure aggratiandi principis evangelici in causis homicidii*, Halle, Salfeld 1707 (repr. 1714, 1720 and 1739); Philip Ludwig Hanneken, *Dissertatio theologica de iure gratiae principis christiani, in reos noxae capitalis*, Wittenberg, 1701 (Jena 1731).

[2] Justus Henning Böhmer, *Jus ecclasisaticum protestantium, usum modernum juris canonici juxta seriem decretalium ostendens, et ipsis rerum argumentis illustrans*, Halle, 1733, vol. 5, lib. 5, tit. 12, § 2.

century and added a death penalty for unnatural sexual intercourse—i.e., sodomy/bestiality. In practice only some of these death penalty provisions were used.

Denmark experienced a huge wave of witchcraft cases in the 1620s but only a few thereafter.[3] The final blow to the persecution of witches came in 1698, when a pastor who had appealed to the Supreme Court against the acquittal of two women accused of witchcraft was sentenced to forfeit his office and life imprisonment. The verdict and an official interpretation of the case were publicized in a booklet. No subsequent witchcraft cases were brought to trial in Denmark. The witchcraft provisions were, however, used again around 1720, when there were several cases of soldiers who had signed contracts with the Devil. Some similar cases around 1700 had been treated leniently, but now three or four soldiers were executed for the crime. The theologians were divided in their view of the cases, and a couple of orthodox theologians argued that the death penalty in Mosaic Law was not part of the eternal moral law but applied only to Israel before the coming of Christ. Only the death penalty for homicide belonged to the eternal moral law. Since the executions seemed to be actually attracting people who wanted to be executed, the hard-line policy was soon dropped. From the 1730s on the few cases of people signing pacts with the Devil were treated without consulting theologians. They were conducted behind closed doors, and the offenders were punished with a year or two of imprisonment. In Sweden witchcraft cases were very common in the first half of the eighteenth century, but after 1700 death penalties handed out by the lower courts were not confirmed in the courts of appeal.[4] In Lutheran Germany the execution of witches stopped as well around 1700, whereas there are isolated examples of executions of witches in Catholic Germany until 1775.[5] In the 1750s these developments culminated in a public debate in Lutheran Germany about the possibility of demonic possession and ultimately the presence of demons on Earth.[6]

---

[3] Krogh, *Oplysningstiden og det magiske*, p. 119–50.

[4] Per Sörlin, *Trolldoms- och Vidskepelsesprocesserne i Göta Hovrätt, 1635–1754*, 1993.

[5] Behringer, *Hexenverfolgung in Bayern*, p. 344–65; and Katrin Moeller, '"Es ist ein überaus gerechtes gesetz. Dass Zauberinnen getötet werden": Hexenverfolgung im protestantishen Norddeutschland', 2002, p. 96.

[6] Eric Midelfort, *Exorcism and Enlightenment: Johann Joseph Gassner and the Demons of Eighteenth-Century Germany*, 2005, p. 88–94.

In spite of the death penalty provisions in Danish Law, nobody was executed for adultery and bigamy.[7] Until 1720 the Faculty of Theology repeatedly proposed execution in severe cases of adultery and bigamy. From the 1730s, however, it was divided: on the one hand there was an orthodox faction advocating that the king should make an example and use the death penalty sometimes; on the other there was a Pietist faction that did not want to use executions for these crimes. Both sides, however, agreed that the death penalty was not required by God. In Sweden a few executions for adultery took place up until 1740.[8] In Hamburg, Richard Wosnik's list of executions includes one for adultery in 1691 and two for bigamy from 1710 and 1724.[9] In Lutheran Württemberg executions for bigamy were unknown, and the last execution for adultery seems to have been carried out in 1695.[10]

Cases of incest and bestiality were relatively frequent in Norway and Iceland, but rare in Denmark.[11] Several of the Norwegian and Icelandic cases, however, were presented to the Faculty of Theology in Copenhagen by the king. Until 1720 the death penalty was the ordinary punishment, and there was an agreement in the Faculty of Theology that the penalty was a divine requirement. In 1718, however, the jurist Andreas Hojer wrote a dissertation in Latin on incest, which he published in Germany. Hojer was soon to become a leading civil servant. The dissertation argued that incest was not a crime against nature, but only a crime against the rational social order. The leading theologians in Denmark were furious and wanted Hojer punished for his book, but Hojer had powerful friends and his arguments could not be brushed aside. Until then leading theologians had justified their recommendations of the death penalty solely by referring to the Mosaic Law. Now they were forced to make explicit the forensic character (i.e., belonging to the forum of the Jewish community before the coming of Christ) of at least parts of the Mosaic Law.[12] In the years that followed, references to Mosaic Law in theological statements about the death penalty were supplemented by references to the New Testament and

---

[7] Krogh, *Oplysningstiden og det magiske*, p. 153–7.

[8] Erik Anners, *Humanitet och rationalism: Studier i upplysningstidens strafflagsreformer–särskilt med hänsyn till Gustav III:s reformlagstiftning*, 1965, p. 161–3.

[9] Wosnik, *Beiträge zur Hamburgischen Kriminalgeschichte*, p. 24–51.

[10] Schnabel-Schüle, *Überwachen und Strafen im Territorialstaat*, p. 304, 297–9.

[11] Krogh, *Oplysningstiden og det magiske*, p. 158–62.

[12] Krogh, *Oplysningstiden og det magiske*, p. 163–71.

with allegations that the penal provisions were in accordance with Natural Law.

In the 1730s statements by the Faculty of Theology about cases involving incest and bestiality were in most cases divided in two. One came from the orthodox faction, arguing for the maintenance of the death penalty, and the other from the Pietist faction. The Pietists argued that the penal provisions in the Mosaic Law were given by God to the Jewish community at that time and did not belong to the eternal moral law.[13] The disagreement in the Faculty of Theology reached a climax in 1742, when the Pietist Jeremias Reuss wrote a statement in a bestiality case in which he completely declined to give advice about which penalty should be used, stating that all death penalty provisions in the Mosaic Law were of a forensic nature. The use of the death penalty was thus a question for the secular authorities, and not for theologians. This radical opinion, however, was not generally shared by the leading Danish theologians, but from then on the kings only rarely consulted the professors of the Faculty of Theology. The debates coincided with a growing reluctance on the part of the Supreme Court judges especially to pass sentence of death for incest and bestiality. The level of proof required was also increased considerably, so that only a few death sentences were brought before the king to confirm. The last execution for incest in Denmark was in 1739, and the last death sentence for bestiality was carried out in in 1751. The king, however, continued to confirm death sentences from Norway and Iceland, the last instance being a father in Iceland who was executed for incest in 1762. In Sweden executions for incest and bestiality were still frequent in the 1770s.[14] The Hamburg execution list cites one case of a death sentence for bestiality from 1726.[15] In Württemberg several people were executed for bestiality in the first half of the eighteenth century. Penal practice in cases of incest in the eighteenth century is not presented by Schnabel-Schüle, but she mentions a case from 1761 where the Faculty of Law of the University of Tübingen advised that a man guilty of incest with his stepdaughter should be sentenced to six years' hard labour, reasoning that today more lenient principles were used to judge such cases.[16]

---

[13] Krogh, *Oplysningstiden og det magiske*, p. 175, 199–201.
[14] Anners, *Humanitet och rationalism*, p. 165, n. 32.
[15] Wosnik, *Beiträge zur Hamburgischen Kriminalgeschichte*, p. 24–51.
[16] Schnabel-Schüle, *Überwachen und Strafen im Territorialstaat*, p. 314–7, 311.

The mandatory death penalty for murder had a special, inviolable position and was not questioned until about 1750. In 1749 a murder case provoked internal debate in the Danish central administration.[17] A drunken soldier had quarrelled with a parish bailiff and in the ensuing scuffle had drawn his rapier and stabbed the bailiff fatally in the eye. The soldier was sentenced to death, but the army wanted him pardoned. The judge advocate general first obtained a statement from the Faculty of Law at the University of Copenhagen. The professors took up the question of the mandatory nature of the death penalty. They stated that the divine requirement of the death sentence for deliberate murder was not a universal law but should be considered particular and forensic. Nevertheless, the professors ended up advising the king to confirm the death sentence, as they found the killing deliberate. This statement did not satisfy the leading generals, and they ordered the judge advocate general to obtain a statement from a university in Germany, where such cases were usually treated more leniently. He chose the University at Halle. The statement from the university argued in detail that the king had the right to overturn a death sentence even in murder cases and found many arguments against the idea that the death penalty in Mosaic Law should be considered as eternally valid. The university found sufficient extenuating circumstances to recommend a pardon, and the king subsquently overturned the death sentence. In 1752, in a similar murder case, the University of Göttingen was asked for a statement.[18] The Göttingen professors recommended a pardon but were more guarded in their arguments. They cited an alternative translation of certain passages from the Pentateuch and from this deduced that Mosaic Law exempted not only killing in self-defence or by accident but also killing in anger. In addition they wrote that trustworthy theologians and jurists believed that there were no limits at all to the royal right to overturn the death sentence. In 1755 the Faculty of Law in Copenhagen recommended that a soldier who had killed his opponent in a duel should be reprieved.[19] The generals had put pressure on the Faculty to reach such a verdict. Just as in 1749, the professors doubted that any there were any religious limits to the royal right to quash death sentences.

---

[17] Krogh, *Oplysningstiden og det magiske*, p. 201–4.
[18] Krogh, *Oplysningstiden og det magiske*, p. 206.
[19] Krogh, *Oplysningstiden og det magiske*, p. 206–9.

Judging from these statements, one might assume that there had been a general change in Danish penal practice, but the change had taken place only in military cases. The majority of the judges in the Supreme Court and the secretaries in the Chancellery still believed that the death penalty was mandatory at least for homicide. Not until the 1760s did royal pardons begin to reduce the number of cases of the death penalty in cases of infanticide and cases of killings in fights or under the influence of alcohol.[20] It is difficult to establish whether a similar development took place in other Lutheran countries, because many individual cases have to be examined in order to determine when practice changed. The two statements from the universities in Halle and Göttingen, however, show that the faculties of law of the two progressive German universities were more or less in line with the law professors in Copenhagen when it came to the divine nature of the death penalty. Furthermore, the statement from Halle to the Danish king was published in 1775 in a collection of the legal opinions of the Halle jurist J.T. Carrach. This publication was not unique. The Göttingen jurist C.F.G. Meister published two volumes of legal opinions in 1771–75, and in 1779 the Danish jurist P. Kofod Ancher published a collection of opinions from the 1740, '50s and '60s.[21] The purpose of these publications was to present penetrating juridical arguments, but also to document the fact that in their confidential opinions in the preceding decades the jurists had argued that the penalty clauses in the Mosaic Law were not binding, and had advised that the death penalty in the criminal codes for religious and sexual offences as well as for manslaughter need not be imposed. Such opinions had been new and daring at the time when they were given.

The overall picture of the status of the mandatory divine death penalty thus shows that penal practice in relation to the crimes in question

[20] Infanticide: Maren Nielsdatter pardoned by a royal edict of 2 December 1763 (Rgsk. 1763 voucher 126–26). Dorthe Cathrine Nielsdatter pardoned by royal edict 28 February 1766 (Rgsk. 1766 voucher 116–17). Killings in fights: Morten Berentsen, a sailor pardoned by royal edict 20 July 1764 (RA, Generalauditøren,(Søetaten), betænkninger 13 July 1764). Jens Christian Larsen Lund pardoned by royal edict 26 January 1769 (RA, gen.aud. (Søetaten), betænkninger 29 December 1768).

[21] C.F.G. Meister, *Rechtliche Erkenntnisse und Gutachten in Peinlichen Fällen größten Theils im Nahmen der Göttingischen Juristen-Fakultät ausgearbeitet*, 1771–75. J.T. Carrach, *J.T. Carrachs rechtliche Urtheile und Gutachten in peinlichen Sachen im Namen der Hallischen Juristen-Fakultät*, ed. H.J.O. König, 1775. P. Kofod Ancher, *Svar paa nogle Spørgsmaale til Det Juridiske Fakultet*, Copenhagen, 1779.

changed considerably in the first half of the eighteenth century. The death penalty had already stopped being used in cases of witchcraft and contracts with the Devil, bigamy and adultery. Executions for incest and bestiality became increasingly rare, and around 1750 there was generally more lenient punishment in murder cases. At the root of this development was a growing unease among the Supreme Court judges, the professors and the leading civil servants about the automatic death penalty irrespective of extenuating circumstances and without regard to the actual efficacy of the penalty in deterring crime. At a theoretical level the biblical foundation of the dogma of the mandatory death penalty was questioned. At first only some of the death penalty provisions were questioned, but from the middle of the century all the death penalty provisions in the Pentateuch were deemed to be forensic and therefore not binding in modern society. The Danish example, however, also shows that, although progressive theologians and jurists argued against the eternal nature of the death penalty provisions in the Pentateuch and thus managed to have some death sentences overturned, they also met with opposition from other parts of the ruling élite, especially in relation to the death sentences for homicide.

These debates and changes in the interpretation of the Mosaic Law were not expressed in public until the 1770s, however. They took place only in learned disputations in Latin and in confidential statements to the king. The death penalty provisions remained on the statute book all over Europe and were not debated publicly until Beccaria took up the question in his famous book *Dei delitti e delle pene* ('On Crimes and Punishments'), from 1764.

Henrik Stampe's Proposal

The changes in Danish penal practice did not affect the suicide murders directly, as the death penalty was not questioned for such premeditated murders of innocent victims. Indirectly, however, the changes did increase the focus on the murders. In the first decades of the eighteenth century executions for suicide murders had taken place alongside executions for infanticide and for other murders/manslaughter as well as instances of the death penalty for other offences. But from 1750 executions for suicide murders completely dominated the instances of punishment as a public spectacle in Copenhagen. The annual accounts for 1750–59 from the city judge document the execution of ten suicide murderers and only two executions for other crimes.[22]

The executions took place on a permanent scaffold erected at Nytorv, in the middle of Copenhagen. It was just outside the windows of the more affluent citizens, and the municipal corporation became increasingly uncomfortable with the bloody scenes enacted there. In 1761 the king permitted the permanent scaffold to be taken down. From then on whippings and brandings took place at a stake erected for each

Figure 8. Woodcut depicting the execution of Johanne Hansdatter on the permanent scaffold at Nytorv, from the ballad 'En sindriig aandelig Sang forfattet som en Tale af en bodfærdig Synderinde navnlig Johanne Hansdatter', 1756 (Jens P. Sørensen private collection). The small square with the houses close to the scaffold is well illustrated. (Appendix, case 1756:1)

[22] RA, Reviderede regnskaber, Københavnske regnskaber, Byfogedregnskaber 1749–59.The two other cases were Andreas Truelsen, who was executed in 1751 for murdering his brother, and Simon Bendsen, executed in 1759 for assaulting and robbing a mail courier.

occasion and taken down again afterwards. Executions were moved out of town, to the gallows.[23]

Suicide murders thus increasingly emerged as a most pressing criminal problem, and the brutal punishments of the suicide murderers was increasingly seen as revolting and out of step with the times.

In early 1757 no fewer than three suicide murders were committed in the course of three weeks. This caused the government to act once again. The king requested the permanent Commission for the Revision of the Law to consider what penalties could deter this type of murder.

Before the discussions in the commission commenced, Henrik Stampe, a member of the commission and chief legal adviser to the king, came up with a truly revolutionary proposal.[24] His argument was strictly utilitarian. The purpose of punishment was to achieve public safety and calm, so the punishments should therefore, first, prevent the perpetrator from repeating the crime and, second, deter others from committing the same crime. The same punishment should not be applied for all crimes; rather, in each case the punishment should be designed according to the psychological make-up of the specific perpetrators. Most people considered the death penalty the worst punishment and therefore the most effective deterrent. In the case of the suicide murderers, however, the opposite was the case. According to Stampe suicide murderers were melancholy, depressed people who considered life not as something precious but as a heavy and unbearable burden. To sentence such people to death was to their way of thinking not a punishment but rather a fulfilment of their wish, a reward for the crime they had committed. Therefore the most effective punishment for these people was not the death sentence but the continuation of the life of which they were so tired, and making this life as unbearable as possible. They would now properly feel the torments that they had previously only imagined.

For these reasons Stampe suggested a different punishment. The murderers should be branded and whipped. Every year, on the anniversary of the murder, they should be brought to the place where the murder had been committed and whipped again. In prison they should perform the most strenuous and ignominious work. Finally, when they

---

[23] Gerhard L. Grove, 'Skafottet og kaget på Nytorv ved midten af det attende århundrede', 1903–05, p. 160–76.

[24] Henrik Stampe, *Erklæringer breve og forestillinger generalprokurørembedet vedkommende*, vol. II, 1794, p. 153–62.

died, their body should be taken to the place of execution by the night man's men and buried there.

Stampe's proposal graphically exposed the futility of the death penalty as a deterrent for potential suicide murderers, but it did not even mention the central issue of the time in discussion relating to punishment. The sole purpose of punishments in Danish Law was not, as Stampe claimed, to ensure public safety. Most cases of the death penalty were seen as divine requirements of Christian society, as we saw earlier. Stampe's proposal suggested the abolition of the death penalty for murder: the most important case of divine command. The divine requirement of the death penalty was being discussed at the time of Stampe's proposal, but only in secret statements to the king. What Stampe was suggesting was in effect a public decree announcing, so to speak, to the whole kingdom and to the whole of Christianity that the Danish king would no longer follow the divine commands about punishment laid down in the Bible!

Stampe's proposal received some support in the Commission for the Revision of the Law.[25] The majority in the commission, however, while admitting that the suggested punishment should fit the nature of the crime, found it absolutely necessary to obtain the opinion of the Faculty of Theology as to 'whether it may be considered to be in accordance with the revealed Word of God that he who had shed innocent blood, his blood should not again be shed'.[26] Furthermore, the members of the commission questioned the effect of the new punishment and feared that it might be abused. They found it likely that people who committed murder for other reasons would make use of such a decree and claim that they had been motivated by the desire to lose their life, thinking that by saying so they would now escape the death penalty.

In the 1740s the Faculty of Theology had lost its role as the king's adviser in cases of reprieves of the death penalty. This late demand for their opinion was a reminiscent of the days when the theologians were the guardians of the biblical foundation of criminal law. The Faculty answered that the death penalty for murder was part of God's natural

---

[25] The statements of the Commission as well as that of the Faculty of Theology and the contributions to the king's council are in Danish National Archives, DK, Indlæg til sjællandske registre 1767/673.

[26] Danish National Archives, DK, Indlæg til sjællandske registre 1767/673, the Commission's report of 26 November 1767: 'Om det kand holdes for at være overensstemmende med Guds aabenbarede Ord, at dend som havde udgydet uskyldig Blod, hans Blod skulde icke igien udgydes.'

or moral law and was applicable not just to Jews in the time of Moses' time but to every Christian society and permanently. They could accept a brief postponement of the death penalty, but not its abolition. Finally, Stampe's proposal was raised in the king's council and managed to split the four ministers of state as well. The Minister for Foreign Affairs, Count Bernstorff, supported the new punishment, but the three others could not accept the abolition of the death penalty for murder.

The debate in 1757–58 thus did not lead to any changes. The suicide murders continued, and so did the harsh executions. In 1763 the minister of state J.L. Holstein, who for nearly thirty years he had been in charge of juridical as well as religious affairs, died. Holstein had been one of the main bulwarks against changes in the religious foundation of criminal law. Then in 1766 Christian VII ascended the throne. He had a more enlightened way of thinking, but as he had mental health problems he created considerable uncertainty within the government. A few years into his reign he became mentally ill, and his personal surgeon, J.F. Struensee, seized power. Struensee introduced many enlightened reforms, the most important of which was freedom of the press. His position was, however, based solely on his control over the king and the intimate relationship that he enjoyed with the young queen. In 1772 Struensee was removed in a conservative-led *coup d'état* headed by the dowager queen, and was executed for *lèse-majesté*.

In 1766 and 1767 a new wave of no fewer than nine suicide murders alarmed the city. In the summer of 1767 Anne Christophersdatter, a housemaid, angry at her mistress's accusations, chose to take a friend's nine-month-old child to the hall in the mistress's house and cut its throat with a knife.[27] The courts sentenced her according to the decree of 1749, but her mother submitted a petition to the king asking for her daughter to be pardoned from the pinching with red-hot tongs and the exhibition of her dead body. Christian VII, who at that stage was still competent mentally, responded that 'As experience shows that the present decree does not impede such inhuman fanaticism, the Chancellery shall present a new decree on these instances.'[28]

[27] Appendix, case 1767:3.

[28] 'saasom Erfarenheden viser, at den nuværende Forordning ikke hemmer en saa umenneskelig Fanatismus; saa skal Kanzelliet foredrage en nye Forordning om slige Tilfælde', petition 17 October 1767, in Danish National Archives, DK, indlæg til sjællandske registre 1767/673.

The Chancellery returned to Stampe's proposal. This time only one secretary argued against it. After brief consideration the proposal, with minor changes, was presented to the king and approved. The decree of 18 December 1767 stated that anyone who murdered another person without reason, other than to do harm and thereby lose his life, should:

1. Be branded and whipped.
2. Every year on the anniversary of the murder, dressed in the ordinary clothes he wore daily in prison, without hat or cap and bare-headed, with a halter around his neck, and with hands tied—to insult him the more—he should be brought to the place where the murder had been committed in the night man's carriage and whipped again.
3. In prison he should perform the most strenuous and demeaning work.
4. After this death, have his body taken to the place of execution by the night man's men, have his head and hand cut off there, his body placed on the post and wheel, with the head as well as the hand nailed to the pole over the body.

The only secretary opposing the new decree, Henrik Hielmstierne, had suggested that the suicide murders could instead be prevented by reducing the religious content of the execution ceremony. This led to a change in the clerical presence at executions prescribed in the Church ritual. A royal prescript to the bishops on 22 April 1768 forbade the pastors to accompany the convict on his or her way from the prison to the place of execution, and no prayers or singing of psalms were allowed on the way. The pastor should meet the convict at the place of execution and there 'without any public speech should only try to keep the sinner in as much devotion and silence as possible, until he is dead'. This change was brought about by the need to

> deprive the common man of the false and not uncommon fantasy, which can lead many to do evil, namely that it is such a blissful death, and that nobody can be better prepared for death, and salvation cannot fail when the pastor walks along with the sinner saying prayers and singing.[29]

The decree of 1767 was epochal in a Lutheran context, with its public break with the mandatory and divinely ordained death penalty for

[29] Order to the bishops of Denmark 22 April 1768, in Danish National Archives, DK, 'Indlæg til sjællandske tegnelser 1768/310: Uden at holde nogen offentlig Tale alene søge at holde Synderen i mueligste Andagt og Stilhed, indtil hand er død'; 'betage den gemene Mand den urigtige og ikke usædvandlige Indbildning, som kand føre mange til at gøre ondt, nemlig at det er saa lyksalig en Død, og ingen kand være bedre bered til Døden, og Salighed ikke kand feyle, hvor Præsten gaaer ved Synderen med Bøn og Sang.'

murder, and indeed it represented a landmark throughout Europe in prescribing a penalty other than the death sentence for premeditated murder. It is remarkable that the vexed question of the divinely ordained duty to execute a murderer, which had determined the fate of the proposal ten years earlier, was not mentioned at all in the discussions in 1767. No theologian was asked whether the proposal was in accordance with society's obligations to God. It might be supposed that the king and his advisers would have felt it necessary to present their reasons for this break with God's law as it had been interpreted for the last two and a half centuries. But this was not the case. Instead of a religious argumentation for the abolition of the death penalty being developed, thereby defining the new position in a religious context, the question was treated as non-existent. One might argue that the position of the Mosaic Law had already been undermined by the growing number of royal reprieves of the death penalty for religious and sexual crimes as well as for manslaughter and infanticide. But this development was related to specific cases, and the arguments about Mosaic Law not being binding for the modern Christian state that were put forward in statements to the king were not made public. Now a public decree had in effect abolished the idea of an automatic and divinely ordained death penalty for murder. The reason for the absence of any religious argument is probably that a public Lutheran theological position denouncing the concept of a divine mandatory death penalty for murder had not yet been developed. A public discussion of the position of the divine mandatory death penalty took place in the 1770s in a broader Lutheran context. I shall return to this debate in the next chapter.

The decree of 1767 was also innovative in presenting a new type of punishment. The annual public whippings as regular public reminders of the harsh fate awaiting criminals seem to have been Stampe's own invention, and so too the posthumous exhibition of the body at the gallows.

It could be assumed that the decree was an early consequence of Cesare Beccaria's *Dei delitti e delle pene* ('On Crimes and Punishments'), which was published in 1764. Beccaria's book, with its questioning of the rationality of the death penalty, quickly became well known all over Europe, including in Copenhagen.[30] Stampe's proposal was in many

[30] A Danish scientist informed Beccaria of the new decree a few weeks after it came out. See Ditlev Tamm, 'Hvorfor læse Beccaria?', in *Cesare Beccaria: Om forbrydelse og straf*, Copenhagen, 1998, p. 213.

ways in the spirit of Beccaria's utilitarian view of punishment. Beccaria argued that many people were not afraid of death:

> There are many who can look upon death with intrepidity and firmness, some through fanaticism, and others through vanity, which attends us even to the grave; others from a desperate resolution, either to get rid of their misery, or cease to live: but fanaticism and vanity forsake the criminal in slavery, in chains and fetters, in an iron cage, and despair seems rather the beginning than the end of their misery.[31]

It is quite possible that Beccaria's ideas had sown the seed for the revival of Stampe's proposal in 1767, but the proposal was actually written in 1757, eight years before the publication of *Dei delitti e delle pene*. The penalty given in the 1767 decree was the first and for many years the only example in Europe of a punishment designed to be worse than the death penalty. As a practical example of Beccaria's ideas on punishment, the penalty became a reference point in the penal debates in the following years.

The decree was part of a brief blossoming of enlightened policies in Denmark. One of Struensee's reforms was to abolish the only death penalty for crimes against property in Denmark: that imposed for burglary and for stealing cattle or horses. After Struensee's fall in 1772, the new conservative government overturned several of his reforms, but the freedom of the press and the abolition of the death penalty for offences against property remained in force, and so did the decree of 1767.

Effects of the Decree of 1767

The government had taken a leap into the unknown with this daring initiative. Now it waited for the effects, but the first years were not promising. Between 1769 and 1771 five people were sentenced to the punishment prescribed in the decree of 1767. Two of them, both navy personnel, had only attempted suicide murder, but the naval courts had dealt with no fewer than seven suicide murders in the 1760s.[32] The navy feared a new wave of murders and wanted to frighten off possible murderers.

---

[31] Cesare Beccaria, *On Crimes and Punishments*, Chapter 28, here cited from an internet version: http://www.constitution.org/cb/crim_pun.htm.

[32] See Appendix.

A case in 1772 revealed the limitations of the new decree. A day-labourer called Hans Jørgen Carl had cut the throat of an old match-seller. The old man was totally unknown to him. Carl stated that he had decided to commit a crime, but he denied that he had done it because he was depressed and wanted to lose his life. As there were no witnesses to the murder, the city court chose to sentence him to be beheaded by sword. He declared himself satisfied with the sentence and would not appeal against it to the Supreme Court. A royal letter confirmed the verdict unless he appealed, but once again Carl refused to request an appeal.[33] The use of the new punishment was thus dependent on the murderer's confession of a specific motive. If the murderer denied that his intention had been to be executed, the decree could not be employed.

With five suicide murders and with an example of a suicide murderer circumventing the decree and obtaining the death he probably wished for, the new decree was not a striking success in the first five years it was in force. But after 1772 it finally began to appear that it was having an impact on crime: over the next four years no murders occurred.

The city was not allowed to forget the murders and the new punishment, however. Every year the five local perpetrators sentenced according to the 1767 decree received their annual whipping. To these five were added suicide murderers from the rest of the country sentenced pursuant to the 1767 decree. They were taken to the Spin-house or to the so-called Slavery—the military prison—to do their strenuous and shameful work, and as they were now some way from the places where the murders had been committed, their annual whipping took place in Copenhagen as well.

The whippings were impressive and expensive: the night man turned up with his carriage in front of the Spin-house in order to carry out the defiling and shameful task of transporting the convict. Another, finer, carriage transported the city court judge, who was to announce the sentence and supervise the punishment. A force of a hundred men from the corps of nightwatchmen was called out in order to secure law and order. They were headed by the chief and the lieutenant of the corps.[34] This procession now moved through the city to the place where

---

[33] Appendix, case 1772:2.

[34] The punishment was expensive and caused internal discussion in the government including over details of the punishment. See Danish National Archives, DK Indlæg til Kancelliets brevbøger 1777/1407.

the murder had been committed. Here the executioner waited with a bucket full of water to keep the nine birch rods supple. The murderer was to receive twenty-seven strokes, three with each rod. The sentence was read aloud by the judge, and the murderer received his punishment.

In 1777 the government decided that the annual punishments should be limited. The prison boards were informed that convicts with a record of good behaviour could apply to be excused from their annual whippings.[35] The decision had the effect that, after they had been whipped annually for a few years, the murderers were absolved of this part of their punishment.[36]

The following year the city court judge asked if the macabre treatment of the corpses of the murderers, when they had died, really needed to be carried out. According to the decree of 1767, the corpse had to be taken to the place of execution by the night man's men with a great deal of publicity. Here the head and the hand were supposed to be cut off and the body placed on the post and wheel, with the head and the hand nailed on the pole over the body. After six years with only one suicide murder in Copenhagen, however, the need for solemn exemplary punishments was not felt so urgently. One of the secretaries in the Chancellery wrote that he had found it almost unbearable even to read about it. Another found that this 'butchering of a dead body could very well be abolished'. The government decided that if the murderer had received a pardon from the annual whippings, a simple burial at the place of execution would be enough. If he or she had not been pardoned, the government should be consulted in each case.[37] With these limitations in its actual use, the new punishment was still the worst punishment for those criminals who were allowed to live, but the macabre, publicly performed cruelties were reduced.

After four years of calm, a new suicide murder took place in 1777, followed by one in 1779, another in 1783 and a fourth in 1789. But these murders had changed in character. When in 1783 the musketeer

---

[35] Danish National Archives, DK, Indlæg til Kancelliets brevbøger 1777/155.

[36] All the murderers sentenced according to the 1767 decree in the years 1769–72 and who served their penalty in the Spin-house received a pardon from the annual whipping in 1776–77. Hans Terkelsen, sentenced in 1777, received such a pardon in 1781 (Appendix, case 1777:1). Svend Jensen, sentenced in 1779, received a pardon in 1789 (Appendix, case 1779:1).

[37] Danish National Archives, DK, indlæg til Kancelliets brevbøger 1778/570 and 1779/1346.

Johann Friedrich Geneser cut the throat of his own small child, he explained that he had been drunk and always did harm when he was drunk. But he denied having been 'fed up with life' and depressed. This clear denial saved him from the new punishment. Instead he was sentenced to death according to the 1738 decree. As probably the last person in Denmark to suffer this punishment, still alive, he was broken on the wheel. Afterwards he was discreetly strangled by the executioner when being placed on the wheel to die.[38] Two ballads were written about Geneser, and both dwelt on the fact that he had long refused to repent of the murder and had even threatened to murder fellow prisoners. Only a short time before his execution he had repented and turned to God. It is likely that Geneser had feared that his much-desired death penalty was in danger. He had to hide the truth not only from the judges and the prosecutor but also from his spiritual adviser, as well as from interested members of the general public.

In 1789 a dragoon, Friderich Warnicke, from Odense, killed his seven-year-old son and, just like Johann Friedrich Geneser, denied that he done it because he was depressed. This time, however, in his presentation to the king the judge advocate general argued that Warnicke's denial should not be accepted. Among other things, the adviser argued, 'that his denial of having committed the murder because he was bored with life could have happened precisely for the purpose of losing his life'. He accordingly obtained the king's approval to sentence Warnicke to the punishment prescribed in the decree of 1767.[39]

A few months later a deserter, corporal Daniel Kiranni, on his way to give himself up, chose to murder another soldier whom he did not know by shooting him in the back just outside Copenhagen. Kiranni also denied having murdered 'in order to lose his life'. Once again the judge advocate general argued that Kiranni had shaped his confession in order to avoid the punishment in the 1767 decree and to obtain the death penalty instead. He therefore wanted him punished according to the 1767 decree. The king, however, sentenced Kiranni to have his hand and head cut off with an axe and then impaled on a stake, and the body buried at the place of execution.[40]

---

[38] Appendix, case 1783:1.

[39] Danish National Archives, Generalauditøren (landetaten), Justitsprotokol 1789, p. 299, and originale relationer 3 July 1789.

[40] Appendix, case 1789:1.

The punishment prescribed in the 1767 decree seems to have been instrumental in drastically reducing the frequency of the suicide murders. The new decree was not able to put a complete end to suicide murders in the first twenty years of its existence, but it certainly made it more difficult to commit suicide through killing somebody else. Previously, a depressed or violently angry person could commit a murder and afterwards candidly describe her feelings and motives to the court and to the pastor preparing her. She could expect a pastor who was eager to save her and a community that passionately and perhaps a little enviously followed her conversion from a desperate person blinded by Satan through remorse and repentance to the calm and happiness of being reborn.

The death penalty alone could still be given to suicide murderers, but this required a long period of lying to suspicious prosecutors and judges as well as to pastors urging one to be honest before God and not deny the sins one had committed. Only resolute soldiers with the ability to hide their intentions during the questionings and in court obtained death. But even this strategy no longer could no longer ensure the much sought-after certainty, as Warnicke's case showed.

CHAPTER THIRTEEN

MEASURES TAKEN AGAINST THE SUICIDE MURDERS IN GERMANY

It was not only in Denmark that the religious basis for the suicide murders had captured the attention of the government and the public. In Prussia the role of the clerical preparation and the execution scenario for the suicide murders began to be publicly debated and were met with legal initiatives in 1769. When it came to enlightened initiatives and the rationalist battle against old prejudices, Prussia was the leading German state in the second half of the eighteenth century. The Prussian king, Frederick the Great, took a special interest in reforming the judicial system. His reign is characterized by many decrees concerning specific legal topics and by a general reform of the judicial system in the Allgemeines Landrecht ('General State Laws of the Prussian States'), which came into force in 1794, six years after Frederick's death.

In February 1769 the rationalist theologian Gothilf Samuel Steinbart published a booklet entitled *Is it Advisable that Malefactors should be Prepared for their Death and Accompanied to their Execution by Clergymen?* The booklet was written in Berlin and dedicated to the Prussian minister for justice, Baron Münchhausen.[1] Henrik Stampe had exposed the failure of the death penalty to combat suicide murders, and Steinbart, with the same ruthless cogency, exposed the responsibility of the clergy for the suicide murders. When the religious motivation of the suicide murderers had been commented on in the Danish discussions, it had been called a 'delusion' and 'fanaticism'. Steinbart, however, singled out the clerical preparation for criticism.

He started by criticizing the core element in the preparation by many pastors: the belief that the sins of the prisoner would be forgiven and that it was certain that his soul would go to Heaven if he repented and turned to God just before being executed. This was not the belief in early Christianity, he said. At that time:

---

[1] Gothilf Samuel Steinbart, *Ist es rathsam Missethäter durch geistliche zum Tode vorbereiten und zur Hinrichtung begleiten zu lassen?*, Berlin, 1769.

> the nature of being Christian was still true honesty and the practising of all the sublime virtues of love for mankind, and no one had yet conceived the idea of believing that Heaven should be the reward for a few feelings of remorse and good thoughts, which fear had instilled in the dying.[2]

Steinbart described the preparation by such pastors in terms very similar to the Pietist narratives of the salvation of convicts presented in Moser's collection (see p. 71–5). When the criminal awaiting execution had been brought to repent of his many bad deeds, then, writes Steinbart, the cleric

> shows the delinquent, through a lot of Bible texts taken out of their context, that precisely such persons who find their sins gross and despicable repent them, and judging themselves unworthy of all mercy yet longing for it, are given the most wonderful promises in the Gospel.[3]

Now the criminal began to await Heaven with great confidence. Some pastors even urged the delinquent to die joyfully, thereby publicly bearing witness to his salvation, and—adds Steinbart—bearing witness to the praiseworthy diligence of his confessor as well.

On the day of the execution, when the crowd, in horror and pity, awaited a wretched, miserable criminal, what then did they see?

> A hero steps up with a jubilant look: all the terrible preparations for the most disgraceful and horrible death do not interrupt his cheerfulness; he smiles at them and dies in triumph.[4]

The crowd was astonished, but a print told of the beautiful conversion of the executed criminal, and a ballad called on the crowd to follow his example. Shortly afterwards a pamphlet would be published in which, in the shape of a sermon, the wonder of mercy showing itself in the quick conversion of the former criminal is dealt with. Here his

---

[2] Steinbart, *Ist es rathsam*, p. 6: 'Da man noch das Wesen des Christenthums in Wahre Rechtschaffenheit und in die Ausübung aller erhabenen Tugenden der Menchenliebe setzte, und noch nicht darauf gefallen war, Den Himmel für die Belohnung einiger durch Furcht erweckten reuvollen Empfindungen und guten Gedanken der Sterbenden zu halten.'

[3] Steinbart, *Ist es rathsam*, p. 12: 'zeigt dem Delinquenten durch eine Menge aus dem Zusammenhange angeführter Sprüche der Schrift, dass eben solchen Personen, die ihre Sünder für gross und abscheulich hielten, solche bereueten, sich aller Gnade unwürdig schäzten, doch aber darnach sehneten, die herrlichsten Verheissungen im Evangelio ertheilet wären.'

[4] Steinbart, *Ist es rathsam*, p. 13–4: 'Ein Held tritt herauf mit frohlockender Mine: alle furchtbaren Vorbereitungen zum schimpflichsten und grauvollesten Tode unterbrechen seine Heiterkeit nicht, er lächelt sie an und stirbt im Triumph.'

resolution in the face of death is seen as a foretaste of Heaven, and his salvation is judged to be true.

Executions taking place like this were what led to the suicide murders, Steinbart wrote. Ordinary people with no great powers of thought would see things as follows:

> My preacher tells me … my eternal destiny depends on my state of mind at the hour of death. As of now, however, I cannot know when or how I am going to die, and whether at that time I will have sufficient time, or understanding, or guidance necessary to create the right frame of mind. … A much more certain way, however, it would be if I, just like the executed delinquent who died redeemed, suddenly was torn away from all my responsibilities and put in gaol. Then I would not be diverted by any financial difficulties, and not prompted to any offences. … The clergymen would visit me frequently, whereas I cannot so easily expect consoling words from them in my present healthy state. And who knows whether I will be so lucky as to see my confessor on my death-bed. … Accordingly I am in constant danger of losing my salvation if I wait for my natural death; on the other hand, heaven is certain if I am executed in a violent manner: so I will kill the first person that comes along.[5]

Steinbart suggested that clerics should in general be forbidden to accompany delinquents to the place of execution and to be present there. In cases of delinquents who had murdered in order to be executed, he suggested a swift execution and no preparation by clerics at all. These were radical suggestions, and the booklet met with several critical responses.[6] The responsibility of the Church to take care of all souls up to the last moments of life was essential to Christian belief, and although Steinbart's vivid description of the close connection

[5] Steinbart, *Ist es rathsam*, p.16–7: 'Mein Prediger sagt mir … mein ewiges Schicksal von meinen Gesinnungen in der Stunde des Todes abhängen wird. Nun kann ich aber nicht wissen, wenn oder wie ich sterben werde, und ob ich als denn noch hinlängliche Zeit oder Verstand, oder Anweisung haben möchte, mich in die rechte Gemüthsfassung zu setzen. … Weit sicherer aber wäre es, wenn ich so, wie der hingerichtete selig verstorbene Delinquent, auf einmal aus allen meinen Verbindungen herausgerissen und in ein Gefängniss gesetzt würde. Dann würde ich durch keine Sorgen der Nahrung zerstreuet, und zu keiner Vergehung angereitzt. … die Herren Geistlichen besuchten mich fleissig, dagegen ich jetzt in gesunden Tagen so leicht keinen Zuspruch von ihnen erwarten kann. Und wer weiss ob es mir auf dem Sterbebette so gut werden möchte, meinen Beichtvater bey mir zu sehen. … Folglich laufe ich immer Gefahr, die Seligkeit zu verlieren, wenn ich meine natürlichen Tod abwarte; dagegen ist der Himmel mir gewiss, wenn ich gewaltsam hingerichtet werde: ich will also den ersten den besten umbringen.'

[6] Martin Bergman, *Dödsstraffet, kyrkan och staten I Sverige från 1700-tal till 1900-tal*, 1996, p. 108–15. Bergman describes the debate initiated by Steinbart's publication.

between the religious framework of the executions and the suicide murders was convincing, his opponents claimed that worldly reasons should not obstruct the duty of the pastor to assist the criminal until his last moment of life. As one opponent argued, the secular authorities had the right to execute criminals in painful ways, but they had neither the power nor the right to send their souls to Hell.[7]

Steinbart's ideas, however, were taken up by the Prussian government, but in a more modest form. A decree of 3 July 1769 forbade pastors to accompany criminals to the place of execution and also forbade the presence of a pastor there, but only for criminals of the Lutheran confession and only in the case of those being executed for crimes against public safety and for murder. The reason given for this provision was that the purpose of the punishment was to deter, and the presence of the pastor militated against this. In an internal note on the letter approving the provision Frederick the Great wrote that the provision was intended to prevent suicide murders, as he believed that the absence of a pastor would have more effect than the gallows and the wheel.[8] These Prussian provisions were more radical than the Danish advice to the bishops of 1768. First, Danish pastors were allowed to be present to comfort and pray with those sentenced to death in their last moments of life, and secondly, the Prussian provision discriminated between the death convicts. When the precepts forbidding the pastors to be present at the execution were not in place, Prussian pastors were still allowed to be present at the place of execution. In this way the absence of a pastor acted as a supplementary punishment, which could reasonably be interpreted as implying that the state wanted to make the perpetrator's path to salvation harder than that of other people sentenced to death. I do not know how many murderers were sentenced to endure their last hours without clerical assistance.

The debate started by Steinbart and supported by the Prussian decree continued in the following years. In Hamburg a public debate among the pastors of the city took place in 1784 about the expediency of clergymen being present at the place of execution. The reason was that plans were afoot to follow the example of Prussia. In June 1784 the Senate of Hamburg changed the execution ceremonial. It forbade the pastors of the city to accompany delinquents to the place of execution

[7] The riposte of August Ernst Renthe 1769, quoted in Bergman, *Dödsstraffet,*, p. 111.

[8] The decree of 3 July 1769 and its prehistory are described in Bergman, *Dödsstraffet*, p. 108–9.

as well as from being present there, with public dialogue and the laying-on of hands and blessing of the criminal. The reason given was that the mob took the solemn rituals performed by the pastors on the way to, as well as at, the execution 'for a publicly granted "safe passage", by which the soul of the malefactor must ascend directly into Heaven.'[9] This had led to the unhappy cases that had been so numerous lately. Just like the Danish regulation of 1768, the Hamburg regulation was general so that anyone sentenced to death was deprived of clerical assistance in their last hours.

The public debates exposed the contribution of the Lutheran clergy to the suicide murders and probably generally helped to tone down the religious ceremonial at the executions. This general effect, combined with the specific initiatives of Denmark, Prussia and Hamburg, may well have had the long-term effect of reducing the religious motivations for the suicide murders. It is questionable, however, if it had the direct deterrent effect spoken of by Frederick the Great, thereby leading to an immediate reduction of the murders. The Prussian decree forbidding any clerical presence at executions may have reduced the frequency of suicide murders, but it did not completely stop them. In the period 1776–90 I have found evidence of thirteen suicide murders in Prussia.[10]

The sentencing of the suicide murderers to life imprisonment with hard labour was a much more direct attack on the motives of the murderers. The provisions of the Danish decree of 18 December 1767 quickly became known in Germany. On 21 December 1767 a similar decree was issued in a German version for Schleswig-Holstein and the rest of the German territories under the Danish king. In the 1770s and 1780s the provisions were recommended in German juridical

[9] Jürgen Martschukat, 'Einen Freitod durch die Hand des Henkers', 2000, p. 72: 'als einen öffentlich erteilten Freybrief, wodurch die Seele des Missethäters snurgrade zum Himmel auffahren musste.' Martchukat describes the public debate in Hamburg as well as the Senate's intervention. The initiative is also mentioned in Bergman, *Dödsstraffet*, p. 113.

[10] Von Weber, 'Selbstmord als Mordmotiv', p. 165–6, tells of seven cases from 1786–90 described in Klein, *Annalen*. Three cases from 1776–82 are described in Hymmen, *Beiträge zu der juristischen Litteratur*, vol. 4, 1780, p. 307–8 (case from 1776), vol. 6, p. 336–7 (case from 1779), vol. 8, 1785, p. 210–1 (case from 1782). Finally, I have found three ballads about soldiers committing suicide murders in Berlin: 'Zuverlässige Nachricht des Delinquenten Christian Hahn', 1777 (Staatsbibliothek zu Berlin); 'Traurige Bericht von dem Delinquenten Namens Christian Gottlieb Carl Schmidt' (Staatsbibliothek zu Berlin); and 'Warnende Nachricht von der vorsetzlichen Mordthat, welche der Canonier Gottlieb Carl Michael Engel', 1786 (Staatsbibliothek zu Berlin).

literature, and the new punishment for suicide murders became part of the Prussian Allgemeines Landrecht of 1794:

> § 831. If it is detected, that somebody ... out of fanaticism, or else with the intention to be executed, commits a killing: Then the said should not achieve his objective.
>
> § 832. But he should be kept for life in the strictest imprisonment under special surveillance, and at certain fixed times be publicly punished.[11]

Similar provisions formed part of drafts for criminal law reforms in Saxony and Bavaria at the beginning of the nineteenth century but were not part of the final legal codes.[12]

[11] Allgemeines Landrecht für die Preußischen Staaten von 1794, 1970, p. 699, § 831: 'Ist aber ausgemittelt, dass jemand ... aus Schwärmerei, oder sonst in der Absicht hingerichtet zu werden, einen Todschlag begangen hat: so soll derselbe zwar seinen Endzweck nicht erreichen'; § 832: Er soll aber lebenslang im engsten Gefängnisse unter besonderer Aufsicht bewahrt, und zu gewissen bestimmten Zeiten öffentlich gezüchtigt werden.'

[12] Von Weber, 'Selbstmord als Mordmotiv', p. 172–4.

CHAPTER FOURTEEN

THE ROLE OF SUICIDE MURDERS IN THE PENAL REFORM DEBATES

The debates and initiatives on penal reform in Lutheran Europe in the 1770s and 1780s were primarily focused on initiatives to combat infanticide. The main events were the penal reform of Sweden in 1779 and a huge debate in 1780 on the prevention of infanticide in Germany. The suicide murders were not mentioned explicitly in these debates, but when looking closer at the arguments and the proposed penalties, it is obvious that much of the critique of the death penalty was inspired by its failure to reduce the number of suicide murders and that the proposed alternative penalties were inspired by the penalty provisions in the Danish decree of 1767.

In Sweden a penal reform in 1779 limited the use of the death penalty.[1] The reformist king Gustav III wanted wide-ranging limitations in the legally allowed death penalties, but the focal point of his argument was the death penalty for infanticide. He found that the death penalty were not having a sufficient deterrent effect, because when the crime was discovered, the exposed mother would long for death to hide her shame in the oblivion of eternity. Furthermore, the punishment did not create the sought-for abhorrence of the crime. Instead, the clerical preparation and the compassion of the spectators would be focused on the way she died. And afterwards the spectators would speak of the happy outcome that she died so well prepared. Gustav opposed the idea that provisions for the death penalty could not be changed without departing from religious doctrine and claimed that that doctrine could be changed without undermining the true and beneficial foundations of that religion.[2] For these reasons the king proposed the abolition of the death penalty not only for infanticide but also for witchcraft, adultery, bigamy, incest, bestiality, theft, robbery and murder. In cases of infanticide, robbery and murder he found that the perpetrators deserved a punishment worse than death. He proposed that they

[1] The reform is exhaustively analysed in Anners, *Humanitet och Rationalism*.

[2] Anners, *Humanitet och Rationalism*, p. 230–1.

should be whipped, put to hard labour and, each year on the anniversary of the crime, be exposed to the public for a couple of hours and whipped again. Erik Anners thinks that this penalty is a result of Beccaria's influence. This may well be true at a theoretical level, but it seems obvious that the idea of annual whippings was inspired by the Danish decree of 1767. The radical proposal was put before the Assembly of the Estates of the Realm, where it met considerable opposition. The new punishment provisions for infanticide and murder, in particular, were criticized on the grounds that the abolition of the death penalty would be against God's law. The final reform ended up totally abolishing the crime of witchcraft and abolishing the death penalty for bigamy, adultery, rape and theft, where the Assembly of the Estates did not find that God demanded the death penalty. In addition, the death penalty for concealment of a birth when the child died was abolished, but the death penalty for infanticide remained in force when there was clear evidence that the child had been murdered.

In Germany the question of how to prevent infanticide was the subject of a prize competition in a German journal in 1780, and the 400 or so entries were published widely.[3] The debate primarily revolved around the issue of how to prevent unmarried pregnant women from committing infanticide. In this debate society's own responsibility for the murders was a dominant issue. Mothers of illegitimate children were publicly punished and shamed by the Church as well as by the courts. Voltaire and the *Sturm und Drang* writers of the 1770s wrote in defence of young mothers betrayed by their lovers and threatened with punishment and condemnation for having an illegitimate child. In this part of the debate the practical example frequently emphasized was a Prussian decree of 1765, which abolished all penalties for intercourse between unmarried people and forbade all derogatory behaviour towards women with illegitimate children.[4] In 1778 a similar decree was issued in Sweden.[5]

The penalty for infanticide was debated as well. One might assume that the death penalty would have been criticized for its cruelty.

[3] It was the so-called 'Mannheimer Preisfrage' issued by the journal *Rheinischen Beitrage zur Gelehrsamkeit*. The entries are analysed in Otto Ulbricht, *Kindsmord und Aufklärung in Deutschland*, 1990, p. 217–328, and Kerstin Michalik, *Kindsmord: Sozial- und Rechtsgeschichte der Kindstötung im 18. und beginnenden 19. Jahrhundert am Beispiel Preussen*, 1997, p. 295–339.

[4] Michalik, *Kindsmord*, p. 229–36.

[5] Anners, *Humanitet och rationalism*, p. 207–228.

Such views were very rare, however. Criticism of the death penalty as cruel and inhumane did not appear until the 1790s.[6] Here in 1780 the critique of the death penalty was rationalist, focusing on its deficiencies in deterring people from committing the crime. Another important issue was whether it was against divine law not to execute a murderer. One of the arguments frequently put forward against the death penalty was that the murderers were attracted to the publicity around the executions and to the clerical preparation, and that some even would commit infanticide in order to obtain the death.[7] The authors thus found that the women committing infanticide had suicidal motives fully in analogy with the suicide murderers. To my knowledge it has not been studied whether suicide motives were actually present in cases of infanticide.[8] The imputation of a suicidal motive in infanticide cases could, of course, be an unfounded suspicion on the part of the authors. In that case it must have been the suicide murders that influenced the debate and led to a general distrust in the deterrent effects of the death penalty.

Those in favour of preserving the death penalty referred only rarely to divine law as a justification, but several of those arguing against the death penalty used many pages to explain why the death penalty could be abolished without violating divine law. Here they were able to draw on the recent work of the orientalist and theologian Johann David Michaelis. Between 1770 and 1775 Michaelis published a book about Mosaic Law, in six volumes.[9] He used his historical and linguistic knowledge to document the idea that the law was created by the young people of Israel as a successor to nomadic customary law, and he argued that the law could not bind the Christian states of his own time. Michaelis's scholarly arguments in addition to his efforts to maintain the divine origin of the Bible gave his thoughts wide resonance.

The fact that only very few people referred to divine law in their defence of the death penalty might lead one to think that the concept of a mandatory divine death penalty had lost its hold in Lutheran

[6] Michalik, *Kindsmord*, p. 345–52.

[7] Ulbricht, *Kindsmord und Aufklärung in Deutschland*, p. 310.

[8] Otto Ulbricht calls the argument a weak one which was nevertheless frequently put forward: *Kindsmord und Aufklärung in Deutschland*, p. 310. Neither he nor Kerstin Michalik considers it as a true motive in their analyses of motives for infanticides.

[9] J.D. Michaelis, *Mosaisches Recht*, 1771–75.

Germany. I think that is a misinterpretation of the debates, however. The traditional view of the binding nature of the death penalty for homicide, in particular, still had many followers. In her book on penal practice in Württemberg, Helga Schnabel-Schüle describes a debate that took place in Lutheran Baden. In 1779 the government requested the opinion of the leading council of the church (the Kirchenrat) on the punishment for infanticide. The council, with the almost unanimous support of the deans, stated that Genesis 9 was still binding on the Christian prince, and that accordingly the death penalty was of divine origin and therefore unavoidable.[10]

Returning to the infanticide debate, a majority of the writers advocating the abolition of the death penalty wanted the alternative punishment to be harder than death. Murderers should not only be sentenced to hard labour for life, but they should also be whipped or even branded and then, in order to have the greatest deterrent effect, be shown off publicly and whipped once a year on the anniversary of the murder, with a dishonourable burial at the gallows after they died.[11] It seems obvious that again it is the Danish decree of 1767 that provides the practical example of a penalty worse than death.

To sum up, the logic of the suicide murders had a significant presence in the public debate about the death penalty. Mothers committing infanticide were suspected of having suicidal motives and thereby being satisfied with the death penalty, and when an alternative punishment was looked for, the punishment laid out in the Danish decree of 1767 was the favourite suggestion. The reason that the death penalty was retained in spite of deep misgivings about its deterrent effect seems to have been the continued influence of Mosaic Law. Governments obviously preferred the use of mitigating interpretations and royal pardons to the direct abolition of the death penalty. This created a discrepancy between law and practice, which the jurists did not like, but which allowed the religious building to remain formally untouched. And princes and governments avoided having to reach a public decision on the difficult religious issues while at the same time preserving the formal immutability of their faith.

---

[10] Schnabel-Schüle, *Überwachen und Strafen im Territorialstaat*, p. 205–11.

[11] Ulbricht, *Kindsmord und Aufklärung in Deutschland*, p. 312–3.

CHAPTER FIFTEEN

FROM SALVATION TO INSANITY

In the last third of the eighteenth century, as we have seen, there was a general recognition of the phenomenon of the suicide murder and its causes, along with new radical steps to combat it. But this was also a period when there were profound changes to the religious and cultural framework in which the murders took place. The religious beliefs sustaining the suicide murders all came under attack. In Denmark we have seen that the religious motivation for the death penalty, still upheld in the debate in 1757–58, was suppressed in the discussions leading to the 1767 decree. The public debate in Germany in the 1770s provided the religious arguments against the idea of the death penalty as part of divine law. All these changes facilitated the abolition of the death penalty for suicide murders in Denmark and Prussia.

In religious life, orthodoxy and Pietism were challenged by a rationalist theology. Here reason became the essence of divine order, and the mysterious and miraculous elements in religion were rejected. Gothilf Steinbart's attack on the preparation of criminals is a good example of rationalist theological thought. Instead of the mysterious importance attributed to the last-minute conversion, Steinbart emphasized a moral and virtuous life on Earth as the means of achieving eternal life in Heaven.

The morality of suicide was also the topic of much debate. Goethe, along with other poets, defended the right to suicide. Physicians argued that suicide was a result of mental illness. These positions challenged the condemnation of suicide by the Church, and important Lutheran theologians such as Johann David Michaelis also argued against the religious condemnation.[1]

These changes affected the religious discourse of the suicide murders. Seen from the point of view of the murderers, the religious 'guarantee' of eternal life in Heaven as long as one turned to God at the last minute faded away, meaning that execution as a short cut to Heaven

[1] Lind, *Selbstmord in der frühen Neuzeit*, analyses the German discourse on suicide at p. 45–152. Michaelis's position is described at p. 107–9.

was no longer present. At the same time the fear of eternal damnation if one killed oneself lost some of its foundation. It is doubtful, however, whether these altercations in the debates of the enlightened élite affected the inclination to commit suicide murders, as the murderers generally came from the lower classes. In 1792 the Copenhagen jurist J.J. Gudenrath discussed the disappearance of suicide murders. He argued that, rather than being a response to the decree of 1767, the decline in the number of suicide murders was simply due to the fact that people had become less religious and that the soldiers were not flogged as much as before.[2] Following Gudenrath, it could be said that religion gradually lost its position in the popular understanding of life. People became less concerned with the afterlife. They still feared death, but the persistent fear of the terrors of Hell lost its grip.

Seen from the point of view of the judges imposing the death penalty and the civil servants administering the royal pardons, the fading away of the religious framework for the suicide murders not only made them feel freer to dispense with the death penalty but also left the field open for psychological and mental explanations of criminal behaviour. In the first half of the eighteenth century judges and civil servants could grumble about the notion expressed by suicide murderers that one was sure to be saved if one died at the hands of the executioner, but they could not claim that the idea was wrong. Around 1800 this reasoning had become unbelievable and illogical, opening the way for verdicts of *non compos mentis*. If the murderer explained her deed on these religious grounds, this was in itself proof that she was out of her senses.

My in-depth study of penal practice in Copenhagen stops in 1789, by which time suicide murders had become rare. Therefore I have less copious evidence to substantiate the later developments. The punishment provisions in the 1767 decree were used probably for the last time in1806.[3] A decree of 1833, among other penal extenuations, abolished

[2] J.J. Gudenrath, *Mine skrupler om selvmords moralitet og dets strafværdighed efter de borgerlige love*, 1792.

[3] According to the prisoner registers, the last person ordered to be punished after the provisions in the 1767 decree was the Rasp-house prisoner Jochum Ernst Simon Petersen, who murdered a fellow prisoner with an axe because he was 'bored with life' (Danish National Archives, Højesteret, Voteringsprotokol, 1806, case no. 248, the Provincial Archives of Zealand, Tugt-, Rasp-, og Forbedringshuset på Chrisianshavn, Mandtalsbøger). In a dubious case from 1815 a male servant declared to his master his intention to commit suicide with a pistol and locked himself in a room. The master had some soldiers sent for. When they forced the door open, he turned his gun on the first soldier and shot and killed him. The courts discussed whether the killing was

the branding, the annual whippings and the shameful exhibition of the body after death as stipulated in the 1767 decree. The Chancellery was prompted to introduce milder penalties by a changed mentality. The purpose of the decree had been to create a penalty worse than death. This had been necessary because of the not uncommon belief in those days that by murdering another human being and being sentenced to death one could secure a blessed death. This prejudice had now disappeared, and in the rare cases where the 1767 decree would still be applicable, the murderers were mentally ill and close to a condition where they should be declared insane and not responsible for their actions.[4] The Chancellery had considered repealing the whole of the decree, but this had met with opposition, especially from the chief constable of Copenhagen, who still feared an outbreak of suicide murders in the capital.

As late as 1848 the courts considered using the 1767 decree, in a case where a father and a mother had killed their three children.[5] The father had what we would now call learning difficulties and was completely dominated by the mother, who was described as being very religious. She gave different reasons for the killings, but ended up stating that she was depressed and had been obsessed by the idea that the children would go to Heaven if she killed them, and that she also would be blessed if she suffered the death penalty for the deed. Her confession testifies that the hopes of the Chancellery fifteen years earlier, that the religious motivation for the suicide murders had disappeared, had been in vain. The high court sentenced her according to the 1767 decree, and some of the Supreme Court judges wanted to do the same. The majority, however, found that she had been mentally ill at the time and therefore sentenced her to be held in custody by the authorities. It appears that her religious motive was deemed an outdated prejudice and therefore simply contributed to support the verdict of *non compos mentis*.

The use of the death penalty was in general decline in the nineteenth century in Denmark. The Danish penal system underwent

---

intentional or not, but ended up sentencing the servant according to the 1767 decree. The king pardoned him from the branding and the annual whippings (*Collegialtidende*, 1815 p. 769–79).

[4] *Collegialtidende*, 1833, p. 638–9, 662–3.

[5] Danish National Archives, Højesteret, Voteringsprotokol E 1848 (6 and 7 April), case against Erik Hansen and his wife, Ane Kirstine Hansdatter. I am grateful to my collegue Anders Sode-Pedersen for bringing this case to my attention.

comprehensive review in a new criminal code from 1866. Many outdated definitions of crime and penal provisions were repealed, among them those of the 1767 decree. Nevertheless the suicide motive accompanied executions in Denmark right through to the last case that prompted a death penalty, which took place in 1892.[6] The offender, Jens Nielsen, had been sentenced to life imprisonment for robbery. In the penitentiary he tried several times to murder a guard, hoping as a result to be given the death penalty. He was sentenced to death, but the Supreme Court recommended a royal pardon the first and second time. The third time, however, a majority of the Supreme Court judges voted against a royal pardon. The two judges still in favour of a pardon used, among other arguments, a reference to the 1767 decree stating that a perpetrator murdering with the intention of obtaining a death penalty should not be sentenced to death.[7] Nielsen, however, had no religious motive for wanting the death penalty. In the days up to the execution and at the scaffold in the penitentiary yard he turned down the assistance of the pastor.[8]

Outside Denmark also, suicide murders seemed to become rarer. According to von Weber, the suicide murder phenomenon faded away in Prussia during the nineteenth century. The new Prussian penal provisions of 1794 were used very rarely, and, just as in Denmark, the cases where they were used became more dubious.[9] The use of the death penalty was declining all over Germany in the nineteenth century. In Prussia there were no executions between 1868 and 1878,[10] and in Hamburg the number of executions fell as well. Thus no executions took place between 1823 and 1855. Hamburg had changed the execution procedure in 1784 in order to prevent the ceremony being seen as a certain way to go to Heaven, but the death penalty for murder remained unchanged. The change was followed by child murders that were not infanticides in 1784 and 1786, then one in 1804, three in 1808–09 and isolated cases in 1818, 1865, 1878 and 1890. We know of

[6] In a penal reform of 1933 the death penalty was abolished. In 1945 the death penalty was reintroduced, but only for crimes committed during the German occupation 1940–5, and during the next five years forty-six people were executed.

[7] Danish National Archives, Højesteret, voteringsprotokol 1892, no. 279, 10 June 1892.

[8] Reported in *Horsens Folkeblad*, 9 November 1892.

[9] Von Weber, 'Selbstmord als Mordmotiv', p. 174.

[10] Evans *Rituals of Retribution*, p. 352–3. On the general decrease see p. 327–9 and 351–2.

these murders because the murderers were executed.[11] It appears that the willingness of the Hamburg courts to carry out the death sentence for murder maintained the phenomenon of the suicide murder in the city, although it became much rarer than in the eighteenth century.

This fragmentary evidence thus indicates that the suicide murder became much rarer in northern Europe in the nineteenth century, but apparently singular cases could still be found. The decline in frequency seems to be a result of specific legal measures combating the logic of the murders, changes in Lutheran doctrine and in its position in society, a growing inclination to issue verdicts of *non compos mentis* in such cases and the generally growing reluctance to use the death penalty. One reason why the murders did not disappear totally, one could suspect, was that the narrative of people being tempted by the Devil to commit murder but afterwards turning to God and dying saved before the eyes of the whole city was so strong that it lived on in folk mythology and therefore continued to inspire people on the verge of suicide.

Another probable reason is, however, as mentioned earlier, that the use of the death penalty in a society will always attract people who wish to die but who shrink from taking their own life. Thus the last Dane executed, Jens Nielsen, had no religious motive for his wish to die at the hands of the executioner. This explanation is supported by the fact that suicide as a motive for committing murder is seen in the US in the twentieth century as well. In their article from 1999 the sociologists Katherine van Wormer and Chick Odia presented an investigation based primarily on legal literature,[12] where they found twenty-two cases in the US between 1959 and 1996 of murderers who killed in the hope of being sentenced to death. The best-known example is probably that of James French. In 1958 French murdered a motorist who picked him up while he was hitch-hiking. He told the court that he had committed the murder in the hope that he would be executed. His attorney, however, defended him so skilfully that he only received life imprisonment. Three years later French strangled his cellmate, and when tried for murder again he urged the court to sentence him to

[11] Wosnik, *Beiträge zur Hamburgischen Kriminalgeschichte*, p. 48–50.

[12] Katherine van Wormer and Chick Odia, 'The Psychology of Suicide-Murder and the Death Penalty', 1999, p. 361–70. See also Richard Strafer, 'Volunteering for Execution', 1983, p. 860–912. Both articles define two types of suicidal attraction to executions: the rare suicide murders and the more common problem that criminals on death row oppose efforts by attorneys and third parties to continue fighting against the death penalty because they cannot bear the long wait to know their destiny.

death. French was declared sane and executed in 1966. Van Wormer and Odiah's investigation is very provisional, implying that there may be more cases than they have found.

As an explanation of such murders, van Wormer and Odiah suggest on the one hand that the drama and publicity of an execution provides a major attraction for the suicide murderer. Following this causal connection, it could be assumed that the intense public debate about the death penalty in the US, combined with the great publicity surrounding the prisoners on death row, serves to give the same allure to being at the centre of the highly public and solemn execution ceremony as I found in parts of eighteenth-century Europe. The causes for the publicity in the two periods are, of course, not the same. On the other hand, van Wormer and Odiah suggest that a better understanding 'of suicide murder may help explain the futility of capital punishment as a deterrent to murder'. By this they probably mean that the mere presence of the death penalty as a penal provision in a state's arsenal of punishments provides a constant attraction for some people wanting to end their life.

CHAPTER SIXTEEN

CONCLUSION

From the last decades of the seventeenth century the phenomenon of the suicide murder increased drastically in the Lutheran countries. Official religious beliefs provided extraordinary fertile soil for the murders. Luther's and Calvin's wish to return to the Bible as the ultimate authority led them to turn to several provisions from the Mosaic Law, which had been created more than two thousand years earlier by nomadic tribes in the Middle East. The divine mandatory death penalty for murder and certain sexual offences became one of the distinguishing features of the Protestant countries. The notion of the authorities being the sword of God here on Earth obtained a prominent place in the conduct of religion. By enforcing the divine death penalty in accordance with Mosaic Law, the authorities protected the country against the wrath of God and contributed to the common salvation of the people. This belief presumably led to striking differences in the use of the death penalty in Europe between Lutheran and Reformed countries on the one hand and Catholic and Anglican countries on the other.

The preparation of the criminals condemned to death in the Catholic and Reformed confessions told the criminal that by willingly submitting to the punishment he or she made the execution an edifying warning to others not to sin in the same way. Thereby—in the Catholic understanding—the criminal pleased God and alleviated some of His wrath. The Lutheran preparation contained this element as well, but there was more emphasis on the punishment being described as ordered by God as part of His strategy to save the criminal's soul. It was to open her eyes to the sins committed and thereby pave the way for conversion and salvation of the soul.

The extraordinary Lutheran focus on the preparation of criminals sentenced to death and the creation of the highly religious execution ceremony had its origin in distinguishing features of the Lutheran faith. The Lutheran soteriology stressed that salvation followed the acknowledgment of one's sinfulness and required the sinner to turn to God in remorse. This, combined with the belief that it was never too late to convert—and to sin—heightened the focus on the last moments of life and gave everybody the same possibility of saving themselves in this moment, irrespective of their previous life.

The Pietists developed the execution ceremony into a great emotional narrative in their pious eagerness to save even the most flagrant sinners of this world and in their eagerness to spread the edifying message of divine mercy. The execution ceremony became an important religious event expressing divine punishment and divine mercy, leading to the salvation of the criminal's soul, a salvation the spectators hoped would be granted to their souls as well when they faced the decisive last moments of life.

It was this fascinating emotional narrative that depressed or desperate women and men expanded on. They added the common fatalistic view of man as a powerless pawn in the hands of the princes of Good and Evil. If Satan had already laid his traps, there was not much one could do. Anybody could go wrong when tempted by such a force. Some murderers saw themselves as combating the greater evil of suicide. Many diminished the sin by choosing a child whose soul was certain to ascend to heaven and by choosing a method of killing that was the least painful for the child. When the murder was committed, God demanded the sinner's life, but neither God nor the Christian community expelled the sinner. She could walk to her divine punishment as a heroine, certain that her soul would be saved. She could expect to be sympathetically written about in religious ballads and to receive the full attention and the blessing of the Church. The vain could dress for the occasion in a white gown with black ribbons, and the eloquent could make speeches and say prayers that were listened to by the crowd with devout attention.

Suicide murders haunted Lutheran Europe in the eighteenth century. Once the narrative was constructed, not even the harshest additional punishments to the death penalty could stop them. It was a painful process for the states and the Lutheran churches to realize that the murders were nourished by certain key elements of the Lutheran faith.

The numerous murders in Copenhagen led to an early break with the concept of the divine mandatory death penalty in the Danish decree of 1767, which at the same time provided a unique example of a penalty worse than death, in the spirit of Beccaria. In Denmark and Prussia and later in Hamburg the religious logic of the suicide murders was countered with changes in the execution rituals, and in 1794 Prussia copied the Danish penalty. In the general penal debate a recurrent argument against the death penalty was the claim that the suicide motive lay behind many murders. In Sweden and in the German penal debate the new Danish penalty was not mentioned directly, but the combination of hard labour and annual public whippings was seriously considered as an alternative to the death penalty for a number of crimes. In the end, however, the governments shrank back from publicly pronouncing such a radical break with the divine mandatory death penalty.

The suicide murders and the measures to combat them thus held an important position in the early debate on the death penalty in the Lutheran areas, but their influence on the debate was indirect, and the initiatives to combat the murders were not directly mentioned in the debate. It is fair to ask why the murders had such a low profile in the debate. And why was the role of the suicide murders overlooked in the historical analyses of penal reforms of the age of Enlightenment?

One might suppose that the Danish government would boast of the 1767 decree as an enlightened reform in the spirit of Beccaria, but the government did nothing to promote the decree internationally. This silence can be contrasted with the promotion of the Swedish penal reform of 1779. The Swedish king had the reform translated into French and presented as an enlightened initiative.[1] The Swedish reform became a point of reference in the German penal debate, and in histories of the death penalty it is frequently mentioned as the earliest penal reform inspired by Beccaria.

The reason for the Danish silence is probably twofold. On the one hand, the Danish government, although it had found it necessary to break with the divinely mandated death penalty, preferred its action not to be described in those terms. The government did not want to promote the country as having a radical religious stance compared with other Lutheran countries. On the other hand, the suicide murders were not the best case for Lutherans to present to the enlightened Europe. Although the motives of the murderers were referred to as old delusions and prejudices by Danish state officials, it would not be difficult to show, as Gothilf Samuel Steinbart did, that the murders were encouraged by official Lutheran soteriology. To publicize the suicide

[1] Anners, *Humanitet och rationalism*, p. 262.

murders to enlightened Europe would thus, so to speak, risk exposing the dirty linen of the Lutheran confession.

From the 1790s a humanitarian critique developed, which argued not that the death penalty was ineffective, as the rationalists had argued, but that it was cruel. But the humanitarian critique could not refer to the suicide murderers either. They wanted to see the executed as victims of a barbarian penal practice, and the suicide murderers were not the victims but the exploiters of the death penalty. Thus the suicide murderers were forgotten as an inconvenient footnote in history, which none of the positions in the death penalty debate could use for their purpose.

The suicide murders as a large criminal problem came to an end in the last decades of the eighteenth century, and the measures taken to combat them must be credited for at least partly having caused this. The murders did not disappear completely, however. Just as isolated cases were known in the eighteenth century outside the Lutheran areas, so scattered suicide murders can be found in Lutheran areas in the nineteenth century. A systematic knowledge of their distribution in time and space is lacking, but the evidence of their presence in the US today adds to the impression that they must be seen as inseparable from the death penalty. If so, then it is an important fact to be taken into consideration in contemporary debate about the death penalty.

APPENDIX

SUICIDE MURDER CASES IN COPENHAGEN, 1697–1789 INCLUDING ATTEMPTS AND INVENTED MURDERS

Four independent court systems tried criminal cases in Copenhagen in the eighteenth century. The royal court had its own court of justice for employees until 1771, but no suicide murders were prosecuted here.

Other civilians were tried in the City Court (CC), where the city judge together with eight lay judges passed sentence. The court of appeal was the Magistrate (MC), where sentence was passed by the mayors and aldermen. All death penalties had to be taken to the Magistrate's Court, from where cases could be appealed to the Supreme Court (SC), presided over by eight to ten professional judges. Requests for pardon could be submitted to the king, and from 1735 all death penalties had to be laid before the king and thus presupposed a royal resolution (RR) being carried out. In 1771 the Court of the Royal Court and the City Court were merged into the Court of the Royal Court and the City (CCC). At the same time the Magistrate's Court was abolished.

Soldiers and their relatives and servants were prosecuted at a court martial (CM). Each regiment held its own courts martial, where the regimental commander with some officers and privates passed sentence. However, all sentences involving serious corporal punishment, and the death penalties were laid before the king as supreme commander. The cases were presented to the king by the judge advocate general (JAG) in statements suggesting a royal decision.

Sailors in the Navy and their relatives and servants were prosecuted at the Lower Admiralty Court (LA), which in 1747 was merged with the Higher Admiralty Court to form the Admiralty's Combined Court (ACC). Sentences involving serious punishments were laid before the king. Until approximately 1748 statements suggesting royal decisions were made by the Admiralty (AS). After 1748 a newly appointed judge advocate general (JAG) for the Navy made the statements to the king.

Each case presentation below consists of three paragraphs. The first paragraph presents details of the murders and the reasons for the murders stated before the courts. The wording is as close as possible to the wording in the court records. The second paragraph presents the chronology of the cases and the verdicts passed. A verdict under the 1697 decree is explained on p. 47, the 1738 decree on p. 53, the 1749 decree on p. 55 and the 1767 decree on p. 149. The third paragraph consists of references.

The suicide murders are identified by year and arabic numeral (e.g., 1697:1), suicide murder attempts by year and lower-case letter (e.g., 1715:a) and invented suicide murders by year and roman numeral (e.g., 1727:I).

Abbreviations

Types of Verdicts and Statements

ACC	Verdict of the Admiralty's Combined Court (Den kombinerede ret)
AS	The Admiralty's statement to the king (Admiralitetet)
CC	Verdict of the City Court (Bytinget)
CCC	Verdict of the Court of the Royal Court and the City (Hof- og Stadsretten)
CM	Court-martial verdict (krigsretsdom)
JAG	Judge advocate general's statement to the king (Generalauditøren)
LA	Verdict of the Lower Admiralty Court (Underadmiralitetsretten)
MC	Verdict of the Magistrate's Court (Rådstueretten)
RR	Royal Resolution
SC	Verdict of the Supreme Court (Højesteret)
TF	Faculty of Theology statement to the king (Det teologiske fakultet)

Source Reference Abbreviations

Admiralitetet RA, Admiralitetet, generalkopibog (letter book of the Admiralty)

Byting Landsarkivet for Sjælland m.m., Københavns Byting (City Court archive)

Bytingsprot. Landsarkivet for Sjælland m.m., Københavns byting, bytingsprotokol (City Court journal)

KB Det kongelige bibliotek (Copenhagen Royal Library)

Komb.ret RA, Den kombinerede ret, Domssager (The Admralty's Combined Court, verdict files)

RA Rigsarkivet (Danish National Archives)

Gen.aud. RA, Generalauditøren, domprotokol (Judge Advocate General (army), book of verdicts)

Gen.aud. res. RA, Generalauditøren, Originale relationer (Judge Advocate General (army), statements)

Gen.aud. søetat RA, Generalauditøren (Søetaten), betænkninger (Judge Advocate General (Navy), statements to the king)

Mandtalsbog Landsarkivet for Sjælland m.m., Tugt-, Rasp- og Forbedringshuset på Christianshavn, Mandtalsbog for Børne- og Rasphuset samt for Tugt- og Rasphuset 1772–1846 (Census book for the Spin-house and the Rasp-house)

Rgsk. RA, Reviderede regnskaber, Københavnske regnskaber, Byfogedregnskaber (Accounts of the city court judge)

Rådstuen Københavns stadsarkiv, Københavns magistrat, rådstueskriveren (Archive of the Magistrates scribe)

Underadm. RA, underadmiralitetsretten (Lower Admiralty Court archive)

Hø.ret. RA, Højesteret, voteringsprotokol (Supreme Court, journal of judgement considerations)

Sj.t. RA, Danske kancelli, Indlæg til sjællandske tegnelser. (Danish Chancellery, files to royal prescripts concerning Sealand)

Slaverulle Landsarkivet for Sjælland m.m., Københavns Stokhus, Slaverulle 1764–1826 (Census book for the 'Slavery')
Teol.fak. RA, Det Teologiske Fakultet, Kopibog (Letter book of the Faculty of Theology)

Cases

1697:1 Sidzel Chatarina Sivertsdatter, housemaid
During the previous month her mistress and master had accused her several times of stealing, and this Sunday morning they accused her of having stolen two steelyards, which she later found put back in the wrong place. When the master and mistress went to church, she cut the throat of their three-year-old daughter. Afterwards she went to the city judge and gave herself up.

Murder 11/8/1697. CC 6/9/1697 the 1697 decree. MC 17/9/1697 confirms. RR 20/9/1697 pardon from pinching with red-hot tongs. Execution 27/9/1697.

Rgsk. 1697 voucher 142, 163-4, RA, Danske Kancelli, Dokumenter til kgl. Mayt's resolutionsbog udi Danmark 1697/97. NA, Danske kancelli, Indlæg til sjællandske registre 1697/171.

1699:1 Anders Nielsen Rostocker, ship's mate, aged seventy-two
He was the mate on a small vessel and poisoned the three other crew members with white arsenic. He had bought the poison a year earlier with the intention of killing himself. His desire to commit suicide was prompted by his decline from a wealthy man with houses and ships to his present impoverished state. When the three crew got sick, he helped them ashore and tended one of them until he died. He asked the court permission to be buried on consecrated ground.

Murder Oct. 1699. CC 11/12/1699 execution by sword. MC 8/2/1700 the 1697 decree. RR 4/3/1700 pardon from pinching with red-hot tongs.

Rgsk. 1700 voucher 123.

1706:1 Sidsel Hansdatter, housemaid, aged about twenty-nine
Since the age of fourteen she had served at the homes of wealthy and educated people. Two years earlier she had met a soldier and become pregnant. She put the child in care and served for a year as a wet-nurse. She then took her child back but had trouble getting a new job because the child was difficult and she had to sell her clothing to live. She was offered a job where she could not have the child with her. She put it into care again but the foster-mother quickly returned it because it was badly behaved. She then decided to throw the child into the canal. She immediately regretted what she had done and gave herself up. She explained that she had committed the murder because of her unbearable situation where nobody would hire her because of her child's difficult behaviour.

Murder 26/1/1706. CC 1/3/1706 decapitation and head stuck on pole. MC 14/4/1706 confirms. Sidsel appeals, claiming that the murder was committed while she was delirious. SC 16/10/1706 confirms. RR 26/10/1706 that the body after the execution should be anatomized.

Rgsk. 1706 voucher 215-8.

1707:1 Ingeborg Poulsdatter, housemaid
She became pregnant by her master, and he then set her up at a boarding house with a landlady. Here she was put up in the cold loft with just some straw to sleep on. She suffered from frostbite and malnutrition and resented the bad treatment she received from her landlady. She then chose to strangle her eighteen-day-old child. She told the court that the Devil had seduced her into doing the evil deed against her own will. Afterwards she went to the police and gave herself up.

Murder 21/12/1706. CC 28/2/1707 decapitation by axe and head stuck on a pole. MC 14/3/1707 confirms. Execution 5/5/1707.

Rgsk. 1707 p. 54 and voucher 277-80. Rådstuen, domprotokol 1707 p. 921–38.

1710:1 Karen Andersdatter
She had thrown her own four-week-old illegitimate child into the canal. Afterwards she told her brothers and sisters. She pleaded that she had been out of her mind.

Murder 29/6/1710. CC 8/9/1710 decapitation and head stuck on a pole. MC 2/10/1710 confirms. Request for a pardon 26/9/1710 on the grounds that she committed the crime at the instigation of Satan. RR 20/10/1710 decapitation and buried on consecrated ground.

Rgsk. 1710 voucher 153. Rådstuen, domprotokol 1710 p. 105-13. RA, Danske kancelli, Resoutioner skrevne på supplikker 1709-10/460.

1711:1 Jacob Olsen, recently dismissed sailor in the navy
Killed his two-year-old daughter with an axe while she lay in her bed, because his contract period was finished and he would no longer be paid. His wife said that he had been dismissed at Epiphany and had been disturbed ever since: he had not talked to anyone and had not answered when spoken to.

Murder 10/4/1711, LA 30/7/1711 to lose his life.

Underadm., domprotokol 1711 p. 22–6 and vidnebog 1711 p. 206–7.

1713:1 Anna Chatrine Berntsdatter
One night she cut the throat of her mother with a knife. For about eight weeks before the killing she had first been ill and then mentally disturbed, depressed and melancholic. Among other things, she had cried and yelled desperately, saying that she had no soul and no heart, that the Holy Spirit had left her. She had had many moral temptations and religious doubts. She had wanted to commit suicide as well. She stated the reason for the murder as being delirium, but she was able to give an accurate description of the killing.

Murder 17/8/1712. CC 3/4/1713 decapitation and head stuck on a pole. MC 3/7/1713 confirms. Request for a pardon 3/8/1713: she had been ill and in the resulting delirium had committed murder. She is happy with the death penalty if this is the will of her God and her king, but requests that her poor and sinful body may enjoy a burial in consecrated ground. RR 5/8/1713 grants her request. Execution 17/8/1713.

Rgsk. 1713 voucher 134-5, RA, Danske kancelli, Resolutioner skrevne på supplikker 1711–16, fol. 282. Ballad: KB, En ynckelig og smuck ny Sang sunget af en Misdæderinde navnlig Anna Chatrine Berntsdatter.

1714:1 Johanna Kirstine Christensdatter, Spin-house inmate
She had cut the throat of a nine-month-old boy with a knife. She looked after the child for its mother. She considered herself unjustly sentenced to the Spin-house and had resorted to murder out of desperation because she preferred to rather die than live with such hard and unfair work, which she was not phystically able to do. Furthermore, she saw that other inmates who could not cope with the work they were ordered to do were miserably and harshly punished.

Murder New Year's Eve 1713. CC 14/5/1714 decapitation by sword and burial at the gallows. MC 17/7/1714 confirms. Request for pardon 26/9/1714: that her poor body should be buried in the churchyard. Her sister's request for a pardon 10/10/1714: that she be granted her life. RR 23/11/1714 confirms the verdict of the MC. Execution 4/12/1714.

Rgsk. 1714 p. 69. Rådstuen, domprotokol 1714 p. 512-5 and rådstueprotokol 1714 p. 372. Sj.T. 1714/471. Ballad: KB, En ny Klagevise sunget af en Misdæderinde nafnlig Johanne Kirstine Christensdatter …

1714:2 Anna Michelsdatter, unmarried housewife
With her fiancé she had moved to Copenhagen from Jutland but found that work was even more scarce than in Jutland and became depressed. Then she became ill and her depression became worse, and eventually she killed her own five- or six-year-old child by cutting its throat with a knife. A number of witnesses from Jutland testified that she had had such bouts of depression earlier. She asks the court to be buried in consecrated ground.

Murder 5/1/1714, CC 9/7/1714 decapitation and head stuck on a pole. MC 24/9/1714 Confirms. Request for a pardon 1/10/1714: she had been temporarily insane, as proven by depositions. She requests to be buried in consecrated ground. RR 23/11/1714 confirms the verdict of MC. Execution 4/12/1714.

Rgsk. 1714 p. 70. Rådstue, domprotokol 1714 p. 248-53 and rådstueprotokol 1714 p. 375 Sj.t. 1714/471. Ballad: KB, En ynckelig Sørgesang siunget af en Misdæderinde navnlig Anna Michelsdatter …

1715:1 Mette Lauridsdatter, Spin-house inmate
She had been sentenced to the Spin-house for the attempted murder of her own child. In July 1714 she had cut a boy in the stomach with a knife. She had confessed just after the deed, but denied having done it when she appeared before the court. She was put into the city gaol. Here she was given a baby to nurse, but she strangled it with a rope.

Murder ?? CC 10/12/1714 decapitation by sword and burial at the gallows. MC 27/2/1715 Confirms. SC 19/6/1715 confirms. Execution 9/7/1715.

Rgsk. 1715 voucher 36. SC voteringsprotokol 1715A fol. 167. Ballad: KB: En samtale mellem en Synderinde og Jesus og tillige afskedstale med Verden fremsat af Mette Lauridsdatter …

1715:a Anne Chatrine Christophersdatter, Spin-house inmate [ATTEMPT]
Seven years previously, at the age of eleven, she had been sentenced to the Spin-house for arson. She now tried to cut the throat of a child, because she had been ordered to work harder than she could manage, and had been thrashed. She had lost the will to live and had considered suicide.

Attempt 22/5/1714. CC ?? decapitation with the sword. MC?? confirms. TF 9/4/1715: that she could be granted her life, but should be sentenced to whipping and hard labour for life. RR 22/5/1715 according to the Theol. Fac. Statement. Execution of the whipping 27/6/1715.

Rgsk. 1715 voucher 45-6. Rådstuen, domprotokol 1715 p. 20. Teol.fak. p. 837.

1715:b Anne Marie Stephansdatter, Spin-house inmate [ATTEMPT]
She was sentenced to work in the Spin-house for foul language. Here she cut a child's throat and went around telling everyone that she had committed a crime. The child was able to go to work immediately after the attack, however. Five to six weeks before the attempted murder she had been sent to the infirmary as an epileptic. The motive for the crime was the extremely harsh and violent treatment she had suffered, which had led first to physical debility and then to desperation. The defence questioned the genuineness of the murder attempt, citing the fact that many people claimed to have committed a murder in order to lose their life.

Attempt 16/2/1714. CC 1/10/1714 Decapitation by sword. MC 13/2/1715 confirms. TF 24/6/1715: to be set free after a period of punishment in the Spin-house. RR 20/12/1715 to be punished in the Spin-house.

Rgsk. 1715 p. 65. Rådstuen, domprotokol 1715 p. 293-300 Theol.Fak. p. 869.

1716:a Johan Nielsen Rosenquist, Spin-house inmate [ATTEMPT]
He had cut the throat of a twelve-year-old child with a knife. The boy had teased him, laughing at the fact that he was being punished by having to wear a wooden block round his leg. He cut the boy's throat in an attempt to kill him and thereby avoid work in the Spin-house and the punishment awaiting him there.

Attempt 18/10/1714. CC 7/1/1715 decapitation by sword. MC 6/5/1715 confirms. SC 3/7/1716 to be transferred to hard labour at the naval shipyard, Bremerholm.

Rgsk. 1716. Rådstuen, domprotokol 1716 p. 289-93. Hø.ret. 1716 p. 175.

1717:a Anne Margrethe Rudolphsdatter, Spin-house inmate [ATTEMPT]
She had cut a girl's throat with a knife. She had done it not to kill the girl but in order to get out of the Spin-house, and be able to complain about the terrible treatment there. She was mentally disturbed and had once been put in the asylum for eight days.

Attempt 12/11/1716. CC 31/3/1717 for life in the Spin-house. MC 20/10/1717 confirms. Imprisoned 18/1/1718.

Rgsk. 1717 p. 61. Rådstuen, domprotokol 1717 p. 294.

1718:1 Kirstine Pedersdatter, widow of a soldier
She had cut the throat of a four-year-old girl. She explained she had been suffering from chronic depression and psychosis. She had a good reputation and had lived a proper and pious life.

Murder 14/11/1717. CC 24/1/1718 decapitation by sword. MC 31/3/1718 confirms. Request for permission to be buried in the churchyard beside her husband. RR 27/4/1718 grants the request. Execution 14/6/1718.

Rgsk. 1718 p. 31. Rådstuen, domssager 1718 jan.-aug. RA Danske kancelli supplikprotokol 1718 1. halvår no. 267. Ballad: KB, En bodfærdig Synderinde ved Nafn Kirstine Pedersdatter …

1718:a Jens Pedersen, Spin-house inmate [ATTEMPT]
He was sentenced to five years in the Spin-house for stealing from his master. He cut the throat of a young boy, and said he had been motivated by a desire to end his own life. He could not tolerate conditions in the Spin-house and believed he had been imprisoned unjustly.

Attempt 30/12/1715. CC 17/8/1716 to lose his neck. MC 4/11/1716 to lose his life. SC 21/3/1718 to be transferred to Bremerholm. Imprisoned 29/3/1718.

Rgsk. 1718. Rådstuen, domprotokol 1717 p. 70 and rådstueprotokol 1717 p. 318. Hø.ret. 1718 p. 26.

1720:1 Povel Povelsen, grenadier
On 1 February 1720 he had 'cleaved' his own child with his sword. On 13 May 1720 he was pinched with red-hot tongs at two places, his head and hand were cut off with an axe, and his body was placed on the wheel.

Ballads: KB, Et grusom og uhørlig Mord som en Grenadere ved navn Povel Povelsen … KB, En væmodig Begrædelse over Synden og Omvendelse til Gud af en Grenadier ved navn Povel Povelsen …

1720:2 Maren Hansdatter, Spin-house inmate
Had killed a small boy by cutting his throat. She wanted to end her life and escape from the Spin-house regime.

Murder ??. CC 28/8/1719 decapitation by axe and head put on a pole. MC 11/12/1719 decapitation by sword and head put on a pole. Execution 30/1/1720.

Rgsk. 1719 and 1720 voucher 32. Rådstuen, Rådstueprotokol 1719 p. 336. Ballad: KB, Een boedfærdig Synderindes jamerlig Afskeeds-Sang, navnlig Maren Hansdatter.

1720:3 Maren Nielsdatter, Spin-house inmate
Had cut the throat of her own sixteen-month-old daughter with a knife.

Murder 13/8/1719. CC 25/9/1719 Decapitation and head stuck on a pole. MC 11/10/1719 confirms. RR 5/1/1720 that the body as well as the head should be handed over to Johan Buchwaldt for anatomizing. Execution 18/1/1720.

Rgsk. 1719 p. 33 and 1720 p. 40. Rådstuen, rådstueprotokol 1719 p. 305. Sj.t. 1720/2. Ballad: KB, Een grov Misdæderindes dog heel boedfærdig Synderinde navnlig Maren Niels daat …

1720:4 Margrethe Larsdatter, housewife
She had cut the throat of her own two-year-old child while her husband was out. Afterwards she went to the neighbour and confessed the deed. She had nothing against her husband and said that she had done it entirely of her own volition and evil nature. Some years earlier she had been temporarily insane. At the time of the murder there were no sign of insanity, however.

Murder 31/10/1720. LA 19/12/1720 to pay for a life with a life. TF 24/10/1721 cannot recommend any remission from the death penalty.

Underadm. dombog 1720–21 p. 92 f. and vidnebog p. 554 f. Teol.Fak. p. 954.

1721:1 Maria Larsdatter, Spin-house inmate
She had murdered a four-year-old child in the Spin-house.

Murder 14/9/1720. CC 11/11/1720? MC decapitation by sword and head stuck on a pole. Execution 13/2/1721.

Rgsk. 1721 voucher 28-30. Ballad: KB, Misgierninger fordrer Straf idet den angergivne Synderinde Maria Larsdatter … (Karen Brahe IX).

1721:2 Anna Elisabeth Thorsdatter
She had murdered a girl she did not know with a knife. With nowhere to live and nothing to eat, she had resorted to murder in an an attempt to end her life. For this reason she was satisfied with the verdict of the magistrate.

Murder 11/10/1720. CC? to pay for a life with a life. MC 30/6/1721 confirms. Execution 21/8/1721 and the head stuck on a pole despite the verdict.

Rgsk. 1721 p. 31. Rådstuen, rådstueprotokol 1721

1721:3 Dorthea Ernstdatter
She threw her illegitimate child into the canal, out of desperation at her poverty and lack of food. She was satisfied with the verdict.

Murder 27/12/1720. CC ? decapitation by sword. MC 25/6/1721 confirms. Execution 29/7/1721 and the head stuck a pole despite the verdict.

Rgsk. 1721 p. 30, 38–9 and voucher 43. Rådstuen rådstueprotokol 1721 p. 38.

1721:a Niels Jensen Wille, prison inmate [ATTEMPT]
He had been branded twice and had escaped five times from prison at the naval shipyard. He had wounded a fellow prisoner and cut one of the gaolers with a knife. He no longer wanted to go on living because there was no prospect of release from prison and he was bullied by his fellow prisoners. At the time of the crime he would have attacked anybody he met.

Attempt 19/11/1720. LA 16/10/1721 to be whipped and kept in custody.

Underadm. domprotokol 1720–3 p. 525, vidnebog p. 555, retsprotokol p. 578.

1722:1 Marie Sørensdatter, Spin-house inmate
She had cut the throat of a six-month-old child in the Spin-house.

Murder 2/8/1721. CC 13/10/1721 decapitation and head stuck on a pole. MC 23/3/1722 to lose her life. Execution 21/4/1722.

Rgsk. 1721 p. 26 and 41, 1722 p. 35 and 42.

1725:a Anna Dorothea Kletting, Spin-house inmate [ATTEMPT]
She was sentenced to the Spin-house for adultery. She had cut the throat of a seven-year-old child intending to kill it. To the court she stated that if she was sent back to the Spin-house she would commit another crime. Having received the death penalty from the Supreme Court she wrote to the king that the verdict was the result of her foolish statement. Now, however, with the help of the Holy Spirit, her heart no longer listened to the temptations of Satan and had become the abode of Christ. Accordingly, she asked the king to grant her the life. See case 1731:a also.

MC 18/12/1724 to lose her life. SC 31/10/1725 confirms. TF 7/12/1725 to be whipped. RR 15/2/1726 to be whipped in the Spin-house and life imprisonment there.

Teol. Fak. p. 1340, RA, Danske kancelli, Resolutioner på domme 1723–30, p. 701–7.

1726:a Anne Margrethe Andersdatter, Spin-house inmate [ATTEMPT]
At the age of nine she was sentenced to ten years in the Spin-house for theft. After having served nine years of her sentence she decided to cut the throat of a child as a way of losing her own life, but the child recovers. Her motive was anger at her bedfellow's unbearable behaviour, in the form of nagging, slander and other things.

Attempt 1/7/1726. CC 12/8/1726 to lose her life. MC 28/8/1726 confirms. Request for a pardon 12/9/1726. TF 23/10/1726 to be whipped. RR 22/11/1726 to be whipped in the Spin-house.

Teol.Fak. p. 1353. RA, Danske Kancelli, Resolutioner på domme 1723–30, fol. 846–55.

1727:a Karen Danielsdatter, wife of a sailor [ATTEMPT]
In November 1727 she was sentenced to walk with the pillory for three days for using foul and abusive language to her superiors. Angry at this punishment, she decided to throw her own child into the sea. The child was saved, however, but in front of the court she stated that her intention had been to drown the child.

LA ?? to pay with her life. Recommendation of the Admiralty 11/3/1727 to be whipped and imprisoned in the Spin-house for life.

Admiralitetet, generalkopibog p. 557 and 709.

1727:I Kiersten Svendsdatter [INVENTED MURDER]
She claimed to have killed her own illegitimate child. Before the court she cried and admitted that she had lied. In any case, it was proved that the child died from a blow in the presence of witnesses. She wanted to end her life because her friends despised her, and they as well as others criticized her for having had an illegitimate child. She also claimed to have been temporarily insane and to have been treated for mental health problems.

Arrest 22/6/1727 to 13/2/1728, on which date she is forced to make a public confession in the church.

Rgsk. 1728 p. 53 and voucher 83. Bytingsprot. 1727 p. 274.

1727:II Stine Marie Johansdatter, inmate [INVENTED MURDER]
After arriving from Sweden, she had a child and was employed as a wet-nurse. Her child was put out to nurse and died of measles. A year later she was sentenced to three years in the Spin-house for having encouraged some women (to 'loose conduct'). She found the verdict unjust and out of desperation claimed to have strangled her child when it was dying. The City Court judged her allegations to be false.

Arrest 30/9/1727. CC? to be whipped in the Spin-house. Request for a pardon 1/11/1728. RR 14/1/1729 no whipping and reduced stay in the Spin-house.

Rgsk. 1728 voucher 86. Bytingsprot. 1727 p. 352. RA. Danske Kancelli, supplikprotokol 2. halvår 1728 no. 481.

1728:1 Philip Schmidt, musketeer
Sentenced to running the gauntlet sixteen times for theft. In gaol he killed a fellow prisoner with a knife because the other prisoner and an NCO had deliberately terrified him with the descriptions of running the gauntlet. He had lost his mind and wanted to kill everybody.

Murder 2/8/1728. CM 18/10/1728 hand and head to be cut off by axe, and body put on post and wheel with the head on the pole over the body. RR 22/11/1728 confirms.

Gen.aud. 1728–9 fol. 154.

1728:I Barbara Olsdatter, Spin-house inmate [INVENTED MURDER]
She reported having murdered her own child. The doctor at the Spin-house, however, testified that the child had a high temperature and was emaciated. He was surprised that it lived as long as it did. Barbara then withdrew her confession and said that she had turned herself in in order to get out of the Spin-house and avoid the regime there. She would rather lose her life than stay there any longer.

Arrest 31/12/1727. 1/5/1728 The magistrate decided that she should be put back in the Spin-house to serve the punishment to which she had been previously sentenced.

Rgsk. 1728 voucher 89–90.

1728:II Sophia Catharina Rich, Spin-house inmate [INVENTED MURDER]
She was sent to the Spin-house for several years for prostitution. She now reported having murdered her newborn child when living in a brothel and said that the body of a newborn child found at that time close to the brothel was hers. When sentenced to death, she confessed to the pastor and later to the Magistrate's Court that she had invented the murder in order to escape the rigours of the Spin-house and end her life. In the Supreme Court the defence referred to her having stated that she would harm herself or others if she was sent back to the Spin-house.

Arrest 11/10/1728. CC 4/4/1728 death penalty. MC 1/2/1730 public confession in church and one year in the Spin-house. SC 9/5/1730 public confession in church and banishment from the city. Execution 4/6/1730.

Rgsk. 1730, Hø.ret. 1730 p. 189–94.

1730:1 Paul Wissing, private
He had got drunk on schnapps and gone mad; he had loaded his gun and gone out seeking to commit a crime. As he had also absconded from a parade and a drill, his comrades were ordered to arrest him. He then shot one of the comrades, who died.

CM 24/5/1730 decapitation, head put on a pole and the body to be buried at the gallows. RR 14/8/1730 confirms.

Gen.aud. 1729–31 p. 187.

1731:1 Elemina Olufsdatter, housemaid
She had served the family for eight years when she suffocated their eighteen-month-old child. She said her fiancé, a soldier, had beaten her three times with a broom handle and called her a whore and other names. This had made her lose her mind and she committed the murder to put an end to her life.

Murder 15/1/1731. CC 5/3/1731 the 1697 decree. MC 18/4/1731 confirms. SC 14/6/1731 confirms. RR 6/10/1731 cutting off of head and hand and burial in consecrated ground. Execution 30/10/1731.

Rgsk. 1731 p. 58 and voucher 113 and 133–7. Bytingsprot. 1731 p. 156. Sj.t. 1731/378.

1731:a Anna Dorothea Kletting [ATTEMPT]
She was in the Spin-house for life (see case 1725:a). She cut the throat of a boy she knew and liked, attempting to kill him. When the boy begged for his life, she relented. She said she had been badly treated and would rather die than stay in the Spin-house. Afterwards she regretted what she had done with all her heart.

Attempt 29/5/1731. CC 13/8/1731 death penalty. MC 17/10/1731 confirms. SC 19/5/1732 confirms. RR 27/6/1732 to be set free.

Rgsk. 1731 voucher 117–18 and 140. Rgsk. 1732 voucher 189-90. Bytingsprot. 1731 p. 211.

1732:a Christoph Ernst Leo, private [ATTEMPT]
For a long time he had been thinking of shooting someone at random. He had sold some of his military equipment and feared the punishment. When on sentry duty, he shot at a woman walking along the street. The woman was warned by a journeyman mason, however, took evasive action and was only slightly wounded.

CM 27/9/1732 decapitation by axe and head stuck on a pole. RR 27/10/1732 to be branded on the forehead and hard labour for life.

Gen.aud. 1731-3 p. 265.

1732:b Helvig Andersdatter, wife of a sailor [ATTEMPT]
She had been lying with one hand over the face of her child and a knife at its throat. The child was not hurt, however. She had been behaving like a mad person, running around the house completely naked and uttering un-Christian phrases such as she belonged to Satan and not to God, that she

cursed Christianity and the day she was born. She had been quarrelling with her husband and as a result had been sentenced to the pillory.

LA to be whipped in the Spin-house for three days and two years' hard labour there. She send a request for a pardon to the king. The Admiralty explained the case to the king 18/11/1732.

Admiralitetet 1732 p. 1445.

1733:1 Anne Maria Truelsdatter, housewife
She had cut the throat of her own newborn child, because she was mentally disturbed and depressed at her terrible poverty and therefore wanted to end her life. Neither her husband nor anybody else had suspected anything, however. Her husband had been ill for some years, and she already had four children.

Murder 19/5/1733. CC 13/7/1733 death penalty. MC 29/7/1733 confirms. SC 15/10/1733 confirms. Request to the queen to spare her life. TF 9/11/1733 that it is not advisable to grant pardon from the death penalty. Request to the king to be granted burial in consecrated ground beside the child she had killed as well as financial support for her children. The request was supported by the pastor because, with a repentant and believing heart, she was prepared to suffer for the crime she had committed. RR 4/12/1733 granted burial in consecrated ground and freed from paying fines.

Rgsk. 1733 voucher 186 and 188. Bytingsprot. 1733 p. 300. Teol.fak. p. 72.

1733:2 Carl Heinrich Mensing, musketeer, aged thirty
He had served for thirteen years. He shot a sailor at random from behind while walking in the street. He said he was depressed at being demoted from his position as sergeant. He had tried to buy himself out of his commission and offered 30 rix-dollar (rigsdaler). The captain demanded 60 rix-dollar, however. He committed the murder in order to get rid of his life.

Murder 6/9/1733. CM 30/9/1733 hand and head to be cut off and corpse stuck on post and wheel. RR 11/11/1733 confirms.

Gen.aud. 1733–5 p. 258.

1733:a Caspar Arnold, musketeer, aged thirty-five [ATTEMPT]
He had served for one and a half years. He was on sentry duty when a wigmaker and his wife passed by. He shot at them and hit the wife in the thigh. She survived, however. He said he had been denied a position as a *frimand* (a soldier who only has to attend parades etc.).

Attempt 1/5/1733. MC 18/6/1733 hand and head to be cut off and corpse put on post and wheel. RR 7/10/1733 confirms.

Gen.aud. 1733–5, 189.

1733:b Kirsten Pedersdatter, inmate, aged eighteen [ATTEMPT]
She had served three years of a life sentence. A fellow prisoner had threatened to lodge a complaint with the Master Spinner and she feared a severe

punishment. She first decided to murder the fellow prisoner, but as she could not find a way to do this she chose to murder a child instead. She cut its throat, but the child did not die. She said she had wanted to put an end to her unhappy existence.

Attempt 4/4/1733. CC 1/6/1733 to lose her life. MC 1/7/1733 confirms. SC 15/10/1733 confirms. RR 6/11/1733 (on request for pardon) to work in the Spin-house at a place separated from others to prevent further incidents.

Rgsk. 1733 voucher 184. bytingsprot. 1733 p. 280.

1733:I Ingeborg Christensdatter, housemaid, aged twenty [INVENTED MURDER]
She told the court that she had had a baby three years earlier, in the town of Slagelse. On her way to Copenhagen she had suffocated the child because she could not afford to keep it. She had now been ill, had repented of her crime and could not be happy until she had confessed to it. An inquiry at the church where the child was buried revealed that it had actually died from an illness. Ingeborg then confessed to having invented the killing because she was ill and weak and no longer wished to live.

Bytingsprot. 1733 p. 345 (6 July) and 390 (17 August).

1736:1 Hans Hansen, former royal life guardsman
He had strangled his own eighteen-month-old child with a scarf. Afterwards he gave himself up. He claimed no motive other than being tempted with evil thoughts, to which he had succumbed.

Murder 13/3/1736. CC 9/4/1736 the 1697 decree. MC 25/4/1736 confirms. Request from his wife that he be pardoned from the pinching with red-hot tongs. RR 9/5/1736 pardoned from the pinching with red-hot tongs.

Byting, Domsakter 1736 p 361. Sj.t. 1736/234.

1736:2 Anna Knudsdatter, housemaid, aged seventeen
She went out with the intention of murdering the next child she met. She met a five-year-old girl playing. She bought the girl a pretzel, took her in her arms and carried her to the ramparts, to a place where nobody could see them, and there she cut the girl's throat. She said she had been engaged to a musketeer for two years. He had made her leave her service and go to his colonel, who he said had promised him permission to get married. The colonel, however, denied this. Two days later the musketeer took a cloak from her and said he would never give it back. Because of this Anna went out of her mind. She got a knife and committed the murder.

Murder 4/6/1736. CC 26/6/1736 the 1697 decree. MC 18/7/1736 confirms. Request for a pardon 26/7/1736: the musketeer had stolen her property and denied that he had promised to marry her, and she had been badly treated by his colonel. She asked for an ordinary decapitation. RR 10/8/1736 confirms but she shall be pinched with red hot tongs only once.

Rgsk. 1736 voucher 187. Sj.t. 1736/333.

1736:3 Karen Andersdatter, housemaid, aged twenty-six
Her illegitimate child was in custody while she was in service. She went and fetched the child from its foster-mother and threw it into the sea, where it drowned. She said her mistress treated her harshly, saying her work was never satisfactory. She wanted to find another position, but her mistress threatened to put her in the pillory and would not let her leave. She was not satisfied with the way the foster-mother treated her child either. These things had all been too much for her and had caused her to commit the crime in order to end her life.

Murder 25/6/1736. CC 30/7/1736 the 1697 decree. MC 15/8/1736 decapitation and head stuck on a pole. Request for pardon 20/8/1736 to be granted ordinary decapitation and burial in consecrated ground. RR 23/11/1736 confirms the Magistrate's Court verdict.

Rgsk. 1736 voucher 189. Sj.t. 1736/379.

1736:4 Ludvig Jørgen Petersen, tailor
He cut the throat of a random eight-year-old girl. He said that until Shrovetide he had led a God-fearing life, singing and praying morning and night. Then he began to have strange thoughts and doubted God's mercy. A doctor declared him melancholic. He had visited his pastor several times—the last time being on the morning of the day of the murder.

Murder 30/6/1736. CC 6/8/1736 the 1697 decree. MC 22/8/1736 life for life. SC 18/10/1736 confirms. RR 23/11/1736 confirms and burial in consecrated ground.

Bytingsprot 1736 p. 388. Sj.t. 1736/533.

1736:a Christen Povelsen [ATTEMPT]
He had stabbed a mate in the chest with a knife. He was sentenced to hard labour at the naval shipyard, Bremerholm, for another attempted murder. He said that he did it to be given the death penalty. The Faculty of Theology advised the king to pardon him from the death penalty and deport him out of the country.

Teol.fak. p. 409. RA, Holmens chef (søetaten), bog over fangerne 1714–39 no. 23.

1736:b Johann Christopher Riesen, private, aged thirty-four [ATTEMPT]
He tried to shoot a cook for no reason. He said that after an illness the previous winter he had been suffering from depression. He had shot the cook while partly delirious, and he felt that somebody had pushed him into doing it.

Attempt 3/4/1736. CM 7/4/1736 decapitation by sword. RR 23/4/1736 hard labour for life.

Gen.aud. 1736 p. 717.

1736:I Mette Nielsdatter, housemaid, aged twenty [INVENTED MURDER]
She reported having thrown a child into the sea. A week later she retracted her self-accusation. She said she had been out of her mind and was bored with life.

Report 23/10/1736. Denial 29/10/1736. CC 12/11/1736 six months in the Spin-house.

Rgsk. 1736 voucher 203-4. Bytingsprot. 1736.

1736:II Kirstine Sigvartsdatter, housemaid, aged twenty [INVENTED MURDER]
She reported having thrown a young girl whom she did not know into the sea. She said she had been accused of stealing. She was fed up with life but had done it at the instigation of Satan. She wanted to drown herself, but then chose to drown the girl instead. A fortnight later she admitted that the story was not true.

Report 8/10/1736. Denial Oct. 1736.

Bytingsprot. 1736 p. 479 and 1736 p. 3.

1737:1 Anne Marie Nielsdatter, Spin-house inmate, aged twenty-six
She had cut the throat of a six-year-old girl in the Spin-house. She said that two years earlier she had been whipped and put in the Spin-house for immoral behaviour. The mother of the child had informed against her. After the murder she went to the work area and asked for some water to wash the blood off her hands. The mother then asked if Anne Marie had murdered her child. She said she had and that, because the child's mother had hurt her, she had now hurt the mother.

Murder 26/3/1737. CC 15/4/1737 to lose her life. MC 8/5/1737 decapitation and head stuck on a pole. RR 7/6/1737 confirms and adds that the execution shall be conducted in the square outside the Spin-house.

Rgsk. 1737 voucher 163–4.

1737:2 Zacharias Ebenetter, grenadier
Standing sentry in the middle of the city, for no reason he shot and killed a girl passing by. He had loaded his gun the night before with the intention of carrying out a crime of this sort. He had had similar evil thoughts before.

CM 20/9/1737 the 1697 decree. RR 4/10/1737 confirms.

Gen.aud. 1737 p. 477.

1737:a Carl Thaysen, private [ATTEMPT]
He had been arrested and was awaiting his punishment of running the gauntlet when for no reason he stabbed a fellow prisoner from behind. The victim survived, however. He said he was motivated simply by boredom.

CM 5/10/1737 decapitation by axe and head stuck on a pole. RR 30/12/1737 running the gauntlet eight times and hard labour for life.

Gen.aud. 1737 p. 590.

1737:I Povel Christensen, ordinary seaman [INVENTED MURDER]
He had deserted and he turned himself in for having killed a boy with a stone just outside Copenhagen. No body had been found after five months, and no report had been received of a missing boy.

ACC ?? keelhauling for desertion and six months' hard labour for the murder allegation. AS 22/8/1737 to be exempted from the six months' hard labour.
Admiralitetet 1737 p. 1011.

1738:1 Lene Sørensdatter, housemaid, aged twenty-nine
She had taken a small girl and deliberately thrown her into the sea. She said she was bored and disturbed because a soldier to whom she had been engaged had cheated on her.
Murder 24/6/1738. CC 14/7/1738 decapitation and head on a pole. MC 30/7/1738 confirms. RR 5/9/1738 confirms.
Rgsk. 1738 voucher 219. Sj.t. 1738/518.

1738:2 Hinrich Wendt, private, aged forty-two
He had come across two Frenchmen. When they spoke to him in French, he demanded that they spoke to him in German. As they did not say anything, he stabbed and killed one of them with his rapier. After the murder he stated that he would do it again if he were freed. He wanted the wounded Frenchman to die and he was well aware of the punishment he would be given.
Murder 12/10/1737. CM 30/10/1737 Decapitation by axe and head stuck on a pole. RR 7/1/1738 confirms.
Gen.aud. 1738 p. 628.

1738:a Hans Michael Gattmann, private, aged thirty-two [ATTEMPT]
He had been short of money and in desperation decided to shoot the first person passing his sentry post. This was a sailor, whom he shot from behind but only wounded in the arm.
Attempt 18/1/1738. CM 5/2/1738 the 1697 decree. RR 10/3/1738 confirms.
Gen.aud. 1738 p. 770.

1738:b Anne Sophie Wangs, housemaid, aged seventeen [ATTEMPT]
She asked the mother of a baby to fetch her some schnapps. While the mother was away, she tried to strangle the baby with a cloth, but the returning mother and another woman saved the baby. She said that, mainly, she was depressed because her nose had been broken six years previously. Recently she had been quarrelling with a sailor's wife, had been reprimanded by her mistress and was drunk.
Attempt 26/3/1738. CC 5/5/1738 has forfeited her life. MC 11/6/1738 confirms. SC 4/10/1738 confirms. RR 12/12/1838 to be whipped and in the Spinhouse for life.
Rgsk. 1738 voucher 202-3. Bytingsprot. 1738 p. 415.

1738:I Anne Marie Andersdatter, yarn spinner, aged eighteen [INVENTED MURDER]
She reported having thrown a child into the canal. She had been in the Spinhouse for a year and had been released just before Christmas. A fortnight later she confessed that the murder was an invention. She said she could not get into service without bail and her father would not stand bail for her. She could

not stay at her lodgings any more because a new decree forbade women to live alone without a proper job, and so she had made up this story in order to lose her life.

Bytingsprot. 31/3/1738 p. 415 and 14/4/1738 p. 418.

1739:1 Michel Blödorn, musketeer, aged forty-two
Michel was drunk on the last day of Easter. His landlord refused him a tankard of beer because he was drunk and it was forbidden at Mass time. Then Michel fetched his gun and, apparently for fun, did some drill practices but ended up shooting the landlord. At first he claimed that it was an accident, but then he said that Satan had taken hold of him by the throat and he had committed the murder for no reason.

Murder 31/3/1739. CM 7/4/1739 the 1738 decree. RR 27/4/1739 confirms. Gen.aud. 1739 p. 217.

1739:2 Hinrich Puffvogel, musketeer, aged fifty
He had sold his equipment and was also suspected of having stolen some socks. He fetched his gun to shoot his sergeant. When he could not find the sergeant, he decided to shoot the first person he met. He then followed a sailor and shot and killed him.

Murder 9/9/1739. CM 19/9/1739 the 1738 decree. RR 2/11/1739 confirms. Gen.aud. 1739 p. 315.

1742:1 Margrethe Christensdatter, housemaid, aged twenty-three
She threw a nine-year-old girl into the canal just before Christmas. A week later the girl was reported missing at church. This prompted Margrethe to go to the warden of the gaol and give herself up. She said she had left her job a fortnight before the murder for no reason. She had been dreaming that she would commit a crime like this, and from then on she had been tempted by such thoughts. The defence asked her why she had not turned to God when undergoing such temptation, but Margrethe answered that she was so disturbed that she could not follow the word of God.

CC 5/3/1742 life for life. MC 15/3/1742 confirms. RR 6/4/1742 confirms because Margrethe has stated that she is happy with the verdict.

Rgsk. 1742 voucher 184. Stj.t. 1742/161. Memoirs: Henrik Gerner: Nogle Merkværdigheder som angaaer Henric Gerner fordum Stiftsprovst i Siellands Stift … hans Vita og Fata …, Copenhagen 1772, p. 98–109.

1742:a Anne Jensdatter, sailor's wife [ATTEMPT]
Another man's wife had accused her of something. She feared she would be punished and became distressed. She took an eighteen-month-old child from a doorstep and threw it into the canal, but the child was saved. Anne stated that it had been her intention to drown the child so that she could end her own life. She was pregnant.

ACC 28/8/1742 she forfeited her life when she gave birth to her child. AS 3/9/1742 confirms. TF 28/9/1742 Spin-house for life. RR 26/10/1742 Spin-house for life.

Teol.fak. 1742 p. 1000-5. RA, Søkrigskancelliet, kgl. res. Søetaten vedk. 26/10/1742.

1744:1 Cicilia Johansdatter, housemaid, aged twenty-two
She cut the throat of her own fifteen- to eighteen-week-old child. She was engaged to a guardsman named Friedrich Christian. The child had been conceived since they got engaged. The guardsman was refused permission to marry, however. Six weeks before the murder he had started acting more coldly towards her and stopped visiting her. After the murder she put her hands on the head of the child and said that she had once died for it and now she would die for it again and with pleasure.

Murder 25/2/1744. CC 16/3/1744 decapitation and head stuck on a pole. MC 9/4/1744 confirms. RR 1/5/1744 the city court judge stated that CJ accepted the verdict without appeal but asked the king to allow her to be buried in consecrated ground. The king allowed her to be decapitated by sword and buried in consecrated ground. Execution 26/5/1744.

Rgsk. 1744 voucher 253–4 and 327. Sj.t. 1744/225. Ballads: KB En meget ynkelig Viise hvorudi en Synderinde … Cicilia Johans Dotter …. KB En angerfuld Synderindes sidste Svane-Sang eller Afskeeds-Tale componeret i fiire aandelige og meget gudelige Arier.

1744:2 Karen Jensdatter, Søkvæsthus inmate, aged forty-two
She was arrested for begging in 1737 and put into the Søkvæsthus, the navy infirmary and workhouse for the poor. For a month she had planned to kill a child, to be freed from the workhouse regime. Her prayers to God had prevented her from doing so until Good Friday, when, pretending to be fond of him, she lured a small boy from his mother, took him to the privy and tried to cut his throat. When the boy cried out, she threw it into the privy, where it died.

ACC 14/4/1744 the 1697 decree. Karen asked the king for permission to be buried in consecrated ground. AS 16/4/1744 confirms. RR 1/5/1744 confirms, except for the exhibition of the body on stake and wheel. Instead the body to be buried at the gallows. Execution 26/5/1744.

Admiralitetet 1744 p. 177. RA, Søkrigskancelliet, kgl. res. Søetaten vedk. 1/5/1744. RA, Søkvæsthuset, Mandtalsbøger over fattige m.fl. 1733–45 p. 323.

1745:1 Martin (Karl) Friedrich Vogels, musketeer, aged twenty-two
He had been short of money, stolen clothes from his comrades, sold them and got drunk on the money. He loaded his gun in order to shoot the colonel. His sergeant came to take him to the colonel to explain the theft of clothes. On the way Martin suddenly turned around and shot and killed a nine-year-old boy who was walking behind them.

Murder 9/6/1745, CM 26/6/1745 the 1738 decree. RR 6/8/1745 confirms. Execution 16/10/1745.

Gen.aud. 1745 p. 262. RA, Generalauditøren, Originale relationer 1745 fol. 215. Ballad: KB, Der bewegliche doch hoffentlich seelige Abschied des Delinqventen Karl Friedrich Vogels …

1746:1 Catharina Kaas, housemaid, aged twenty-one
She had persuaded an eight-year-old child to follow her outside the city ramparts, and there she killed it by stabbing it in the neck. She said she had been arguing with her mistress and another woman about receiving Holy Communion.

Murder 16/3/1746. CC 2/5/1746 life for life. MC 16/6/1746 confirms. SC 12/10/1746 decapitation and the corpse to be put on the post and wheel. RR 25/11/1746 Catharina made a sad request to be allowed a burial in consecrated ground. The king allowed her to be beheaded by axe and buried in consecrated ground. Execution 1/12/1747.

Bytingsprot. 1746 p. 266. Hø.ret. 1746 p. 265. Sj.t. 1746/198 and 1746/224. Ballad: KB, Sidste Afskeeds-Ord af én veemodig Synderinde ved Navn Catharina Kaas …

1746:a Johan Jochumsen, sailor [ATTEMPT]
He stabbed a boy in the chest, but the boy survived. He claimed that he had acted on a sudden impulse to commit a murder.

Attempt 15/9/1746. ACC 15/12/1746 decapitation by sword. AS 19/12/1746 hard labour for life. RR 5/1/1747 Hard labour in irons for life.

Admiralitetet 1746 p. 40. RA, Søkrigskancelliet, Kgl. eksp. Søetaten vedk. 5/1/1747.

1747:1 Sidsel Andersdatter, housemaid, aged twenty-four
She lured a nine-year-old boy away from his mother and cut his throat in a gateway. She had been dismissed from her job at the executioner's. She lived for two days at a night man's outside the city, whose son she was engaged to. She then returned to Copenhagen mad and deranged as she did not know where to go. She claimed that she did not remember anything about the killing.

Murder 18/11/1747. CC 20/3/1747 to lose her life. MC 20/4/1747 confirms. SC 26/6/1747 decapitation and the corpse displayed on post and wheel. RR 18/8/1747 confirms. Execution 31/8/1747.

Bytingsprot. 1747 p. 449. Hø.ret. 1747 p. 298. Sj.t. 1747/428.

1747:I Martin Hansen, Spin-house inmate [INVENTED MURDER]
In the Spin-house he reported having killed his brother. In the City Court he denied the confession. An examination revealed no such murder. Same person as in case 1757:2.

Confession 3/9/1747. CC 12/9/1746. MC 19/9/1747 hard labour in irons for one year.

Rgsk. 1747 voucher 266–68.

1748:1 Anne Lovise Pedersdatter, Spin-house inmate
After being found guilty of theft in 1738 she had been whipped, branded and sent to the Spin-house for life. There she killed a thirty-week-old baby with a knife. After the killing she went to the work hall and said that she was now 'a free man'. She said she no longer wanted to live because of the length of her sentence.

Murder 8/7/1748. CC 15/7/1748. MC 10/9/1748 decapitation and the corpse displayed on post and wheel. She died in gaol. RR 6/12/1748 that her body should be buried at the gallows by the night man.

Bytingsprot. 1748 p. 438 and 481. Sj.t. 1748/546.

1748:2 Birthe Cathrine Jørgensdatter, housemaid, aged twenty-one
With cherries she lured a small boy to go with her to the Jewish churchyard, sat him on her lap and cut his throat with a knife. She said she had lost her mind because she had been beaten on her head by her master.

Murder 3/8/1748. CC 23/9/1748 decapitation and corpse stuck on post and wheel. MC 10/10/1748 confirms. SC 23/12/1748 confirms. RR 31/1/1749 confirms. Execution 20/2/1749.

Rgsk. voucher 254 and 300-1. Bytingsprot. 1748 p. 460. RA. Danske kancelli, sjællandske registre 1749/28.

1748:3 Maren Jensdatter, sailor's wife
She had killed her own daughter with a knife because she felt guilty at having been unfaithful to her husband.

Murder 3/7/1748. ACC the 1697 decree. AS 30/7/1748 confirms.

Admiralitetet 1748 p. 844.

1748:a Sidsel Anders Hansen Weydes, Spin-house inmate, aged sixty-two [ATTEMPT]
She had tried to cut the throat of an eighteen-month-old child, but the attempt had failed. She had been in the Spin-house for four years for begging. She had been at the infirmary for a year and carried out the murder attempt because she was mentally disturbed as a result of illness and grief.

Attempt 3/11/1747. CC 8/1/1748 forfeited her life. MC 25/1/1748 confirms. SC 30/3/1748 Spin-house for life in careful custody.

Rgsk. 1748 voucher 277. Bytingsprot. 1747 p. 259.

1748:b Anne Marie Skades, musketeer's daughter, aged fifteen [ATTEMPT]
She met a six-year-old child on the street and tried to cut its throat with a jack-knife but did not succeed. She said her mother had sworn at her and so she decided to do a mischief.

Attempt 8/8/1748. MC 10/10/1748 to be beaten with rods inside the Spin-house and to work there for three years.

Rgsk. 1748 voucher 298. Bytingsprot 1748 p. 468.

1749:1 Kirstine Schiønsted, housemaid, aged seventeen
She killed her master's three-year-old son with a knife while he was asleep. The only season she gave was that the Devil had seduced her as a young person.

Murder 5/12/1748. MC 6/2/1749 the 1697 decree. SC 2/4/1749 confirms. RR 9/5/1749 confirms but she shall only be pinched with red-hot tongs once at the scaffold. Execution 29/5/1749.

Rgsk. 1749 voucher 305. Bytingsprot. 1748 p. 60. Hø.ret. 1749 p. 107. Sj.t. 1749/275.

1751:1 Ingeborg Svend Gunnersens, inmate, aged sixty-two
She cut the throat of an eight-year-old girl. She said she had been ordered to pay a debt but could not. She had beome desperate and murdered the innocent child, whom she loved dearly.

Arrest 25/7/1750. CC 30/8/1750 the 1749 decree. MC 1/10/1750 confirms. SC 23/11/1750 confirms. RR 29/1/1751 confirms and refuses a request from Ingeborg only to be pinched once with red-hot tongs. Execution 18/2/1751.

Bytingsprot. 1750 p. 42. Byting, ekstraretsprotokol 1750 p. 139. Hø.ret. 1750 p. 453. Sj.t. 1751/38. Ballad: KB, Sidste afskeeds-Ord af én vemodig Synderinde ved Navn Engeborre Jens Gunnersen …

1752:1 Ane Olsdatter, Spin-house inmate, aged thirty-three
She cut the throat of a four-year-old boy. She had been in the Spin-house for eleven years. Three months earlier she had secretly given birth to a stillborn baby, and had also been punished by the Master Spinner. Since then she had intended to do an evil deed. She had chosen the boy because his mother had scolded her the previous summer. The father of her stillborn child was Martin Hansen (see case 1747:I and 1757:2).

Murder 27/12/1751. CC 6/3/1752 the 1749 decree. MC 27/3/1752 confirms. SC 17/5/1752 confirms. RR 28/7/1752 confirms. Execution 10/8/1752.

Byting, ekstraretsprotokol 1752 p. 372. Hø.ret. 1752 p. 194, Sj.t. 1752/354.

1753:1 Søren Kieldsen, sailor, aged thirty-two
He persuaded an eight-year-old boy to go into a field with him and then killed him by cutting his throat. Afterwards he gave himself up. He had been engaged to a girl and had two children with her, both of whom had died. Then he had been at sea for some years. When he returned from sea, the girl was with somebody else and he became depressed. On the day of the murder he had been told that the girl was happier now than when she lived with him. Witnesses said that he had behaved strangely, and some days before the murder the doctor had bled him.

Murder 4/7/1753. ACC 25/8/1753 the 1749 decree. JAG 9/11/1753 Decapitation by axe. RR 12/11/1753 Head and hand to be cut off with an axe.

Komb.ret. 1753 B-25, Gen.aud, søetat 1753.

1754:1 Anna Magdalena Jansdatter, fruit seller, aged forty
She lured a six-year-old boy playing on the street down into the cellar where she lived. She asked for the names of his parents and his age, and then she cut his throat with a knife. Afterwards she went to the city gaol and turned herself in. Two years previously she had been accused of stealing a silver candlestick. The candlestick incident had been mentioned again in a conversation with somebody the previous summer, and this had hurt her deeply.

Murder 29/12/1753. MC 1/5/1754 the 1749 decree. SC 27/6/1754 Confirms. RR 9/8/1754 confirms. Execution 20/8/1754.

Rgsk. 1754 voucher 127. Bytingsprot. 1754 p. 346. Hø.ret. 1754 p. 275. Ballad: Dansk folkemindesamling, Poenitenzes taare fældede af en bodfærdig Synderinde Anna Kirstine Mühlsteinsdatter … (Rothmans samling 1906/6b:3).

1754:2 Christen Eskildsen, prisoner, aged twenty-five
He had been branded and sentenced to hard labour in irons for life. He tried to escape several times and threatened to kill somebody. On 7 February 1754 he suddenly stabbed and killed a 72-year-old sergeant from behind. The motive was partly revenge, partly fear of a punishment that was awaiting him and partly the fact that he was tired of life and preferred to die rather than live such a miserable life.

CM 21/5/1754 the 1749 decree. RR 15/7/1754 confirms.

Gen.aud. 1754 p. 169.

1754:a Johan Carl Freyvaldt, grenadier, aged forty-one [ATTEMPT]
He had been a soldier for nineteen years. He had a wife and a child on Funen. He was upset because he could not pay for them to come to Copenhagen. He had been drinking and got confused and desperate. He cut the throat of his landlady's nine-year-old daughter with a knife twice, but she survived. He claimed it was an accident.

CM 28/5/1754 the 1738 decree. RR 15/7/1754 running the gauntlet eighteen times and hard labour for life.

Gen.aud. 1754 p. 171.

1755:1 Isidorus Eichenberger, musketeer, aged thirty
He was a Catholic; he had been in the army for six years and was a *frimand*, a rank that meant he only had to attend parades. He found out that his landlady had tricked him into a debt and he decided to shoot her. On his way he took a jug of beer. As he could not pay for it, he shot the innkeeper dead. Afterwards he gave himself up, saying that besides the unfair debt he felt guilty about his bad lifestyle, and had been troubled with desperate thoughts. This made him drink, and he committed the murder when drunk.

Murder 28/4/1755. RR 13/5/1755 the 1738 decree. RR 10/7/1755 confirms.

Gen.aud. 1755 p. 32. RA, Generalauditøren (Landetaten), originale relationer 1755 no. 160.

1756:1 Johanne Hansdatter, housemaid, aged nineteen
She persuaded a ten-year-old child to go with her to a bridge, and then pushed the child into the water so that it drowned. She said her fiancé, a smith's journeyman, had broken off their engagement right in front of his new girlfriend.

Murder 8/1/1756. MC 5/5/1756 life for life. RR 17/5/1756 confirms because Johanne was satisfied with the verdict. Execution 22/6/1756.

Rgsk. 1756 voucher 165. Bytingsprot. 1756 p. 330 and 346. Sj.t. 1756/339. Ballad: Jens Sørensen's private collection, En sindriig aandelig Sang og Vise forfattet som en Tale af en bodfærdig Synderinde navnlig Johanne Hansdatter …

1756:2 Karen Corneliidatter, Spin-house inmate, aged thirty-four
She had been whipped and branded and put in the Spin-house for life for theft. She cut the throat of an eight-week-old baby whom she knew and looked after.

After the murder she said that now they could not threaten her any more, because now she was 'a free man'. She had been under so much pressure of work that she had to pay someone to help her, and said that the inspector of the prison, Master Jacob, was responsible. She explained to the defence that the Spin-house was a terrible place, with physical force being used and unchristian treatment.

Murder 16/2/1756. CC 19/5/1756 the 1749 decree. MC 26/5/1756 confirms. SC 29/6/1756 confirms. RR 30/7/1756 confirms. Execution 17/8/1756.

Rgsk. 1756 voucher 172–73. Bytingsprot. 1756 p. 362. Ballad: KB, En bodfærdig Synderindes Samtale med Gud forestillet i en gudelig Sang og Viise over Delinqventinden Karen Cornelidotter.

1757:1 Marie Lisbeth Johansdatter, Spin-house inmate, aged seventeen
In September 1756 she was sentenced to one year in the Spin-house at the wish of her parents for immoral behaviour and petty theft. She cut the throat of a three-year-old boy whom she knew. She said the master wanted her to do more work than she could manage and he beat her. The defence questioned the master and an inmate who worked with Marie. Both denied that Marie had been forced to work too hard.

Murder 26/1/1756. ACC 19/5/1756 the 1749 decree. JAG confirms.

Komb.ret. 1757 B-39.

1757:2 Martin Hansen, Spin-house inmate, aged twenty-six
He had been in the Spin-house for ten years with short periods of freedom. He strangled a one-year-old child with a piece of rope. His request to leave the Spin-house had been turned down, so he committed the murder as a way of escaping. The same person as case 1747:1 and probably the father of the stillborn baby mentioned in case 1752:1.

Questioning 7/2/1757. CC 21/3/1757 to be beheaded by sword. MC 20/5/1757 the 1749 decree. SC 29/6/1757 confirms. RR 8/9/1758 confirms.

Rgsk. 1758 voucher 90–91. Bytingsprot. 1757 p. 113.

1757:3 Maria Elisabeth Conradsdatter, Spin-house inmate, aged forty
She had been branded for theft. She cut the throat of a three-year-old child because of the hard work she was made to do in the Spin-house, the little they got to live on (she had been near starvation several times) and because she was bored with the world. The defence blamed the inhumane management of the Spin-house, with its unreasonable workloads and severe punishments.

Murder 12/2/1757. CC 21/3/1757 to be beheaded by sword. MC 20/4/1757 the 1749 decree. SC 28/6/1757 confirms. RR 8/9/1758 confirms. Execution 3/10/1758.

Rgsk. 1758 voucher 92–93. Byting, domsakter 1757 p. 344.

1757:a Kirstine Eliasdatter, soldier's wife, aged forty-eight [ATTEMPT]
She had thrown a three-year-old child into the canal. It survived and was rescued after a few minutes. She drank and had probably been threatened by her

husband. Just after the attempted murder she said that she was tired of life and wanted to die. In court she claimed to have had visions and to have believed that it was a dog that she had thrown into the water.

CM 31/3/1757 the 1749 decree. RR 11/5/1757 life in the Spin-house.

Gen.aud. 1757 no. 102, 2. Gen.aud. res. 1757 no. 102, 2.

1757:b Carl Friedrich Vielguth, musketeer, aged twenty-six [ATTEMPT]
He had been arrested and was awaiting punishment of being forced to run the gauntlet over three days. He dug a stone out of the prison wall and used it to beat a fellow prisoner on the head, but the other prisoner survived. Vielguth did not know the other prisoner and said that, if it had not been him, he would just have attacked someone else. His motive was fear of punishment and the fact that he was tired of living.

Attempt 2/5/1757. CM 13/6/1757 the 1738 decree. RR 13/7/1757 to be whipped and in the Slavery's department for defiled prisoners for life.

Gen.aud. 1757 p. 150. Gen.aud. res. 1757 VI, 1.

1758:1 Dorthea Pedersdatter, Spin-house inmate, aged fifty-one
She had been whipped and branded for theft and had been in the Spin-house for eleven years. She cut the throat of a four-year-old boy with a knife. Her long prison sentence had made her come up with the evil idea of harming somebody.

Murder 8/7/1758. CC 4/9/1758 the 1749 decree. MC 20/9/1758 confirms. SC 29/11/1758 confirms. RR 15/12/1758 confirms. Execution 11/1/1759.

Rgsk. 1758 voucher 113-14. Bytngsprot. 158 p. 36 and 51.

1758:2 Wilhelm Olsen, Slavery inmate, aged thirty
He had earlier tried to shoot a sergeant. He stabbed a fellow prisoner who was unknown to him in the stomach. The stab was not directly lethal, but the fellow prisoner died of the wound in connection with a liver illness. Olsen said he had little hope of ever getting out of the Slavery and that this had given him ideas. He also said that his life had been pointless and that Satan had persuaded him to do it.

Murder 15/2/1758. CM 28/2/1758 the 1738 decree. RR 19/7/1758 the 1749 decree. Execution 11/8/1758.

Gen.aud. 1758 p. 86. Gen.aud. res. 1758 XXX, 1.

1758:a Kirstine Pedersdatter, aged thirty [ATTEMPT]
She had thrown a child into the moat with the intention of killing it and thereby putting an end to her life.

Attempt 26/7/1758. CC 18/9/1758 the 1749 decree. MC 18/10/1758 forfeited her life. SC 29/11/1758 Spin-house for life.

Rgsk. 1758 voucher 115.

1758:b Hans Jensen, private, aged forty [ATTEMPT]
He stabbed a sleeping colleague in the stomach and in the back, but did not kill him. He said the colleague had harassed him and he had had his wages cut

as a punishment. Both claims were shown to be false, however, and later Hans confessed that he had acted out of desperation.

Attempt 5/3/1758. CM 30/9/1758 the 1738 decree. RR 31/10/1758 running the gauntlet eighteen times and life in the Slavery. Execution 4/11/1758.

Gen.aud. 1758 p 138. Gen.aud. res. 1758 XXXV, 1.

1759:1 Kirstine Jørgensdatter, no income, aged about thirty
She was married to a hatter but had been living apart from her husband for three years. She had lived by pawning her clothes while she still had some. She lodged for two nights with a sailor's wife. On the day of the murder she sent the sailor's wife out to buy schnapps and while she was out she cut the throat of the woman's small boy. She said she was bored with her life and anyway she had been drunk when she did it.

Murder 30/10/1758. CC 11/12/1758 the 1749 decree. MC 17/1/1759 confirms. SC 5/3/1759 confirms. RR 6/4/1759 confirms. Execution 26/4/1759.

Bytingsprot. 1759 p. 126. Hø.ret. 1759 p. 7. Sj.t. 1759/252.

1759:2 Anna Andersdatter, housemaid, aged thirty
She had lured a six-year-old boy into a stable at the house where she worked and cut his throat. She said a man had been flirting with her, but he had then left town without saying goodbye to her. She thought that he was cheating on her and did not want to stay with her. As a result she became deranged and did not know what she was doing until after the crime had been committed.

Murder 4/5/1759. CC 11/6/1759 the 1749 decree. MC 27/6/1759 confirms. SC 2/10/1759 confirms. RR 9/11/1759 confirms but waives the pinching with red-hot tongs. Execution 29/11/1759.

Rgsk. 1759 voucher 101–03. Bytingsprot. 1759 p. 259. Hø.ret. 1759 p. 227.

1759:a Wilhelm Nielsen, Slavery inmate, young [ATTEMPT]
In the Slavery he stabbed another slave several times trying to kill him but did not succeed. He had been beaten for several days by another slave because of an unpaid debt. Fearing the beating would continue, he planned to carry out a crime.

Attempt 29/11/1759. RR 21/12/1759 the 1738 decree. RR 27/2/1760 Flogging with fifty lashes each day for three days in the Slavery attended by the other slaves and continued stay in the Slavery at the king's mercy. Execution 4/3/1760.

Gen.aud. 1759 p. 69.

1760:I Johan Jacob Sommer [INVENTED MURDER]
A child was found drowned, and Sommer claimed that he had thrown it into the water. There were no witnesses. During the trial he first denied and then confessed to the deed several times. He had been disturbed and depressed for a long time.

MC 27/10/1760 the 1749 decree. SC 24/12/1760 to be offered his family to be taken into custody or being taken into custody by the authorities.

Rgsk 1760 voucher 98. Hø.ret. 1760 p. 358.

1761:1 Abelone Johanne Greifkesdatter, prisoner
She was arrested on suspicion of theft. While under arrest she confessed to having killed her own newborn child and thrown the body into the sea. It was documented that she had been pregnant, but the child was not found. The king waived the death penalty and condemned her to the Spin-house. When she was still in the gaol, however, she killed a nine-month-old boy by throwing him into the privy. She said she had made up the story of the murder of her own child in order to be executed. The Supreme Court judges were very angry at the shocking response to the royal pardon and considered recommending to the king a punishment worse than those laid down in the decrees.

Possible infanticide 10/4/1760. CC 30/9/1760 the 1749 decree. MC 28/10/1760 the Spin-house for life. SC 7/1/1761 decapitation and head stuck on a pole. RR 20/2/1761 Spin-house for life.

Murder 24/2/1761. CC 20/4/1761 the 1749 decree. MC 29/4/1761 confirms. SC 8/6/1761 confirms. RR 3/7/1761 confirms. Execution 23/7/1761.

Rgsk. 1760 voucher 97, 1761 voucher 124 and 172-74. Hø.ret. 1761 p. 156.

1761:2 Peter Christian, rifleman in the Navy, aged thirty
He had been separated from his wife because of constant arguments, but then he returned home to her. The next morning he lured her out of the house and then cut the throat of their child with a knife while it lay in its cradle. Afterwards he gave himself up. He confessed to having deliberately lured his wife away from home in order to be able to kill the child. He claimed he was addicted to a debauched lifestyle, had absconded from his service several times and had sold his equipment. For this he feared he would be punished and had resorted to this deed in desperation.

Murder 1/11/1760. ACC 24/1/1761 the 1749 decree. RR 6/4/1761 confirms.

Komb.ret 1760–2. Gen.aud. søetat 28/3/1761.

1762:1 Oluf Svahn, lieutenant's servant, aged twenty-one
He had stolen from his master and was afraid of being found out. He decided to commit suicide and locked himself in a room with several guns. When the door was forced open, he shot at the people outside, hitting three of them. Two survived, but the third died of complications.

Murder 25/2/1762. CM 29/4/1762 the 1749 decree. RR 26/5/1762 hand and head cut off by axe and body buried at the gallows. Execution 30/6/1762.

Gen.aud. 1762 p. 237. Gen.aud. res. 1762 XCIX, 1.

1762:2 Michel Hansen, sailor, aged twenty-one
He persuaded the neighbour's seven-year-old child to go with him and then cut the child's throat. Afterwards he told everybody he met about the murder. He claimed he had deserted from his ship a couple of days earlier and had committed the murder in order to lose his life.

Murder 22/6/1762. ACC the 1749 decree. RR 15/10/1762 confirms.

Gen.aud. søetat. 11/10/1762.

1763:1 Anna Lisbeth Greisdatter, sailor's widow
She cut the throat of her own seven-year-old son. She said she had been brooding over her own poverty and worried about how to support her child. She therefore wanted the child to die and wished for her own death. She told the pastor that she was prepared to die but hoped for a less severe punishment.

Murder 30/8/1762. ACC the 1749 decree. RR 24/2/1763 confirms.

Gen.aud. søetat 23/2/1763.

1763:a Johannes Jensky, grenadier, aged forty-four [ATTEMPT]
He had been arrested and sentenced to run the gauntlet twelve times. He stabbed a fellow prisoner in the belly with a knife while the prisoner was asleep. The prisoner recovered, however. Jensky claimed he was tired of life and did not want to go on living. He denied being afraid of running the gauntlet.

Attempt 3/5/1763. CM 12/10/1763 the 1738 decree. RR 24/12/1763 running the gauntlet eighteen times and in the Slavery for life under special custody.

Gen.aud. 1763 p. 265. gen.aud. res. CXXVII, 1.

1764:1 Christoph Gottfriedsen, fusilier, aged twenty-five [INVENTED MURDER]
A dead man was found in the canal. Gottfriedsen said that he was responsible for pushing him into the water. He said he had been quarrelling with his landlady, had become desperate, got drunk and then pushed this man, whom he did not know, into the water. Later he denied the confession.

RR The Slavery for life. RR confirms.

Gen.aud. res. 1764 no. 137.

1765:1 Gertrud Jensdatter, ship's carpenter's wife
She killed a four-year-old child, whom she did not know, with a knife after talking to it and given it biscuits. Afterwards she told several people what she had done. She gave no reason for her actions except that she felt depressed. She decided to kill the child as soon as she saw it. The day before she had sought medical treatment and had been bled.

Murder 3/6/1765. ACC 6/7/1765 the 1749 decree. RR 26/7/1765 decapitation by axe.

Gen.aud. søetat 28/7/1765.

1766:1 Marie Jensdatter, wife
She cut the throat of her own two-year-old girl. She said she lived in miserable circumstances and was tired of life. Her pastor said she had been depressed for a long time.

Murder 28/4/1766. CC 30/6/1766 decapitation and head stuck on a pole. MC 23/7/1765 confirms. SC 11/10/1766 life for life. RR 7/11/1766 Spin-house for life because of her depression.

Rgsk. 1766 voucher 117-9. Hø.ret. 1766 p. 204.

1766:2 Barbara Andersdatter
She cut the throat of a small girl with a knife. The defence in the Supreme Court argued that she had been drunk.

CC 30/6/1766 the 1749 decree. MC 16/7/1766 confirms. SC 8/10/1766 confirms. RR 8/5/1767 confirms. Execution 19/5/1767.

Rgsk. 1767 voucher 120–1 and 200-1. Hø.ret. 1766 p 196.

1766:3 Hans Friedrich Junghans, sailor
He killed a nine-month-old child with a knife. He fled but then returned and apologized for the murder to the father, whom he knew slightly. He said that things had been going badly for him, and so he had decided to do a mischief.

Murder 2/4/1766. ACC the 1749 decree. RR 12/6/1766 confirms.

Gen.aud. søetat 29/5/1766.

1766:4 Knud Reinholdtsen, sailor, aged twenty-three
He sent his wife out for something to drink and then cut the throat of his own nine-month-old child. He had been brooding over his poverty and feared punishment for absconding from his ship. He therefore decided to kill anyone he could find.

Murder April 1766. ACC the 1749 decree. RR 14/8/1766 confirms but waives the pinching with red-hot tongs.

Gen.aud. søetat 9/8/1766

1766:5 Johannes Hermansen, former sailor and road sweeper
He was injured in the arm and then started begging in order to be arrested and taken to the Søkvæsthus, the navy infirmary and workhouse for the poor and indigent. Here he recovered from his injury, but the infirmary directors would not let him go. He told several other inmates that he would get out one way or another and decided to commit a crime. He then killed an 82-year-old inmate with a stone. Several witnesses testified that he was not mentally competent.

Murder 9/6/1766. ACC the 1749 decree. RR 28/1/1767 confirms.

Gen.aud. søetat 23/1/1767.

1766:a Andreas Jensen, Musketeer, aged twenty-seven [ATTEMPT]
He had been arrested and was waiting to run the gauntlet. He stabbed a fellow prisoner, whom he did not know, in the stomach with a knife. The man recovered, however. On his way to the punishment he made a false confession of a murder. His motive was simply that he was afraid of the punishment awaiting him.

Attempt 8/8/1766, CM 5/9/1766 the 1738 decree. RR 6/12/1766 running the gauntlet eighteen times and the Slavery for life.

Gen.aud. 1766, p. 151.

1766:b Peder Aagesen, sailor [ATTEMPT]
He had been brooding over an unsuccessful proposal to a girl and a quarrel with a relative. When walking with his seven-year-old son he suddenly threw

him into the moat. A sailor working in the moat saved the boy from drowning. The boy said that the father had threatened to cut his throat the same day, but Peder Aagesen denied this.

Attempt June 1766. ACC forfeited his life. RR 2/10/1766 given fifty lashes each day for three days and in the Slavery for life.

Gen.aud. søetat 26/9/1766.

1766:I Nicolaus Henrch Betzner, fusilier, aged twenty-two [INVENTED MURDER]

He reported having thrown a girl in the water and drowned her. However, no girl was missing and no body was found. He then explained that he had made a false confession out of fear of a punishment awaiting him and because he was tired of life.

JAG 25/1/1766 running the gauntlet sixteen times and the Slavery for life. RR 16/4/1766 confirms.

Gen.aud. 1766 p 73. Gen.aud. res. 1766 no. 156.

1767:1 Hans Jørgen Førster, sailor

He cut the throat of a three-year-old child as it lay in bed. He claimed to have intended to commit a murder for a long time and suffered from depression.

Murder 13/6/1767. ACC 1749 decree. RR 4/9/1767 confirms but waives the pinching.

Gen.aud. søetat 20/8/1767.

1767:2 Anders Pedersen, sailor, aged eighty

He took a walk and then decided to commit a crime. He walked home and stabbed his eight-year-old daughter in the chest, killing her. He said he was angry because his neighbour had accused him of theft in public.

Murder 27/6/1767. ACC the 1749 decree. RR 22/8/1767 confirms.

Gen.aud. søetat 22/8/1767.

1767:3 Anne Christophersdatter, housemaid

She asked for permission to look after the nine-month-old child of a friend and took it to her mistress's hall and cut its throat with a knife. She claimed she was angry at accusations made by her mistress and at the way she was treated.

CC 22/6/1767 the 1749 decree. MC 15/7/1767 confirms. SC 15/10/1767 confirms. RR 13/11/1767 confirms but waives the pinching.

Rgsk. 1767 95–96 and 172–4. Hø.ret. 1767 p. 303.

1767:4 Christen Olsen Upsal, musketeer, aged fifty

He could not pay his rent. He went out and tried unsuccessfully to borrow the money. He wandered around in a strange mood and had a few drinks. He thought of killing himself but gave up the idea. Then he grabbed a child of three or four and stabbed it in the throat with his sword. He handed himself in, saying that the Devil had told him to commit a crime. He said that afterwards he tried to kill himself, but that it was as though somebody had ordered him to stop, in order to save his soul.

Murder 11/10/1767. CM 17/10/1767 the 1738 decree. RR 22/1/1768 to be given twenty-seven lashes and in the defiled department of the Slavery be put to the toughest work and watched closely. For the next two years to be whipped once a year. He dies in the Slavery 27/9/1791.

Gen.aud. res. 1767 XXXV, 1. Slaverulle 1774-91.

1769:1 Peter Christian Fallenkamp, musketeer
He killed his landlord's eleven-month-old child with his bare fists. He explained that he was tired of life and of being a soldier.

Murder 15/11/1769. CM 24/11/1769 the 1767 decree. RR 3/1/1770 confirms.

Gen.aud 1769 p 354. Gen.aud. res. 21/12/1769.

1769:a Hinrich Hansen, musketeer, aged thirty-six [ATTEMPT]
While working in the countryside on holiday, he persuaded a girl selling bread to come into his room and then beat her on the head several times with a stone. She managed to survive. He said he blamed himself for not having respected his parents and their advice in his youth. He had read in the Bible that 'the ravens shall peck the eyes out of disobedient children'. This had shocked him so much that he could not rest until he had done the evil deed. The judge advocate general described him as melancholic and said he had become disturbed by solitude and his reading of religious books.

Attempt 25/12/1768. CM 5/1/1769 In the Slavery for life. RR 1/3/1769 confirms.

Gen.aud. 1769 p. 310. Gen.aud. res. 22/2/1769.

1769:b Asmus Asmussen, slave, aged eighteen [ATTEMPT]
A fellow slave accused him of stealing, and he decided to commit a crime because he was tired of life. He cut another fellow slave's throat, but only wounded him.

Attempt 24/9/1769. CM 2/10/1769 the 1767 decree. RR 15/11/1769 to be given fifty lashes a day for three days, and to continue his punishment of hard labour.

Gen.aud. 1769 p. 341. Gen.aud. res. 8/11/1769.

1769:c Lars Rasmussen Pleyel, sailor [ATTEMPT]
He tried to cut the throat of a 3½-year-old child whom he did not know. The child's father stopped him, and the child was not seriously hurt. He claimed he was afraid of being punished for absconding from his ship and was angry because his wife had pawned his linen. He also said he had not been responsible for his actions because he was drunk. The judge advocate general feared that he would start a new wave of similar crimes in the navy, and therefore recommended punishment according to the new decree.

Attempt 13/6/1769. ACC the 1767 decree. RR 12/10/1769 confirms.

Gen.aud. søetat 6/10/1769.

1769:d Dorothea Theresia Pedersdatter, inmate, aged thirty-one [ATTEMPT]
She tried to cut the throat of an eleven-year-old girl. The girl resisted and and received several lacerations before being saved by two women. Dorothea claimed she was depressed. The pastor confirmed that she had been deranged and had thoughts of hurting herself and others. She had earlier made a false confession to the murder of a child.

Attempt 12/10/1768. CC 5/6/1769 life for life. MC 6/7/1769 in safe custody in the Spin-house. SC 3/10/1769 confirms.

Rgsk 1769 voucher 152.

1770:a Johan Friderich Nicolaus Leo, musketeer, aged thirty-six [ATTEMPT]
He lured a ten-year-old boy to a bridge and threw him into the canal. The boy was saved, however. He claimed he had been unjustly accused of theft and was depressed.

Attempt 26/12/1769. CM 12/12/1770 the 1767 decree. RR 30/1/1771 to run the gauntlet sixteen times and in the Slavery for life.

Gen.aud. 1771 p. 408. Gen.aud. res. 23/1/1771.

1770:b Carolina Kirstina Nielsdatter, fusilier's wife [ATTEMPT]
She was trying to cut the throat of a five-year-old girl but was prevented by the mother and another woman. Her explanations for her actions varied, and she tried to have herself declared temporarily insane. The judge advocate general found the explanations incredible and ruled that she was motivated by problems such as alcoholism and homelessness.

Attempt 10/10/1769. ACC the 1767 decree. RR 26/4/1770 confirms. Waiving of the annual whipping 19/6/1776. Dies in the Spin-house 20/7/1787.

Gen.aud. søetat 21/4/1770. Mandtalsbøger

1771:1 Elisabeth Frandsen
She pushed a child into the moat, where it drowned. She said she had unsuccessfully attempted the same crime once before. She explained that she was tired of life and wanted to commit a crime. In a pardon request she claimed to have been temporarily insane. The warden and the pastor confirmed that she had been delirious.

CC 24/9/1770 the 1767 decree. MC 3/10/1770 confirms. SC 17/1/1771 confirms. RR 25/2/1771 confirms. Public whipping and branding 28/2/1771. Waived the annual whipping 22/8/1777. Dies in the Spin-house 18/5/1815.

Rgsk. 1771 voucher 75 and 168. RA, Danske kancelli, supplikprotokol 1771 no. 46 and 159. Mandtalsbøger.

1771:2 Franz Diderich Rubst, Spin-house inmate, aged nineteen
He had earlier attempted to cut a child's throat and was put in the Spin-house. He killed a six-year-old child with an axe. He said he was tired of life.

Murder 27/6/1771. CCC 3/10/1771 the 1767 decree. SC 23/12/1771 confirms. Public whipping and branding 20/2/1772. Waived the annual whipping 30/7/1777. Dies in the Spin-house 11/1/1797.

Rgsk. 1772 voucher 48 and 283. Mandtalsbøger.

1771:a Johann Ludwig Schwermann, defiled slave, aged twenty-three [ATTEMPT]
He was put in the Slavery for attempted murder. He threw an eight-year-old boy into the moat. When the boy tried to get out, he pushed him back into the water but ran off when somebody came along, and the boy was saved. He said he was tired of life. He chose a child because it could not defend itself and because it had not committed any great sins like an adult.

Attempt 3/8/1771. CM 18/9/1771 the 1767 decree. RR 11/11/1771 to be given fifty lashes a day for three days and put to hard work in secure custody, so that he could not harm anybody. Execution 18/11/1771.

Gen.aud. 1771 p 8.

1772:1 Ulrica Nordberg
She threw a four-year-old boy in the sea, where he drowned. She claimed she felt she had been humiliated by a neighbour. The defence said she suffered from epilepsy, but she had not been having a seizure at the time of the murder. A minority of the Supreme Court judges found that it had not been proven that the motive for the murder was a desire to be executed. Consequently they would only sentence her to the Spin-house for life.

Murder 13/2/1772. CCC 17/8/1772 the 1767 decree. SC 17/11/1772 confirms. RR 14/1/1773 to the Spin-house for life.

Rgsk. 1773 voucher 69-70. Hø.ret. 1772 p. 596.

1772:2 Hans Jørgen Carl, dismissed sailor and day labourer
He had been drinking and quarrelling with his brother and some other men. The brother ran off, afraid that Carl would stab him with a knife. Carl then met an old match-seller and killed him by cutting his throat. He said he had been wanting to commit a crime all day, but he denied being bored with life.

Murder 30/5/1772. CCC 27/8/1772 decapitation by sword, Carl would not appeal. RR 12/11/1772 confirms if Carl again refused to appeal. Execution 22/12/1772.

Rgsk. 1772 voucher 105-6 and 290-5.

1776:a Anne Larsdatter [ATTEMPT]
She cut her own child's throat, intending to kill it. The child had done nothing to offend the mother. She was depressed virtually to the point of delirium.

CCC 18/3/1772 the Spin-house for four years.

Rgsk. 1776 voucher 115.

1777:1 Hans Terkelsen, prison inmate
He cut the throat of a two-year-old child with a knife. He had only three weeks left of a two-year sentence of hard labour rasping wood. He had been ordered to do another kind of work and had been quarrelling with a fellow prisoner. This had made him deranged and made him wish to end his boring life, and so he killed the child. A plea of insanity was turned down in court.

Murder 26/4/1777. CCC 4/8/1777 the 1767 decree. RR 15/10/1777 confirms. Public whipping and branding 28/10/1777. Pardoned the annual whipping 21/4/1781. Died in the Spin-house 20/8/1810.

Rgsk. 1777 voucher 144-145. Mandtalsbøger

1777:a Jens Hansen, slave [ATTEMPT]

He stabbed a sleeping guard in the thigh and the chest with a bayonet. He only intended to wound the guard. He said he wanted the death penalty, because he would rather die than stay in the Slavery.

Attempt 10/7/1777. CCC 29/9/1777 to work in the Rasp-house as long as he had the strength necessary.

Rgsk. 1777 voucher 158.

1779:1 Svend Jensen, sailor, aged thirty-four

He hit the head of his nine-week-old child against the bedpost, and it died two days later. He claimed to have absconded from his ship and to be afraid of his punishment. He sent his wife out to buy schnapps. While she was out, the child started crying. He picked it up and then threw it back into the bed. It kept crying. Then he threw it into the bed so hard that the baby's head hit the bedpost. Immediately after the incident he said he wanted to kill the child, but later he said that it had been an accident.

Murder 19/2/1779. ACC 15/5/1779 the 1767 decree. RR 2/9/1779 confirms. Pardoned the annual whipping 13/2/1789. Died in the Spin-house 25/5/180?

Komb.ret. 1779-80. RA, Admiralitetet kgl. resolutioner 2/9/1779. Mandtalsbøger.

1779:a Maria Margaretha Engelsdatter, musketeer's wife, aged thirty-six [ATTEMPT]

She attempted to cut the throat of her own six-year-old daughter, but was interrupted by a musketeer. She claimed to have been very intoxicated.

Attempt 31/12/1778. CM 14/1/1779 the Spin-house for life. RR 3/2/1779 the Spin-house at the king's mercy.

Gen.aud. 1779 p. 110.

1780:a Christoph David Haack, musketeer, aged thirty-one [ATTEMPT]

He threw a seven-year-old boy into the canal in an attempt to drown him, but the boy was rescued. He claimed to be depressed and had wanted to commit a crime in order to end his life.

Attempt 2/10/1780. CM 21/11/1780 the 1767 decree. RR 31/12/1780 hard labour in the Rasp-house as long as he is able to work, then in the Slavery.

Gen.aud. 1780 p. 139.

1781:a Marthe Kirstine Nielsdatter, Søkvæsthus inmate [ATTEMPT]

She tried to strangle a three-year-old boy with some yarn, but the mother stopped her. She had already tried unsuccessfully to escape from the Søkvæsthus. Seeking to avoid the everlasting stay and fed up with life she had had been planning for a month to do a mischief.

Attempt Aug. 1780. CCC 16/7/1781 the Spin-house for life in safe custody. Rgsk. 1781 voucher 87.

1781:b Friedrich Christian, sailor, aged twenty-one [ATTEMPT]
When he woke up in the morning, he had a vision: a man came to his bedside and told him to kill one of the small children in the house. He got up and stabbed a seven-year-old girl in the throat with a knife. She recovered, however. He denied having any motive other than the vision.

Attempt 9/1/1781. ACC 12/6/1781 the 1767 decree. RR 13/7/1781 to be given fifty lashes a day for three days and life in the Slavery.

Komb.ret 1781–82. RA, Generalauditøren (Søetaten), Indkomne sager 13/7/1781.

1783:1 Johann Friedrich Geneser, musketeer
He sent his wife out and cut the throat of his own small boy as he lay in bed. Then he gave himself in to the authorities, saying he had been desperate and drunk. He said he was always inclined get into trouble when he was drunk. He denied being bored with life or suffering from any kind of depression or melancholy.

Murder 1/9/1783. CM 22/9/1783 the 1738 decree. RR 12/11/1783 confirms. Execution 3-13/12/1783.

Gen.aud. 1783 p. 187. Gen.aud. res. 1783 CLIII, 1. Ballads: KB, Misdæderen Johan Friderich Chineser … hans døende Advarsel og sidste Svanesang, and KB, En opvækkende nye Viise hvorudi Misdæderen Johan Friderich Petersen Kineser … forestilles som sin Synds bekiender og en i Fængslet omvendt og benaadet Synder.

1783:a Jens Andersen, sailor, aged thirty-six [ATTEMPT]
He was arrested and waiting to be flogged. He cut a fellow prisoner's throat with a rusty knife but only wounded him slightly. He claimed he had intended to commit a crime out of fear of the flogging that awaited him.

Attempt 30/1/1783. ACC to be given fifty lashes every day for three days and in the Slavery for life. RR 16/4/1783 confirms.

RA, Admiralitetet, Kgl. resolutioner 1783 no. 25.

1784:a Üte Mortensen, disabled soldier [ATTEMPT]
He walked into a cobbler's and for no reason stabbed the cobbler in the chest with his cobbler's knife. The wound was not serious, however. He claimed that it was a mistake and said that he was drunk.

Attempt 29/5/1784. CCC 18/10/1784 the Spin-house for life.

Rgsk. 1784 voucher 106.

1785:I Johann Lichtmanegger, musketeer, aged thirty-eight [INVENTED MURDER]
While arrested for desertion and theft, he confessed to having murdered a sailor along with another musketeer. Eighteen months later the allegation was proved false. He said he was bored with life.

Confession 12/2/1783. CM 15/11/1784 the Slavery for life. RR 7/1/1785 confirms.

Gen.aud. 1785 p. 214.

1789:1 Daniel Kiranni, corporal, aged forty-nine

He deserted from Elsinore and tried unsuccessfully to get to Sweden. He then went to Copenhagen, and near the city gate he met two privates from another regiment. They had a friendly conversation together. The two men were then walking along in front of him, and he told them there was no need to hurry as the gate was not open yet. Then he shot and killed one of them from behind. He said he thought they had recognized him and wanted to get into the city before him in order to report him and get the reward for apprehending a deserter. The judge advocate general argued that the explanation was unconvincing. The fact that he denied having committed the murder in order to lose his life only proved that he knew the 1767 decree. If he said that he wanted to be executed, then he would not be given the death he sought.

Murder 29/6/1789. CM 16/9/1789 the 1738 decree. JAG 6/11/1789 the 1767 decree. RR 13/11/1789 hand and head to be cut off by axe and stuck on a pole.

Gen.aud. 1789 p. 307. Gen.aud. res. 11/6/1789. Ballad: KB, Jammer-Sang over Granadeer og Desserteur eller Tyrannens afskyelige Mord paa en forbigaaende Landsoldat …

BIBLIOGRAPHY

Primary Sources

Rigsarkivet (Danish National Archives)

Admiralitetet (The Admiralty)
Generalkopibog 1710–1747
Kgl. resolutioner 1710–1747

Danske Kancelli (Danish Chancellery)
Kancelliets brevbøger 1777–1789
Indlæg til Kancelliets brevbøger 1777–1789
Sjællandske registre 1697–1789
Indlæg til sjællandske registre 1697–1789
Sjællandske tegnelser 1697–1789
Indlæg til sjællandske tegnelser 1697–1789
Dokumenter til kgl. majestæts resolutionsbog udi Danmark 1695–1698
Kgl. resolutioner skrevne på supplikationer, domme m.m. 1723–30
Supplikker 1697–1789

Den kombinerede ret (The Admralty's Joint Court)
Sager til justits- og domprotokoller 1748–1789

Det Teologiske Fakultet (The Faculty of Theology)
Kopibog 1697–1758

Generalauditøren (Judge Advocate General for the Army)
Generaljustitsprotokol 1728–1750
Justitsprotokol 1750–1789
Originale relationer 1742–1762
Relationer til kongen 1763–1789

Generalauditøren (Søetaten) (Judge Advocate General for the Navy)
Betænkninger 1748–1789
Indkomne sager 1746–1789

Holmens chef (Commander of the Navy Dockyard)
Bog over fangerne 1714–39

Højesteret (Supreme Court)
Voteringsprotokol 1697–1892

Reviderede regnskaber, Københavnske regnskaber (audited accounts from Copenhagen)
Byfogedregnskaber 1681–1789

Underadmiralitetsretten (Lower Admiralty Court)
Domprotokoller 1706–1747
Vidnebøger 1709–1747

Søkrigskancelliet (Navy Chancellery)
Kongelige resolutioner vedrørende søetaten 1727–1747

Søkvæsthuset (Navy Infirmary and Poorhouse)
Mandtalsbøger over fattige m.fl. 1733–1757

Landsarkivet for Sjælland M.M. (The Provincial Archive of Zealand)

Børnehuset på Christianshavn (the Spin-house and the Rasp-house at Christianshavn)
Mandtal over Børne- og Rasphusets lemmer 1772–1806
Mandtal over Rasphusets årsfanger 1806–1846

Københavns Byting (City Court Archive)
Bytingsprotokol 1722–1771
Domsakter 1728–1771

Københavns Stokhus (the Slavery)
Slaverulle 1763–1826

Københavns Stadsarkiv (The Copenhagen City Archive)

Københavns magistrat, rådstueskriveren (Archive of the Magistrate's Scribe)
Domprotokol 1697–1735
Rådstueprotokol 1701–1735
Domssager 1702–1735

Stockholms Stadsarkiv (The Stockholm City Archive)

Magistratens og rådhusrättens arkiv (Archive of the Magistrate and the City Court)
Tänkebok i renskrift 1651

Primary Printed Sources

Allgemeines Landrecht für die Preußischen Staaten von 1794, Alfred Metzner Verlag, Berlin, 1970

Ancher, P. Kofod: *Svar paa nogle Spørgsmaale til Det Juridiske Fakultet*, Copenhagen, 1779

Anon.: *Als Margaretha Ursula Huberin Burgerliche Balln-Binderin [allhier in Regenspurg Wegen begangenen Kinder-Mords ... zum Tode verdammt] und [darauf den 21. Octobr. 1734] ... hingerichter worden*, Staatsbibliothek zu Berlin (16 in: 4" Fy 7898)

Anon.: *Bewegliche Abschieds Worte womit Johanna Susanna Riedeln als solche wegen verübten Kinder-Mords*, Dresden 1726, Staatsbibliotek zu Berlin (Fy 7910: R)

Anon.: *Danmark og Norgis Kirkeritual*, Copenhagen, 1685 (1985)

Anon.: *Der bewegliche doch hoffentlich seelige Abschied des Delinqventen Karl Friedrich Vogels ...*, Copenhagen 1745, Royal Library Copenhagen (Hielmstierne 3)

Anon.: *Der in der Todt gehende, und seiner eignen Tochter ... antwortende bussfertige Vater oder Arme Sünder Jeremias Bertz ...*, Augsburg, 1740, Württembergische Landesbibliothek (Crim.R.qt.K.46–3)

Anon.: *Die aus der Grabe redende nur 15. Wochen alte Martyrin Maria Magdalene Bertzin, welche von ihrem eigenen Vatter Jeremias Bertz ... ermordet worden ...*, 1740, Staatsbibliothek zu Berlin (FY 7912 R)

Anon.: *Ein erbärmlicher Klaglied von einer sehr erschröcklichen That ... Michael Rohrbach ... der selbig drei seiner eignen Kinder mit seinem Messer die Gurgel abgestochen ... zu Wymiss gerichtet hat ... wie es dann weiters im Lied gnugsam wird vermeldet*, 1638, Deutches Volkslieder Archiv (Bl–a 654)

Anon.: *En angerfuld Synderindes sidste Svane-Sang eller Afskeeds–Tale componeret i fiire aandelige og meget gudelige Arier*, Copenhagen, 1744, Royal Library Copenhagen (Hielmstierne 31)

Anon.: *Een boedfærdig Synderindes jamerlig Afskeeds-Sang, navnlig Maren Hansdatter* ..., Copenhagen, 1720, Royal Library Copenhagen (Hielmstierne 38)

Anon.: *En bodfærdig Synderindes Samtale med Gud forestillet i en gudelig Sang og Viise over Delinqventinden Karen Cornelidotter*, Copenhagen, 1756, Royal Library Copenhagen

Anon.: *En bodfærdig Synderinde ved Nafn Kirstine Pedersdatter* ..., Copenhagen, 1718, Royal Library Copenhagen (Hielmstierne 26)

Anon.: *En gandske nye Viise om det forskreckkelige Mord, som af trende Fod-gardere, Carl Evalt, Baltz Beck, og Frid. Elmhorst* .... Copenhagen, 1727, Royal Library Copenhagen (Hielmstierne 54)

Anon.: *Een grov Misdæderindes dog heel boedfærdig Synderinde navnlig Maren Niels daat.* ..., Copenhagen, 1720, Royal Library Copenhagen (Hielmstierne 12)

Anon.: *En meget ynkelig Viise hvorudi en Synderinde ... Cicilia Johans Dotter* ..., Copenhagen, 1744, Royal Library Copenhagen (Hielmsterne 49).

Anon.: *En ny Klagevise sunget af en Misdæderinde nafnlig Johanne Kirstine Christensdatter*, Copenhagen, 1714, Royal Library Copenhagen (Hielmstierne 9)

Anon.: *En opvækkende nye Viise hvorudi Misdæderen Johan Friderich Petersen Kineser ... forestilles som sin Synds bekiender og en i Fængslet omvendt og benaadet Synder*, Copenhagen, 1783, Royal Library Copenhagen (Hielmstierne 4)

Anon.: *En samtale mellem en Synderinde og Jesus og tillige afskedstale med Verden fremsat af Mette Lauridsdatter* ..., Copenhagen, 1715, Royal Library Copenhagen (Hielmstierne 30)

Anon.: *En sindriig aandelig Sang og Vise forfattet som en Tale af en bodfærdig Synderinde navnlig Johanne Hansdatter* ..., Copenhagen, 1756, Jens Sørensen private collection, Copenhagen

Anon.: *En væmodig Begrædelse over Synden og Omvendelse til Gud af en Grenadier ved navn Povel Povelsen* ..., Copenhagen, 1720, Royal Library Copenhagen (Hielmstierne 13)

Anon.: *En ynckelig Sørgesang siunget af en Misdæderinde navnlig Anna Michelsdatter* ..., Copenhagen, 1714, Royal Library Copenhagen (Hielmstierne 17)

Anon.: *En ynckelig og smuck ny Sang sunget af en Misdæderinde navnlig Anna Chatrine Berntsdatter* ..., Copenhagen, 1713, Royal Library Copenhagen (Hielmstierne 8)

Anon.: *Et grusom og uhørlig Mord som en Grenadere ved navn Povel Povelsen* ..., Copenhagen, 1720, Royal Library Copenhagen (Hielmstierne 11).

Anon.: *Et ynckelig og uhørlig, et forfærdelig og gruelig Mord er udi Helsingør forøvet af et Qvindfolck* ..., 1721, Royal Library Copenhagen (Hielmstierne 20)

Anon.: *Handbook ther uti är författadt huruledes Gudstiensten medh Christelighe ceremonier och Kyrkiosedher uthi wåra Swenska Församblingar skal bliffua hållin och förhandlada*, Uppsala, 1614, Royal Library Copenhagen

Anon.: *Handbok ther uti är författadt huruledes Gudstiensten med Christelige ceremonier och Kyrkioseder uthi wåra Swenska Församlingar skal bliffwa hållen och förhandlad*, Stockholm, 1693 (1716), Royal Library Copenhagen

Anon.: *Jammer-Sang over Granadeer og Desserteur eller Tyrannens afskyelige Mord paa en forbigaaende Landsoldat* ..., Copenhagen, 1789, Royal Library Copenhagen (Hielmstierne 1)

Anon.: *Kurtze Relation und Urtheil die von des h. Röm. Reichs Erb-Marchall- Amts wegen ob commissum infanticidum zu Pappenheim justificierte Eva Ellingerin Betreffend*, Regensburg, 1724, Royal Library Copenhagen

Anon.: *Misdæderen Johan Friderich Chineser … hans døende Advarsel og sidste Svanesang*, Copenhagen, 1783, Royal Library Copenhagen (Hielmstierne 7)

Anon.: *Misgierninger fordrer Straf idet den angergivne Synderinde Maria Larsdatter …*, Copenhagen, 1721, Royal Library Copenhagen (Karen Brahe IX)

Anon.: *Moralische Gedanken als Leonhard Fels … Wegen grausamen verübtem Morde seines Sohnes …*, Augsburg, 1772, Staatsbibliothek zu Berlin (Fy 7912 R)

Anon.: *Poenitensis Taare udøst af en bedrøvet Misdæder Nicolai Marcusøn*, (no place), 1716, Royal Library Copenhagen (Hielmstierne 14)

Anon.: *Poenitenzes taare fældede af en bodfærdig Synderinde Anna Kirstine Mühlsteinsdatter …*, Copenhagen, 1754, Danish Folklore Archives (Rothmans samling 1906/6b: 3)

Anon.: *Reumutiges Klag-Lied des Armen Sünders Jeremias Bertz …*, Augsburg, 1740, Staatsbibliothek zu Berlin (Fy 7912 R)

Anon.: *Rituale romanum Pauli V. pontificus maximi jussu editum et a Benedicto XIV auctum et castigatum*, Ratisbon, 1872

Anon.: *Rostvolles armen Sünderlied der Maria Anna Mayrinn …*, Augsburg, 1783, Staatsbibliothek zu Berlin (G in Fy 7912 R)

Anon.: *Sidste Afskeeds-Ord af én veemodig Synderinde ved Navn Catharina Kaas …*, Copenhagen, 1746, Royal Library Copenhagen (Hielmstierne 21)

Anon.: *Sidste Afskeeds-Ord af én vemodig Synderinde ved Navn Engeborre Jens Gunnersen …*, Copenhagen, 1751, Royal Library Copenhagen (Hielmstierne 27)

Anon.: *Todesurtheil einer ledigen Weibsperson namens Catharina J. … 10. Februarii 1769*, Vienna, Wien Bibliothek (C39975)

Anon.: *Trenne ganska eftertänkeliga Fånga-Visor, den första: Om den botfärdiga Synderskan Anna Lars Dotter, som för begångit barnamord blef halshuggen på Rätteplatsen i Stockholm, d. 17. Julii 1734* (repr. Gefle, 1776), Uppsala Universitetsbibliotek (Zetterströms poetiska samling, p. 12–32)

Anon.: *Trauriger Bericht von dem Delinquenten Namens Christian Gottlieb Carl Schmidt …*, Berlin, 1785, Staatsbibliothek zu Berlin (17 in Fy 7911 R)

Anon.: *Tvende meget sørgefulde Viiser hvori en ynkværdig Synderinde … Charlotta Claudi, som for begangen mord …*, Copenhagen, 1744, Royal Library Copenhagen (Hielmstierne 16)

Anon: *Warnende Nachricht von der vorsetzlichen Mordthat, welche der Canonier Gottlieb Carl Michael Engel …*, 1786, Staatsbibliothek zu Berlin (17 in Fy 7911: R)

Anon.: *Wohlverdientes Todesurtheil nebst einer Moralrede der Margaretha N. vulgo Schilcheten Grödl. Welche auf gnädigsten Anbefehlung eines Churfürstl. Hochlöbl. Hofraths allhier in München heut den 24. May 1783. wegen an einem ihr nicht angehörigen Kind verübten Mordthat auf einem Wagen zur Richtstadt geführet, und alldort durch den Scharfrichter mit dem Schwert vom Leben zum Tod hingericht worden*, Munich, 1783, SUB Georg August Universitätsbliothek, Göttingen

Anon.: *Zuverlässige Nachricht des Delinquenten Christian Hahn …*, 1777, Staatsbibliothek zu Berlin (9 in Fy 7911 R)

Anon.: *Kirchen-Ordnung der Graffschafft Lippe auf Befehl des Grafen Simon Heinrich*, Lemgo, 1684, Copenhagen Royal Library

Aquinas, Thomas: *Summa theologica*, online version in English translated by Fathers of the English Dominican Province: www.newadvent.org/summa

Beccaria, Cesare: *On Crimes and Punishments*, 2nd American edn, Philadelphia, 1819; internet version: http://www.constitution.org/cb/crim_pun.htm

Beckh, Georg Matthäus: *Die von dem barmherzigen Gott hoch-begnadigte Arme Sünderin und Kindes-Mörderin in Nördlingen […] Donnerstags den 22. Augusti, Anno 1715. in der Haupt-Kirchen zu St. Georgen, gehaltenen Bekehrungs- Trost- und Warnungs-Wochen-Predigt Nach der Freytags den 16. Augusti vorgegangnen Enthauptung einer dreyundzwanzig-Jährigen Weibs-Person, die … ihrem … lebendigen Töchterlein, ihr Schnupp-Tuch in den Mund … gestecket, und jämmerlich ersticket*, Nördlingen, 1716, Staatsbibliothek zu Berlin (6 in Fy 7910 R)

Böhmer, Justus Henning: *Jus ecclasisaticum protestantium, usum modernum juris canonici juxta seriem decretalium ostendens, et ipsis rerum argumentis illustrans*, Halle, 1733, vol. 5
Bullinger, Heinrich: *Seelsorge mit Schwerkranken und Sterbenden (Bericht der Kranken 1535)*, trans. Siegfried Müller, http://www.solideogloria.ch/Bullinger/seelsorge.htm
Carrach, J.T.: *J.T. Carrachs rechtliche Urtheile und Gutachten in peinlichen Sachen im Namen der Hallischen Juristen-Fakultät*, ed. H.J.O. König, Halle, 1775
Codex Austriacus III: Supplementum codicis austriaci, Sammlung oesterreichischer Gesetze und Ordnungen …, ed. Sebastian Gottfried Herrenleben, Leipzig, 1748
Collegialtidende, Copenhagen, 1815 and 1833
Die peinliche Gerichtsordnung Kaiser Karls V. (Carolina), 1532 (ed. F.C. Schroeder, Stuttgart, 2000)
Gerner, Henrik: *Nogle Merkværdigheder som angaaer Henric Gerner fordum Stiftsprovst i Siellands Stift […] hans Vita og Fata*, Copenhagen, 1772
Grimm, Johann Melchior: *Als Margaretha Ursula Huberin Burgerliche Balln-Binderin [allhier in Regenspurg Wegen begangenen Kinder-Mords … zum Tode verdammt] und [darauf Den 21. Octobr. 1734] … hingerichtet worden; wurde … / Folgende Rede … gehalten …*, Regensburg, 1734, Staatsbibliothek zu Berlin
Gudenrath, J.J.: 'Mine skrupler om selvmords moralitet og dets strafværdighed efter de borgerlige love', *Iris*, vol. 4, 1792, Royal Library Copenhagen
Hanneken, Philip Ludwig: *Dissertatio theologica de iure gratiae principis christiani, in reos noxae capitalis*, Wittenberg, 1701 (Jena, 1731)
Herzog, Friedrich August: *Sammlung auserlesener responsorum juris criminalis welche von dem berühmtesten juristisch- und medicinischen Facultäten, wie auch Schöppen-Stühlen und gelehrten Männern, über besondere merckwürdige und dubiöse casus cum rationes dubitandi & decidendi sind ausgestellet worden*, Hamburg, 1745
Hielmstierne, Henrik: *55 viser om forbrydere, misfostre og naturmærkværdigheder* 1686–1791 + uden år, Royal Library Copenhagen (1853 F, oktav)
Holberg, Ludvig: *Epistler befattende adskillige historiske, metaphysiske, moralske, philosophiske, item skiemtsomme Materier*, vols 1–5, Copenhagen, 1748–54, published with notes by F.J. Billeskov Jansen; vols 1–8, H. Hagerup, Copenhagen, 1944–54
Horsens Folkeblad, 9 November 1892
Huet, Peter Daniel: *Memoirs of the Life of Peter Daniel Huet, Bishop of Avranches, written by himself, and translated from the original Latin, with copious notes, biographical and critical, by John Aikin*, London, 1810
Hymmen: *Beiträge zu der juristischen Litteratur in den Preussischen Staaten. Eine periodische Schrift*, vols. 4, 6, 8, Berlin, 1780–85
Klein, Ernst Ferdinand (ed.): *Annalen der Gesetzgebung und Rechtsgelehrsamkeit in den preussischen Staaten*, Berlin, 1788–1809
Laffert, H.W.: *Vermehrte relationes et casus criminales cum rationibus dubitandi et decidendi, ingleichen einigen dazugehörigen Königl. Chur- und Fürstlichen Rescriptis sambt andern Beylagen und zugefügten Urtheilen*, ed. A.F. v. Laffert, Zelle, 1721
Meister, C.F.G.: *Rechtliche Erkenntnisse und Gutachten in Peinlichen Fällen größten Theils im Nahmen der Göttingischen Juristen-Fakultät ausgearbeitet*, vols 1–2, Göttingen, 1771–75
Michaelis, J.D.: *Mosaisches Recht*, vols 1–6, Frankfurt an Main (Garbe), 1771–75
Moser, Johann Jakob: *Seelige letzte Stunden 31. Personen so unter des Scharfrichters Hand gestorben: Vor der Welt als Kindes- und andere Mörder, Duellanten, Räuber, jauner, Diebe, Mordbrenner, Viehisch-unzüchtige, falsche Münzer, andere betrügere, und militar-Verbrechere. Vor Gott aber als in dem blute Jesu gerechtfertigt und abgewaschene, oder doch Gnadenhungrige Seelen. Zum Preis der erbarmenden Liebe Gottes, und zu errettung noch mehrere dergleichen Personen, auch anderer rohen und ehrbaren Sünder. Gesammelt und mit einer Vorrede begleitet*, Stuttgart, 1753
Old Bailey Proceedings Online: http://www.oldbaileyonline.org/.
Petri, Olavus: *Samlade skrifter*, vol. 2, Uppsala, 1915

Schmid, P. Jacob: *Trauben der Heiligkeit aus denen Dörnern der Bossheit, oder vervunderliche Bekehrungen allerhand Mördern, Raubern, Zauberern, auch vieler zum Tod verurtheilten Übelthätern oder Maleficanten, welche eintveders noch frühzeitig, oder wenigst vor ihrem Tod herrliche Buss gewürcket. Zu sonderem Nutz der Gefangenen und Übelthätern, sambt einer Weiss für die Seelsorger, die arme Sünder zu einem guten Tod anzuleiten*, Augsburg, 1752 (1738)

Stampe, Henrik: *Erklæringer breve og forestillinger generalprokurørembedet vedkommende*, vol. 2, Gyldendal, Copenhagen, 1794

Steinbart, Gothilf Samuel: *Ist es rathsam Missethäter durch geistliche zum Tode vorbereiten und zur Hinrichtung begleiten zu lassen?*, Berlin, 1769

Thomasius, Christian: *Dissertatio inauguralis iuridica, de jure aggratiandi principis evangelici in causis homicidii*, Halle, Salfeld, 1707 (repr. 1714, 1720, 1739)

Secondary Literature

Almquist, Jan Eric: 'Karl IX och den Mosaiska Rätten', in *Lychnos: Lärdomshistoriska Samfundets Årsbok*, Uppsala, 1942, p. 1–32

Althaus, Paul: 'Die Todesstrafe als Problem der christlichen Ethik', *Sitzungsberichte der Bayrischen Akademie der Wissenschaften, Philosophisch-historische Klasse*, vol. 2, Munich, 1955

Anners, Erik: *Humanitet och rationalism: Studier i upplysningstidens strafflagsreformer – särskilt med hänsyn till Gustav III: s reformlagstiftning*, A.-B. Nordiska Bokhandeln, Stockholm, 1965

Ariès, Philippe: *The Hour of Our Death* (1977), Penguin Books, London, 1987

Avis, P.D.L.: 'Moses and the Magistrate: a Study in the Rise of Protestant Legalism', *Journal of Ecclesiastical History*, vol. 26, no. 2, 1975, p. 149–72

Beattie, John M.: *Crime and Courts in England, 1660–1800*, Oxford, 1986

Behringer, Wolfgang: *Hexenverfolgung in Bayern: Volksmagie, Glaubenseifer und Staatsräson in der frühen Neuzeit*, R. Oldenbourg Verlag, Munich, 1987

Behringer, Wolfgang: 'Mörder, Diebe und Ehebrecher: Verbrechen und Strafen in Kurbayern vom 16. bis 18. Jahrhundert', in R. van Dülmen (ed.): *Verbrechen, Strafen und soziale Kontrolle*, Fischer Taschenbuch Verlag, Frankfurt am Main, 1990, p. 85–132

Behringer, Wolfgang: 'Weibliche Kriminalität in Kurbayern in der Frühen Neuzeit', in *Von Huren und Rabenmüttern: Weibliche Kriminalität in der Frühen Neuzeit*, Böhlau Verlag, Cologne, 1995, p. 63–82

Bergman, Martin: *Dödsstraffet, kyrkan och staten i Sverige från 1700-tal till 1900-tal*, Nerenius & Santérus Förlag, Lund, 1996

Bode, Gustav: 'Kindestötung und ihre Bestrafung im Nürnberg des Mittelalters', diss. Ruprecht-Karls-Universität in Heidelberg, Berlin, 1915

Bosco, Ronald A.: 'Lectures at the Pillory: The Early American Execution Sermon', *American Quarterly*, vol. 30, no. 2, 1978, p. 156–76

Castan, Nicole: *Justice et répression en Languedoc à l'époque des lumières*, Flammarion, Paris, 1980

Castan, Yves: *Honnêteté et relations sociales en Languedoc (1715–1780)*, Libraire Plon, Paris, 1974

Chaunu, Pierre: *La Mort à Paris XVIe, XVIIe et XVIIIe siècles*, Fayard, Paris, 1978

Cheesman, Tom: *The Schocking Ballad Picture Show: German Popular Literature and Cultural History*, Berg, Oxford, 1994

Davis, Nathalie Zemon: *Fiction in the Archives: Pardon Tales and their Tellers in 16th Century France*, Stanford UP, Stanford, CA, 1987

Dülmen, Richard van: *Theatre of Horror: Crime and Punishment in Early Modern Germany*, Polity Press, Cambridge, 1990

Evans, Richard J.: *Rituals of Retribution: Capital Punishment in Germany, 1600–1987*, Oxford University Press, 1996

Freisen, Joseph (ed.): *Manuale Curatorum secundum usum ecclesie Rosckildensis: Katholisches Ritualbuch der dänischen Diözese Roeskilde im Mittelalter*, Paderborn, 1898

Freisen, Joseph (ed.): *Liber Agendarum ecclesie et diocesis Sleszwicensis: Katholisches Ritualbuch der Diözese Schleswig im Mittelalter*, Paderborn, 1898

Freisen, Joseph (ed.): *Manuale Lincopense, Breviarium Scarense, Manuale Aboense: Katholische Ritualbücher Schwedens und Finnlands im Mittelalter*, Paderborn, 1904

Gade, Helmuth: 'Hamburgische Strafrechtspflege im 18. Jahrhundert unter Berücht-sichtigung der Gerichtsverfassung, den Strafprozesses und der Strafvollstreckung', diss. Universität Hamburg, 1956

Gawthrop, Richard: *Pietism and the Making of Eighteenth-Century Prussia*, Cambridge University Press, 1993

Grove, Gerhard L.: 'Skafottet og kaget på Nytorv ved midten af det attende århundrede', in Fra *Arkiv og Museum*, vol. 2, 1903–05, p. 160–76

Hardeland, August: *Geschichte der Speciellen Seelsorge in der Vorreformatorische Kirche und der Kirche der Reformation*, Reuther und Reichard, Berlin, 1898

Härter, Karl: 'Kriminalität und Praxis der Strafjustiz im geistlichen Territorialstaat des Alten Reiches: Sexuelle Delinquenz und Justiznutzung im frühneuzeitlichen Kurmainz', in *Criminalità e giustizia in Germania e in Italia: Pratiche giudiziarie e linguaggi giuridici tra tardo medioevo ed età moderna*, ed. Marco Bellabarba, Gerd Schwerhoff and Andrea Zorzi, Bologna, 2001, p. 101–34

Härter, Karl: 'Zum Verhältnis von "Rechtsquellen" und territorialen Rahmenbedingungen in der Strafgerichtsbarkeit des 18. Jahrhunderts: Vagabondage und Diebstahl in der Entscheidungspraxis der Kurmainzer Landesregierung', in H. Rudolph and H. Schnabel-Schüle (ed.), *Justiz = Justice = Justicia? Rahmenbedingungen für Strafjustiz im Frühneuzeitlichen Europa*, Kliomedia,Trier, 2003, p. 433–66

Härter, Karl: *Policey und Strafjustiz in Kurmainz: Gesetzgebung, Normdurchsetzung und Sozialkontrolle im frühneuzeitlichen Territorialstaat*, Vittorio Klostermann, Frankfurt am Main, 2005

Hehenberger, Susanne: 'Die beleidigte Ehre Gottes auf das empfindlichste zu rächen, in allweg gesonnen: Blasphemie und Sakrileg im 18. Jahrhundert', in *Wien und seine Wienerinnen: Ein historischer Streifzug durch Wien über die Jahrhunderte. Festschrift für Karl Vocelka zum 60. Geburtstag*, Böhlau Verlag, Vienna, 2008, p. 179–201

Hintze, Otto: *Regierung und Verwaltung. Gesammelte Abhandlungen zur Staats- Rechts- und Sozialgeschichte Preussens*, ed. Gerhard Oestrich, vol. 3, p. 1–29 ('Geist und Epochen der preussischen Geschichte', 1903), and p. 255–311 ('Kalvinismus und Staatsräson in Brandenburg zu Beginn des 17. Jahrhunderts', 1931), Vandenhoeck & Ruprecht, Göttingen, 1967

Jannsson, Arne: 'Mörda för att få dö', in Arne Jarrick and Johan Söderberg (ed.): *Människovärdet och makten: Om civiliseringsprocessen i Stockholm 1600–1850*, Stockholmia Förlag, Stockholm, 1994, p. 21–52

Jansson, Arne: *From Swords to Sorrow: Homicide and Suicide in Early Modern Stockholm*, Stockholm Studies in Economic History 30, Stockholm, 1998

Jenkins, Philip: 'From Gallows to Prison: Execution Rates in Early Modern England', in *Criminal Justice History*, 1986, p. 51–71

Jersild, Margaretha: 'Skillingtryck: Studier i svensk folklig vissång före 1800', diss., Stockholm, 1975

Kendler, Marianne: *P. Jacob Schmid S.J.: Ein Bairischer Hagiograph des 18. Jahrhunderts*, TU Druck- und Verlags GmbH, Munich, 1974

Kolderup-Rosenvinge, J.L.A. (ed.): *Samling af gamle danske love*, Copenhagen, 1824

Krogh, Tyge: *Oplysningstiden og det magiske: Henrettelser og korporlige straffe i 1700-tallets første halvdel*, Samleren, Copenhagen, 2000

Krogh, Tyge: 'Henrettelsens fascination: Om selvmordsmord og statsreligiøsitet i 1700-tallet', *Den Jyske Historiker*, no. 105, 2004, p. 19–34

Laqueur, Thomas: 'Crowds, Carnival and the State in English Executions 1604–1868', in A.L. Beier et al. (ed.): *The First Modern Society. Essays in English History in Honour of Lawrence Stone*, Cambridge University Press, 1989, p. 305–55

Lausten, Martin Schwarz: *Kirkeordinansen, 1537/39*, Akademisk Forlag, Copenhagen, 1989

Lenman, Bruce, and Parker, Geoffrey: 'The State, the Community and the Criminal Law in Early Modern Europe', in *Crime and the Law: The Social History of Crime in Western Europe since 1500*, Europa Publications ltd., London, 1980, p. 11–48

Liliequist, Jonas: 'Brott, synd och straff: Tidelagsbrottet i Sverige under 1600- och 1700-talet', PhD diss., University of Umeå, 1992

Lind, Vera: *Selbstmord in der frühen Neuzeit: Diskurs, Lebenswelt und kultureller Wandel am Beispiel der Herzogthümer Schleswig und Holstein*, Vandenhoeck & Ruprecht, Göttingen, 1999

MacDonald, Michael, and Murphy, Terence R.: *Sleepless Souls: Suicide in Early Modern England*, Oxford University Press, 1990

Malling, Anders: *Dansk salmehistorie*, J.H. Schultz, Copenhagen, 1963, vol. 3

Martschukat, Jürgen: 'Ein Freitod durch die Hand des Henkers: Erörterungen zur Komplementarität von Diskursen und Praktiken am Beispiel von "Mord aus Lebensüberdrus" und Todesstrafe im 18. Jahrhundert', *Zeitschrift für Historische Forschung*, Berlin, vol. 27, 2000, p. 53–74

Martchukat, Jürgen: *Inszeniertes Töten: Eine Geschichte der Todesstrafe vom 17. bis zum 19. Jahrhundert*, Böhlau Verlag, Cologne, 2000

Megivern, James: *The Death Penalty: An Historical and Theological Survey*, Paulist Press, New York, 1997

Meinhardt, Karl-Ernst: 'Das peinliche Strafrecht der freien Reichstadt Frankfurt am Main im Spiegel der Strafpraxis des 16. und 17. Jahrhundert', PhD diss., Rechtswissenschaftlichen Fakultät der Johann Wolfgang Goethe-Universität, Frankfurt am Main, 1957

Meye, Albrecht: *Das Strafrecht der Stadt Danzigs von der Carolina bis zur Vereinigung Danzigs mir der preußischen Monarchie (1532–1793)*, Danziger Verlagsgesellschaft, 1935

Michalik, Kerstin: *Kindsmord: Sozial- und Rechtsgeschichte der Kindstötung im 18. und beginnenden 19. Jahrhundert am Beispiel Preussen*, Centaurus-Verlagsgesellschaft, Pfaffenweiler, 1997

Midelfort, H.C. Erik: *Witchhunting in Southwestern Germany, 1562–1684: The Social and Intellectual Foundations*, Stanford UP, Stanford, CA, 1972

Midelfort, H.C. Erik: 'Selbstmord im Urtheil von Reformation und Gegenreformation', in W. Reinhard and H. Schilling (ed.): *Die Katholische Konfessionalisierung*, Achendorffsche Verlagsbuchhandlung, Münster, 1995, p. 298–310

Midelfort, H.C. Erik: *Exorcism and Enlightenment: Johann Joseph Gassner and the Demons of Eightteenth-century Germany*, Yale University Press, New Haven, CT, 2005

Moeller, Katrin: '"Es ist ein überaus gerechtes Gesetz, dass Zauberinnen getötet werden": Hexenverfolgung im protestantishen Norddeutschland', in Beier-de-Haan, R., Voltmer, R., and Irsigler, F.: *Hexenwahn. Ängste der Neuzeit. Begleitband zur gleichnamigen Ausstellung des Deutschen Historischen Museums. Berlin, Kronprinzenpalais, 3. Mai bis 6. August 2002*, Wolfratshausen, 2002

Møller, H.L.: *Kong Christian VI og Grev Christian Ernst af Stolberg-Wernigerode*, Copenhagen, 1889

Nipperdey, Thomas: 'Max Weber, der Protestantismus und die Deutschen: Drei Kommentare zu einer klassischen Thema', in *Von Geschichte umgeben. Joachim Fest zum Sechzigsten*, Siedler, Berlin, 1986, p. 179–99

Olsen, Niels Finn: 'Chr. V.s krigsartikelbrev af 9. marts 1683: En undersøgelse af den danske landmilitære straffelovgivning og process samt en redegørelse for den forudgående og senere lovgivning', PhD diss., Copenhagen University, 1982

Pedersen, J.: 'Pietismens Tid', in *Den Danske Kirkes Historie*, vol. 5, Gyldendal, Copenhagen, 1951

Pohl, Susanna: '"Ehrlicher Totschlag" - "Rache" - "Notwehr": Zwischen männlichen Ehrencode und dem Primat des Stadtfriedens (Zürich 1376–1600)', in B. Jussen and C. Koslofsky (ed.): *Kulturelle Reformation. Sinnformationen im Umbruch, 1400–1600*, Vandenhoeck & Ruprecht, Göttingen, 1999, p. 239–83

Quensel, Oscar: *Bidrag til svenska liturgiens historia*, vol. 1, Akademiska Boktryckeriet, Uppsala, 1890

Radbruch, Gustav: 'Ars Moriendi: Scharfrichter - Seelsorger - Armesünder - Volk', *Schweizerische Zeitschrift für Strafrecht*, vol. 59, Bern, 1945, p. 460–95

Reinhard, W., and Schilling, H. (ed.): *Die Katholische Konfessionalisierung*, Achendorffsche Verlagsbuchhandlung, Münster, 1995

Rodegra, Heinrich, Lindemann, Mary, and Ewald, Martin: 'Kindermord und verheimlichte Schwangerschaft in Hamburg im 18. Jahrhundert', in *Gesnerus*, Vierteljahrschrift, Aarau, 1978, vol. 35, p. 276–96

Schilling, Heintz: *Höfe und Alianzen: Deutschland, 1648–1763*, Siedler Deutsche Geschichte, vol. 6, Berlin, 1994 (1998)

Schilling, Heintz: 'Die Konfessionalisierung von Kirche, Staat und Gesellschaft: Profil, Leistung und Perspektiven eines geschichtswissenschaftlicen Paradigmas', in W. Reinhard and H. Schilling (ed.): *Die Katholische Konfessionalisierung*, Achendorffsche Verlagsbuchhandlung, Münster, 1995, p. 1–49

Schnabel-Schüle, Helga: *Überwachen und Strafen im Territorialstaat: Bedingungen und Auswirkungen des Systems strafrechtlicher Sanktionen im frühneuzeitlichen Württemberg*, Cologne, 1997

Schuhmann, Helmuth: *Der Scharffrichter: Seine Gestalt - seine Funktion*, Algäuer Heimatbücher, vol. 67, Algäu, 1964

Schuster, Peter: 'Hinrichtungsrituale in der Frühen Neuzeit: Anfragen aus dem Mittelalter', in Harriet Rudolph and Helga Schnabel-Schüle (ed.): *Justiz = Justice = Justicia? Rahmenbedingungen von Strafjustiz im frühneuzeitlichen Europa*, Kliomedia, Trier, 2003 p. 213–33

Secher, V.A.: 'Bidrag til Københavns rets- og kulturhistorie 1624–1663', *Historiske meddelelser om København*, ser. 1, vol. 1, Copenhagen, 1907–08, p. 333–84, 569–98

Sehling, Emil (ed.): *Die Evangelischen Kirchenordnungen des XVI. Jahrhunderts*, vol. 5, O.R. Reisland, Leipzig 1913; vol. 6, J.C.B. Mohr, Tübingen, 1955

Sharpe, J.A.: '"Last Dying Speeches": Religion, Ideology and Public Execution in 17th Century England', *Past and Present*, vol. 107, Oxford, 1985, p. 144–67

Sörlin, Per: *Trolldoms- och Vidskepelsesprocesserne i Göta Hovrätt, 1635–1754*, Almqvist & Wiksell, Stockholm, 1993

Spierenburg, Pieter: *The Spectacle of Suffering: Executions and the Evolution of Repression, from a Preindustrial Metropolis to the European Experience*, Cambridge UP, 1984

Strafer, Richard: 'Volunteering for Execution', *Journal of Criminal Law and Criminology*, vol. 74, Baltimore, Md, 1983, p. 860–912

Stuart, Kathy: 'Suicide by Proxy: The Unintended Consequences of Public Executions in Eighteenth-Century Germany', *Central European History*, 41, 2008, p. 413–45

Tamm, Ditlev: 'Hvorfor læse Beccaria?', in Cesare Beccaria: *Om forbrydelse og straf*, Museum Tusculanums Forlag, Copenhagen, 1998, p. 211–8

Thomas, Keith: 'The Puritans and Adultery: The Act of 1650 Reconsidered', in *Puritans and Revolutionaries: Essays in Seventeenth-Century History Presented to Christopher Hill*, Clarendon Press, Oxford, 1978, p. 257–82

Thunander, Rudolf: *Hovrätt i funktion: Göta Hovrätt och brottmålen, 1635–1699*, Nerentius & Santérus Förlag, Stockholm, 1993

Ulbricht, Otto: *Kindsmord und Aufklärung in Deutschland*, R. Oldenbourg, Munich, 1990

Weber, Helmuth von: 'Selbstmord als Mordmotiv', *Monatsschrift für Kriminalbiologie und Strafrechtsreform*, vol. 28, München, 1937, p. 161–81

Weber, Helmuth von: 'Der Dekalog als grundlage der Verbrechenssystematik', in *Festschrift für Wilhelm Sauer*, de Gruyter, Berlin, 1949, p. 44–70

Weber, Max: *Den protestantiske etik og kapitalismens ånd* (1904), Nansensgade Antikvariat, Copenhagen, 1995

Wettstein, Erich: *Die Geschichte der Todesstrafe im Kanton Zürich*, Zürich, 1958

Wormer, Katherine van, and Odia, Chick: 'The Psychology of Suicide-Murder and the Death Penalty', in *Journal of Criminal Justice*, vol. 27, 1999, p. 361–70

Wosnick, Richard: *Beiträge zur Hamburgischen Kriminalgeschichte*, vol. 1, Hamburg, 1926

INDEX

www.ingramcontent.com/pod-product-compliance
Lightning Source LLC
LaVergne TN
LVHW081515300926
849161LV00006B/1186
* 9 7 8 9 0 0 4 2 2 1 1 5 4 *